PLAY AND THE HUMAN CONDITION

THOMAS S. HENRICKS

Play and the Human Condition

UNIVERSITY OF ILLINOIS PRESS

URBANA, CHICAGO, AND SPRINGFIELD

Library of Congress Cataloging-in-Publication Data
Henricks, Thomas S.
Play and the human condition / Thomas S. Henricks.
pages   cm
Includes bibliographical references and index.
ISBN 978-0-252-03907-2 (cloth : alk. paper)
ISBN 978-0-252-08068-5 (pbk. : alk. paper)
ISBN 978-0-252-09705-8 (ebook)
1. Play—Social aspects. 2. Play—Psychological aspects. 3. Self-realization.
I. Title.
HQ782.H386   2015
306.4'81—dc23   2014035455

Contents

Acknowledgments   *vii*

Introduction   *1*

1. *Variations on a Theme*   *19*

2. *Play Compared to Other Behaviors*   *42*

3. *Play as Sense-Making*   *68*

4. *The Psychology of Play*   *90*

5. *Play's Nature*   *116*

6. *Play and the Physical Environment*   *138*

7. *The Social Life of Play*   *161*

8. *Cultural Play*   *184*

9. *The Play of Possibility*   *209*

References   *229*

Index   *243*

Acknowledgments

Like play itself, academic writing draws on many different resources. This is especially true for a book like this one, which features the ideas of several generations of play scholars. In addition to those writers, more proximate persons and organizations have provided support. I thank first Scott Eberle, as well as others at the *American Journal of Play*, for ongoing recognition of my work and belief in its possibilities. I also thank my friends and colleagues at the Association for the Study of Play for their generosity to scholars of every type and for their strong advocacy of play. I am especially indebted to David Kuschner for the many conversations we have had about play and other matters through the years. I signal the role of Jim Johnson, Fraser Brown, John Loy, and Synthia Sydnor in providing encouragement, comments, criticism, and suggestions for resources. I am grateful to administrators, librarians, and faculty at Elon University for their support, including the provision of resources for study and professional advancement. At that institution, special acknowledgment goes to Tim Peeples, Larry Basirico, Anne Bolin, Rissa Trachman, and Tom Mould. I also recognize Lisa Peloquin for our shared commitment to the themes discussed here. Some former professors—Donald Levine, Victor Lidz, Barry Schwartz, Victor Turner, and Mihaly Csikszentmihalyi—should be noted. They helped legitimize the study of play and expressive culture and provided worthy models for others to follow. I salute Brian Sutton-Smith for his restless investigations of play and for his courtesy to those whose viewpoints differ from his own. I thank Laurie Matheson at the University of Illinois Press for her long-standing support of my work, as well as Jane Zanichkowsky, Jennifer Clark, Dustin Hubbart, and Katherine Jensen for their assistance in improving the manuscript and bringing it to publication. I recognize my parents, Marvin and Sylvia Henricks, for their differing models of the scholarly life. My ultimate appreciation goes to my spouse Judy Henricks and to my children Lizzie and David for their inspiring and sustaining my broader life commitments.

PLAY AND THE HUMAN CONDITION

Introduction

How do we discover who we are? How do we determine the character of the world in which we live? And how do we decide what we can do in a world so configured? Such questions, each connected to our lifelong quest for self-realization, are central to this book. Its thesis is that we learn about ourselves and the world—and about the intersection of these two realms—through acts of play.

To claim that play supports the development of creatures is not to make a statement that is striking or new. Indeed, play is commonly portrayed as one way in which individuals generate life strategies. When we play, we explore the limits of the possible. Ideas—about the world and about ourselves—are hoisted aloft. Pertinent skills are readied. And emotionally charged orientations, essentially judgments about what should happen next, are brought to the fore. Players are committed to making their own visions for the world happen, and on those terms they push into new territories. Each of those self-directed forays provides a range of interesting experiences to reflect on and to savor.

This general view—that play is not just pleasing involvement in the moments of life but creative activity that has consequences for other portions of that life—has been proposed by many scholars (see Millar 1968; Ellis 1973; Levy 1978; Spariosu 1989, 1997; Sutton-Smith 1997; Power 2005; Burghardt 2005). Many of these accounts are described in the pages that follow. Although that scholarly literature is wide-ranging, for the most part it emphasizes the significance of play for the physical and mental well-being of *individuals*. In other words, biological and psychological theories prevail. This emphasis is understandable, for play is frequently self-generated activity that occurs with or without companionship. And that vision of behavior is encouraged by a mythology of individualism—replete with ideas about the proper functioning, experiences, skills, and rights of persons—that is central to many contemporary societies. Such beliefs are articulated and sustained by cadres of educators, therapists, recreationalists, and healthcare providers. By such lights, play is a result of personal insight and urgency. Its benefits should be measured in the same terms.

Although this approach to play is important, there are other ways of thinking about play's character and implications. Scholars in social philosophy, folklore, anthropology, history, sociology, and other fields have argued that play is also a commentary on the lives of *communities*. In other words, play's causes and consequences should be seen in terms of the groups that sponsor that activity or even of society as a whole. Although most of us believe that we play just as we wish, those wishes are culturally circumscribed.

Remembering Huizinga's Commitment

One of the most important statements of the second theme was presented by the cultural historian Johan Huizinga. In his book *Homo Ludens: A Study of the Play Element in Culture* Huizinga argues that play has social and cultural, as well as personal, implications. When people agree on the terms of their engagement with one another and collectively bring those little worlds into being, they effectively create models for living. Within those "magic circles," as Huizinga (1955, p. 10) calls them, cultural themes are evaluated, dramatized, and otherwise made real. Of the many curious things that are said and done in those circumstances, some become elements of collective memory and are formalized as institutional domains. As he sees it (p. 173), "[r]itual grew up in sacred play; poetry was born in play and nourished on play; music and dancing were pure play." In much the same fashion, philosophy, warfare, and the customs of noble living are founded on play patterns. What Huizinga asserts, then, is that civilization, at least in its earliest stages, is performed or played. Public play is central to the making of communities. Ideally, those play events manifest a spirit of creative, critical discourse that prepares the way for more settled styles of engagement and, within those contexts, for ongoing assessments of what has been established. Without intending to be, players are agents of change.

This introduction is not meant to criticize Huizinga's ideas about the origin, maintenance, and reformation of societies (for that see Caillois 2001b; Geyl, 1963; Duncan 1988; Henricks 2002, 2006). Instead, his book is discussed for several other reasons. The first is its challenging thesis that people not only reproduce but also produce social and cultural form through acts of play. The second is its daring title. *Homo ludens*—the idea of people as players—is installed beside two more generally acknowledged conceptions of humanity's essence (Huizinga 1955, pp. ix–x).

As the reader might imagine, one of these conceptions is *Homo sapiens*, the view that humans are especially knowing or thoughtful. Like Shakespeare's Hamlet, we ponder the implications of things in our minds. We deliberate before we act. Frequently, we do not act at all. What we cannot stop, however, is the development of a tremendous reservoir of ideas and images, which function as reference points for living. Nor can we prevent ourselves from casting up scenarios of what is happening now, has happened, and may happen in the moments ahead. Humans are fascinated by their own powers of abstraction and by the prospect of making those abstractions real.

The second vision is of people as makers, or *Homo faber*. The wonderful capacities of our brains are rivaled only by the dispositions of our hands. Humans manipulate the environments they inhabit. More impressive still, they create and maintain those environments. As Karl Marx, perhaps the best-known exponent of this thesis, maintained in his *Economic and Philosophical Manuscripts* of 1844, life is at bottom an attempt to transform the materiality of the world to meet the needs of our bodies and minds. However, and in distinction from animals, humans are not prisoners of their circumstances. Indeed, we produce best when we are freed from direct necessity (Marx 1999, p. 102). By making things and then regarding what we've made, we reach conclusions about our capabilities and about our proper standing in the world. The best place to learn about the human condition is not a philosopher's study but a workshop filled with sawdust and sweat (Marx 1964, p. 91).

Can the urge to play be granted a status equivalent to our desires to *know* the world and to respond to its challenges through acts of *making*? Surely play is just a respite from material necessity and from more serious demands of life. Play is indulgence, escape, and fun. It's what we do when nothing more substantial claims our attention.

Huizinga does not reject the first two visions of human nature. He does, however, claim (1955, p. 9) that play's escape from the chain of material consequence, in essence its triviality, is the very reason why play is so important. Players are granted—and not infrequently seize for themselves—opportunities to step back from and reconsider their ways of living. Those acts of reconsideration are what make play special. Understood in that context, his book is an attempt to identify the defining qualities of play and to demonstrate its broadest range of significance.

The third reason for signaling Huizinga's work here is to acknowledge this author's continuing debt to Huizinga's general insights. Although the current writing offers viewpoints that differ significantly from those found in *Homo Ludens*, the spirit of Huizinga's work—in effect, to produce a wide-ranging theory of play—inspires the current undertaking.

Fourth and finally, Huizinga is remembered because he was willing to evaluate and challenge the play events of his time. Although the best-known portion of *Homo Ludens* is its definition of play, perhaps the book's greater legacy is its description of play's historical transformation. In that light, Huizinga's special concern was the set of changes occurring in Western societies during the nineteenth and early twentieth centuries. For the most part, he did not approve of what he saw. In earlier times, or so he (1955, pp. 173–213) argues, public play events articulated important societal commitments, tensions, and group affiliations. Furthermore, the idea of play "grounds" or "settings" was exceedingly broad. Fields of play included tennis courts, courts of law, forums for public debate, battlefields, card tables, riddling contests, and innumerable other settings. Essentially, these were protected spaces where social equals competed in regulated ways. The behaviors produced in these settings—what we think of as battles, sports and games, teasing, ranting, philosophical speculation, artistic display, conspicuous consumption, and rhetorical bombast—were, in his view, forms of sociocultural expression and realignment. On the play ground, new ideas and customs could be explored with relatively few consequences. Individuals could assess their own qualities and character at the same time—and by the same processes—they evaluated those of other people. And groups could make clear their proper placement in society as a whole and the responsibilities of their members to one another.

Like children grown old, modern societies are said to have lost this vital, creative spark. At least, that is Huizinga's thesis. He associates this change with the coming of industrialism, the rise of the bourgeois mentality, and a persistent commercialism. To be sure, contemporary people have not abandoned their fascination with pleasure. But they have forgotten their commitment to open, engaged public discourse. In Huizinga's view, modern times are ruled by the policies and practices of huge, bureaucratically administered organizations in almost every social sphere. These organizations set the tone of life; behavior becomes managed. Emphasis is placed on occupational competence, idealized now as narrowly conceived or technical "excellence." Worse still, in his judgment, is the rise of such expansionist political ideologies as the fascist and communist movements that were prominent in his lifetime. All these factors contribute to a withering of the play spirit and to the rise of a certain style of seriousness. No longer is life held lightly or provisionally, in the style of players. The spirit of the new age demands work—and progress.

Note that *Homo Ludens* was published first in 1938 and that Huizinga died in 1945. Vast social and cultural changes have occurred since then. Furthermore, the reader should be apprised that Huizinga's critique of industrialized modernism stems from that author's fascination with agrarian, hierarchical societies and especially with the European Middle Ages (see Huizinga 1954). Such a view romanticizes the world we have lost more than the benefits of later centuries.

Still, his guiding concern—in effect, what is the character of play in our time?—continues to be essential for play studies. In part, this means confronting play's moral and policy implications. Public understandings of play, like understandings of any important matter, are not only descriptions of *how* people live but also recommendations for how they *should* live. Presumably, some styles of living are better than others. At the very least, the implications of those choices should be evaluated.

Why Study Play?

In 1923 the British explorer George Mallory was asked by a reporter why he chose to make a third and ultimately fatal assault on Mount Everest. His famous, if perhaps apocryphal, response: "Because it's there." For similar if less dramatic reasons, scholars attempt to understand play. And their quest is not to survey some remote or insubstantial territory. Quite the opposite: play looms over the contemporary landscape as one of the most important locations for human behavior and imagination.

In its purest expressions, scholarship—of play or any other topic—occurs because people wish to understand the world and the extent of human capability. Just as mountaineering historically has been motivated by a wide range of interests, however (Hansen 2013), so studies of play have been responses to contemporary concerns and commitments. Two of these concerns, each the basis for a particular narrative about play, are described below.

IN DEFENSE OF CHILDHOOD

Whatever their commitment to broad-based knowledge about the human condition may be, many scholars investigate play because they are interested in matters that are, to them, more important than play itself. One of those overarching concerns is human development, the great set of changes associated with people's moving through the life course. Contemporary researchers, educators, and clinicians understand development to be much more than a gathering of experiences. Instead, that project features stages or sequences that express and consolidate interrelated advances in body, mind, and social condition.

Motivated by such concerns, researchers emphasize a number of play's benefits. To cite the claims presented in some summaries of play's developmental implications (Johnson, Christie, and Yawkey 1999; Frost, Wortham, and Reifel 2008; Pellegrini 2009), play promotes bodily and motor development, neurological change, cognitive growth and complexity, acquisition of language and literacy, and social and emotional progress. Play helps individuals learn how to manage environments with skills they already possess. Then it encourages them to establish better strategies. For Sheng-Hsi Lin and Stuart Reifel (1999, p. 151) play serves as a "laboratory" where "children can learn new skills and practice old ones in preparation for adult life in society." At the same time it is a "social workshop," a place to try out new roles, and even "an area for expression" that is "concerned with the themes and emotions that are experienced in everyday life." In such ways, play contributes to an enterprising life trajectory.

This viewpoint is fundamental to play-based education. It is also central to play therapy (see Winnicott 1971; Schaefer 1992). Setting aside their traditionally authoritarian role, therapists encourage children to express themselves in their own ways. Nonverbal behaviors (such as making artwork, object play, and role play) take precedence over word-based accounts. Therapists listen, inquire quietly, and participate with their patients. As it is for educators, the guiding rationale is that play allows people to express and act out their own understandings of situations. Self-directed behavior, or so it is argued, produces learning and change.

It may be that some of these claims for play's benefits are manifestations of what Peter Smith (2010, pp. 27–28) calls the "play ethos," a "strong and unqualified assertion of the functional importance of play" by those who believe that play, or at least certain kinds of it, should reciever greater emphasis in children's lives. Policy recommendations (for families, schools, governments, media, and other bodies) are driven as much by cherished values as they are by evidence. And play, in part because of a continuing difficulty in defining that subject, has been especially subject to such enthusiasms. Play advocates—a list that includes educators, therapists, camp counselors, playground developers, makers of toys, directors of children's museums, operators of amusement parks, creators of electronic games, leaders of musical groups, and organizers of sports leagues—believe that the world is made better by their activities.

As suggested above, this fascination with the personal utility of play is especially pronounced in certain kinds of societies, especially those dominated by individualistic, middle-class mythologies. Modernizing societies with strong middle classes endorse commitments to self-control, the future, social mobility, material and cultural acquisition, procedural fairness, and education as a pathway to success. Members of such societies are expected to be "reflexive" about their own identities, that is, to continually assess their standing before others and to formulate strategies that adjust those standings (see Giddens 1991; Lash and Friedman 1992). People are encouraged to have a career, that is, a steady self-regulated course through a series of occupational and social levels. They are even expected to display a distinctive personality type. At least, that is the well-known argument of the sociologists Alex Inkeles and David Smith (1974). By that account, modern people are to be open-minded and ready for new experiences, independent of traditional sources of authority such as priests and elders, and possessed of a marked sense of personal efficacy. They are to reject passivity and fatalism and to substitute for these a belief in their own ability to influence the world. They are to be prepared for change and alert to opportunities. They should be energetic. Possessed of such traits, modern people are informed participant-citizens who care about issues beyond the boundaries of their families and local communities and who play active roles in their societies.

To be sure, no single activity builds such enterprising modern people, who begin their ascendancy in the first years of childhood. And it should be acknowledged quickly that modernism's individualistic self is not without its difficulties. However, the "play ethos"—again, the unqualified belief in the personal utility of play—matches well with the values just described. Modern people are expected to move beyond childhood connections and commitments to increasingly widespread, challenging, and complicated involvements. Play, at least in the forms emphasized by developmental theorists, is one manifestation of this encouragement to tinker and transform. The ultimate creation of such behavior is a reflective, activist self.

In traditional societies, childhood leads more directly to adult responsibilities, habits of living, loving, and working that are visible to every member of the community. By contrast, modern societies define childhood as a specialized life stage that is divided into small segments during which people perform distinctive activities in the company of their age-mates (see Erikson 1963). Each of these life segments, like grade levels in school, is understood to be a time when certain kinds of learning take place so that participants can advance to the next set of challenges. Failure to acquire the pertinent skill sets—not only cognitive but also social and emotional—is taken seriously for non-advancement signifies more than a delay in personal and social development. It indicates that one may be ill-equipped for the occupations of an emerging information society, which require effective social communication, flexible personality, abstract symbol manipulation, and technological sophistication. Seen in that context, schooling serves a double function. On one hand, it provides a clearly marked highway for personal advancement. On the other, it is a social and cultural filter, a way of moving some people ahead and leaving others behind.

Most play scholars are strong advocates for the welfare of all children. They also tend to be critics of the very educational and governmental systems that many of them inhabit. Part of that critique focuses on what those scholars understand to be an excessive emphasis on the drilling and standardized test preparation that have become important features of contemporary education (see Johnson, Christie, and Wardle 2004). They argue that development occurs on many fronts (cognitive, emotional, social, and physical), that intelligence is of many sorts, and that educational policies must reflect contemporary research about age-based needs and capabilities (Eberle 2011).

In that spirit, many champion the view that informal, peer-organized interaction, such as that which occurs during informal recreation or in the "freer" styles of learning, not only revitalizes students for their formal studies but also provides lessons different from those received in authority-based teaching. For some of these scholars, informal play, and specifically recess, should be re-established as an important element of the school day (Pellegrini 2005). For others, the self-directed and energizing qualities of play should be brought into the classroom to enhance learning and literacy (Christie 1991). To repeat, such scholars are strong proponents of play. They are even stronger proponents of child betterment.

This preoccupation with child advancement extends to non-school settings, as well. To a degree that previous generations would find difficult to understand, children are now enrolled in all manner of clubs, sports teams, camps, musical ensembles, dance and fitness activities, and civic associations. The good child, or so it seems, is the busy child, or at least the child who is engaged in a range of what were once called extracurricular activities. These endeavors are not equivalent to the neighborhood play of earlier periods. They are formally organized with established (adult) leaders, timetables, supervised competitions, and measurable outputs.

In part, these commitments of the scheduled or "hurried" child (Elkind 2006) are understood to be contributors to his or her physical and psychological development. They are also, however, markers of accomplishment that signify well-roundedness and leadership potential, themes that are valued by prestigious schools at the next levels of education. Building one's résumé, or so it seems, is no longer a preoccupation reserved for working adults. Levels and kinds of play (providing appropriate degrees of challenge, instructors, playmates, and even toys) are matters to be considered carefully. School may still be the child's chief responsibility, but leisure is moving to a position beside it as equally well-organized, instrumentally directed, and status-ridden.

Once again, scholars of children's play have been attentive to these changes in non-school activities. Part of that critique has included a questioning of the pay-as-you-go leisure system found in some societies; another theme has been the role of adults as managers of children's play. In keeping with those concerns, new styles of playgrounds have emerged along with different patterns of adult involvement. For example, in the United Kingdom a new profession, that of the "playworker," has arisen (F. Brown 2003; Wilson 2009). Playworkers are committed to establishing and furnishing with rough materials publicly accessible spaces in cities and towns where children can play in their free time. Playworkers focus on the rights of economically and socially disadvantaged children to use these spaces. And they encourage styles of play that maximize the creative energy of the kids themselves. All this is done in the name of child development and, as its consequence, social benefit.

NEW CHALLENGES FOR ADULTHOOD

As noted above, many scholars are interested in play because of its connection to childhood. But it cannot be denied that play activities are an important feature of life's later stages as well (see Kuschner 2009). Every day, young adults can be seen running along city streets, exercising in gyms and spas, playing vigorous sports, dancing in bars and clubs, playing games on their electronic devices, and otherwise asserting themselves in the name of pleasure. Many older people attempt to keep up with the younger generation in these pursuits. Failing that, they show their commitment to a range of tamer sports, exercises, parties, vacations, gambling, shopping, and other forms of enjoyment. Even those in the last stages of life gather to walk, do water exercises, make arts and crafts projects, play board and computer games, and banter with friends. Cultural images of older people sitting passively to watch young ones play are yielding to visions of active, energetic, creative, and even sexy seniors.

The above-mentioned changes can be associated with advancing health standards and with new understandings of the life cycle. But they are also connected to a more complicated set of social changes, including a new stage of societal development that sociologists call the "late," "advanced," or even "post"-industrial age (see Jameson 1984; Giddens 1991; Roberts 2001). Societies of this type feature economies dominated by technical, informational, and service jobs. Workers in advanced industrial societies are less likely to produce material goods as farmers, factory workers, and manual laborers did in earlier periods. Instead, many contemporary workers now produce and maintain the organizational and informational systems that regulate economic relationships. Those relationships take on global dimensions. Increasingly, material goods are produced, assembled, and shipped from the less wealthy countries. In advanced industrial societies, higher-status workers design, market, and manage social and cultural relationships. At lower levels, they operate the machines expressing this technology and perform personal services for the population as a whole.

Parallel changes include a rise in life expectancy and a shift in the organization of work hours. What this means is that large blocks of non-work time have been created, at least for the favored classes. Because of this shift, advanced industrial countries are sometimes described as leisure-oriented or even as "leisure societies" (Dumazedier 1967). This term is not, however, meant to imply that people have become leisurely but quite the opposite: for twentieth- and twenty-first-century people, leisure becomes problematic (see Riesman 1950; Rojek 1985). Indeed, today people are expected to decorate themselves with activities of this sort. They should know the goings-on of movies, music, and television. No-nonsense approaches to food, drink, clothing, and sex have been replaced by behaviors that indicate reflection and sophistication. Leisure commitments—hobbies, vacationing, support for local sports teams, social skills, home decorating, and the like—become vehicles for the construction and estimation of personal quality (Freysinger and Kelly 2004). In a world featuring tens of thousands of specialized jobs, widespread mobility of populations, vast urban settlements, and the ownership of increasingly abstract forms of capital, it becomes difficult to assess personal identity and capability. Contemporary people are less likely to center their existence in established residential communities, to submit to the judgments of neighbors, or, indeed, to know those neighbors well.

What most of us can judge is whether the people we meet can amuse us at a party or bar, whether they comport themselves well at their chosen recreation, and whether they are able to chat amiably about the commercially sponsored programs that stream across our televisions, computers, and movie screens. More than sixty years ago, Martha Wolfenstein (1951) commented on the emergence of what she called the "fun morality," an ethic that not only encourages fun but makes it obligatory that one do "fun things" and, on that basis, be considered a "fun person." On one hand, this essentially aesthetic sensibility suggests that enjoyment has superseded more serious, contemplative, and worklike modes of being. But, on the other, the combining of pleasure with moral obligation also insinuates a new instrumentalism. People should have fun, not just for its own sake but because they want to be well-regarded by their peers. Being considered "cool," "hip," "hot," "with it," and the like is now a badge of identity pertinent to social acceptance and advancement. The attaining of the pleasured self is not a privilege of the gilded classes alone but a moral imperative that reinforces the orientations of the entire society.

Furthermore, in the new-style jobs focusing on information management and organizational creativity, work and leisure merge (see D. Bell 1976). People who desire upward mobility in today's corporate culture do well to learn the games, tastes, and enthusiasms of that circle's members. Think about a group of businesspeople on the golf course cultivating a network of professional relationships. Are they at work or at play? What if those same persons are coaching a Little League team, leading a troop of scouts, or participating in a local garden club? One need not belong to a country club to appreciate how professional and personal relationships intersect. In a world where chief commodities are a range of social contacts, engaging manners, and self-assurance, play activities are moments of personal revelation. We live in a period that celebrates social and economic entrepreneurship. And the main items for sale are visions of selves.

This linkage between work and play is expressed also in what can be termed "pleasure industries." Visits to spas, health clubs, bars, vacation resorts, restaurants, zoos, art galleries, antique shops, sporting arenas, and the like are now justified as needed getaways or as refurbishments of body and mind in an anxiety-ridden world. Whatever functions these activities fulfill, they are all too frequently commercialized undertakings.

Beyond the specific objects and services that are offered, the principal commerce is the giving and receiving of pleasure. At the same time attendees receive a predictable stream of pleasant sensations they advertise themselves to others as persons who *deserve*—and can pay for—such experiences.

Still another theme is the rise of new "cultural" settings for play, especially those associated with electronic media (see Aarseth 1997; Wolf 2001). The development of satellite communications, the Internet, and miniaturized electronics has meant that people of all ages can now play video games with competitors from across the world. Tens of thousands are playing some of the best-known games at every moment of the day. They are also browsing websites, trawling through social network pages, sending messages (with photos) to one another, and preparing and publishing personal presentations including videos and homepages. Much of this is done in the name of enjoyment. As the sociologist Simon Williams (2001, p. 12) puts it, contemporary people inhabit a "mediascape" society that offers new possibilities for representations of personhood, cultural creativity, and social encounter.

This profusion of expressive possibilities led the play theorist Tilmon Kuchler (1994, p. 1) to declare that humans have reached "the end of modernity and the beginning of play." In that vision of society, people are depicted as moving continually from one culturally informed situation to the next, each featuring a chance-laden intersection of occurrences. Every moment provides its characteristic challenges and enjoyments as well as feelings that are consolidated and then left behind. For the most part, these occasions are not systematically linked. Rather, and somewhat like spiders on a web, people hear reports of distant satisfactions and race off in every direction to become acquainted with these. And just as people are players who prosecute their own enjoyments, so they are "in play" as forces they cannot control swirl around them (see Hans 1981).

To conclude, it is arguably the case that contemporary people live in social circumstances that are highly various, ambiguous, and transitory. Furthermore, the chief contexts for personal orientation have shifted by degrees from the natural and spiritual worlds to social and cultural formations. Although these new formations provide a certain order to public and personal life, they generate problems of their own sorts. That complex of humanly instigated patterns and problems—including contagious diseases, cancers, nuclear threats, crime, pollution, unemployment, and terrorism—has been described by Ulrich Beck (1992) as the "risk society." Modern people seek to identify and manage such risks by a process that involves estimations of the likelihood of each calamity and the garnering of resources to anticipate and respond to it. But people also are fascinated by this specter of humanly induced risk and, indeed, artificially generate it by participating in sports and games, exotic forms of racing, adventurous travel, gambling, drug use, risky sex, and similar behaviors. In other words, many instances of play feature what Norbert Elias and Eric Dunning (1986) call "the quest for excitement." Although people want to be protected from the greatest dangers, many actively court difficulty, opposition, and disorder. Choosing to engage in risky, indulgent, or deviant play displays our defiance of what the world has in store for us. Playing successfully transmutes anxiety.

Developing a General Approach to Play

I have presented two different narratives about why we should study play. Proponents of the first narrative emphasize the important role of play for self-development, what Brian Sutton-Smith (1997, pp. 9–10) calls the "play-as-progress" rhetoric. Scholars committed to this viewpoint rue the decline of play—or at least of certain preferred versions of play—in our bureaucratically managed age. Accordingly, children should be allowed the freedom of expression and home-made pleasures that play advocates experienced when they were young. Children should go outdoors; they should mingle and roam. Skinned knees, bloody noses, and hurt feelings are the appropriate risks of comradeship. That same adventurous, egalitarian spirit should be harnessed for classroom learning. Informality, enthusiasm, and disorder are the allies rather than the enemies of educators and counselors. What contemporary children should not do is wander malls aimlessly, use drugs, stare at television and computer screens, play violent video games, engage in risky sex, buy things they do not need, and fiddle incessantly with their electronic gadgets.

The other, not entirely opposite, view is that contemporary people of all ages live amid a tremendous profusion of play opportunities and that the character of those opportunities is different from what previous generations have known. Vast numbers of people have chances to play (via computers and their hand-held equivalents, sports complexes, arcades, camps, museums, vacation destinations, and the like) in unprecedented ways. This extension of pleasurable and putatively creative possibilities is something to be celebrated. At the very least, such settings are the foundations for new forms of personal expression, occupation, identity, and social connection. In short, play has not declined; people are playing—and learning—frenetically. They find pleasure in rambunctious, disapproved, and sometimes illegal play. It is only a cadre of educators, moralists, and play theorists who are suspicious of their choices.

Amid this disagreement about whether people play too little or too much and about the relative merits of the forms they choose, it is appropriate to reconsider the character and implications of play. Is play amusement of just any sort, or does it exhibit some special qualities that make it different from similar behaviors? Once we have determined what play is, perhaps we can assess its causes and consequences in a more productive way and articulate policies that foster play's benefits and avoid its dangers.

In beginning this project, it is important to emphasize that the two sets of contemporary concerns just presented are only a small, historically situated vision of what play is and can be. Other settings and other theories beyond these must be considered. And it is critical also to stress that social and cultural analysis, an interest that this author shares with Huizinga, is itself a small segment of the many ways of thinking about play. As the dominant tradition in play studies makes plain, play is fundamentally about individual minds and bodies. It is also about the physical environments that people inhabit. In other words, play is not only psychological and sociocultural reconnoitering; it is a much more general confrontation with our capabilities and limitations as individuals and as members of our species. Play transcends time and place and the ideas that we attach to circumstances. One cannot understand play without appreciating its diverse expressions, but it is on the basis of that diversity that a general understanding of play is built. That expanded view of the human condition guides this book's assessment of play's character and possibilities.

Scope of This Book

This book explores the causes, consequences, and contexts of play. That project involves comprehending not only the variation in play's settings and behaviors but also the general themes that unite all forms of play. Accomplishing such broad purposes is impossible if the writer confines himself to the approaches of any one discipline. The contributions of researchers working within the boundaries of psychology, education, sociology, biology, anthropology, folklore, history, leisure studies, philosophy, and other studies are in every case crucial. Understanding play means understanding the intersection of these different contributions.

The broad outlines of the book having been described, it is important to say what the book is not. No attempt is made to survey the entire range of theory and research on play. In part, this is because the literature concerning this subject has grown to such an extent that it cannot be contained by any single volume. The other reason is that there are now handbooks and encyclopedias (see Carlisle 2009; Johnson, Eberle, Kuschner, and Henricks 2015) as well as compendia of play theories like those cited at the beginning of this introduction. Such volumes display admirably the many different approaches to play. Less effectively do they integrate those approaches.

Similarly, the current book is not a polemic, some morally energized viewpoint that proclaims some theories to be right and others to be misdirected or wrong. Detailed criticism of other scholars' work is not this book's ambition. On the contrary, my intent is to show how different classic and contemporary theories of play are true enough in their own fashion. That is, most theories tend to describe well certain aspects of play but neglect or treat poorly other matters that rival approaches emphasize. In that spirit, the book provides introductions to the writing of some important scholars of play. I stress that these introductions are not meant to substitute for the reader's consultation of the original sources. A few paragraphs cannot summarize well an important book, series of articles, or, in some cases, the focus of a career. And readers inevitably interpret others' ideas in their own fashion.

Finally, my intention in this book is to be essayistic in style and integrative in tone. Wherever possible, plain language and commonplace examples are employed. Also evident are the pronouns *I*, *we*, and *you*. Such terminology, or so I believe, is suitable for a topic that celebrates the subjectivity—and intersubjectivity—of persons. Finally, I am not shy about expressing my own views of what play is, how it differs from other forms of human expression, and what meanings surround it. Those declarations are intended to invite readers to think about play and to advance their understandings of it, much as Huizinga's writing has inspired my own reflections. Disagreement with the assessments presented here is part of that process.

So conceived, the book is arranged in the following way. This introduction provides an overview and presents an argument for why studying play matters. The following three chapters address the challenge of presenting a general model of play. Chapter 1, "Variations on a Theme," describes some of the issues that make establishing a working definition of play—and in consequence conducting research on that topic—difficult. In that light, the chapter reviews several contemporary definitions of play. Chapter 2, "Play Compared to Other Behaviors," presents my view that play is different from three other patterns of willfully directed behavior.

Those patterns are ritual, work, and communitas. At chapter's end I offer my own description of play's guiding themes.

Chapter 3, "Play as Sense-Making," identifies play as a special pattern of meaning construction, one way in which people make sense of their qualities and character as they interact with particular elements of situations. The focus of the chapter is the extent to which behavior and experience are contextualized by environmental, bodily, psychological, social, and cultural patterns. Ultimately, the chapter provides a general theory of play which centers on that behavior as a distinctive strategy of self-realization.

The middle chapters of the book explore five different contexts for play. The first of these, Chapter 4, "The Psychology of Play," describes important contributions of psychologists and human development theorists to the study of play. The chapter's special theme is the role of imagination in envisioning life's possibilities.

Chapter 5 is titled "Play's Nature." At its most basic levels, play is a pattern of behavior that is shared across species. When we play, we express ourselves as physical creatures that confront the limitations of our bodies as we move through the world. These limits are both constraints and forms of enablement. Creatures play because their bodies allow them, and indeed encourage them, to do so. In that context, the chapter focuses on the physiological foundations of play and the consequences that it has for those formations.

Chapter 6, "Play and the Physical Environment," analyzes the intersection between active players and material forms. The qualities of our species have not evolved in isolation; they have emerged as responses to changing physical circumstances. Although some of these capacities to recognize and respond are narrowly established, others are more flexible and learning-dependent. The chapter considers the role of play in the development of these dispositions and capabilities. Concluding remarks focus on the so-called playgrounds movement, the study and development of physical environments that stimulate creative play.

Chapter 7 addresses the social life of play. Although some forms of play are solitary endeavors, most involve interactions with other people. People play with objects and ideas, but they also play with one another. Groups and organizations sponsor play activities and benefit from them. And facts of social differentiation such as ethnicity, class, gender, and age influence who is allowed to do what in those settings. In that context, the chapter discusses play as a "social construction of reality." Sub-themes include play's role in facilitating social identities, play's status as a distinctive pattern of social relationship, and opposing views of play's significance for groups and organizations

Chapter 8 is titled "Cultural Play." In order to make possible their interactions with one another, humans develop great complexes of publicly circulated ideas and artifacts. Those symbolic and material creations are more than tools; they are contexts that people rely on to assess their standings as persons and as members of societies. The chapter explores what it means to play culturally, how play events may be read as texts, and how these events are connected to the wider society. Three models of the play-culture relationship are presented.

The ninth and final chapter offers a synthesis of the preceding chapters. It is called "The Play of Possibility." If there is an overarching contribution of play to human affairs, it is to facilitate people's comprehending their own character and capacities in their life-worlds. In that light, the chapter extends the theory of play as self-realization, presented in Chapter 4. Huizinga's challenge to evaluate the role of play in the contemporary era is revisited. Some problematic qualities of play are analyzed; so also are the connections between play and freedom. Such discussions are intended to help contemporary players see more clearly the respective strengths and weaknesses of their undertakings and to encourage the development of play's more beneficent forms.

1   *Variations on a Theme*

Works written about play not infrequently begin with the observation that the topic at hand is extremely variable, elusive, and otherwise difficult to study. Sometimes this difficulty is expressed directly in the titles of those works. Play is said to be "ambiguous" (Sutton-Smith 1997) or even "paradoxical" (Gruneau 1980; Loy 1982; Handelman 1992; Kline 1995). Such claims are based on the view that play exhibits opposing qualities or themes and, indeed, that it revels in such contradiction and irregularity. As Joseph Levy (1978, p. 1) introduced his summary of play scholarship: "To play means to accept the paradox of what is at once essential and inconsequential."

Other paradoxes have been cited. For Huizinga (1955, pp. 5–6) play is marked by its curious combination of the serious and the nonserious. For Gregory Bateson (1972), players carefully establish boundaries between pretense and reality; then they confound that distinction by making their pretenses real. Many have emphasized the way in which play demands, at the same time, adherence to rules and spirited improvisation (Caillois 2001b; Huizinga 1955). In play, order and disorder commingle, becoming both antagonists and allies (Henricks 2009). For such reasons, Brian Sutton-Smith and Diana Kelly-Byrne (1984b, p. 30) argue that play exhibits a fundamental bipolarity. Simultaneously, it "equilibrates" and "disequilibrates." And these acts of constructing, testing, modifying, and destroying are not confined to any one field of behavior or sector of society. Indeed, anything that humans do, or so it seems, can suddenly be dissimulated and reconstituted by play.

As noted in the introduction, compendia of play theory acknowledge this multiplicity of contexts, manifestations, and meanings. And play journals continue to publish streams of articles based on their authors' distinctive assumptions about play's qualities and implications. What readers encounter in those journals may be described as diverse images and issues (Kuschner 2009) or as a polyphony of research, theories, and issues (Cohen and Waite-Stupiansky 2012). Finally, play advocates—from educators exploring active, creative styles of learning to proponents of vigorous outdoor activity to organizers of formal sports leagues to manu-facturers of toys and games—push forward their own visions of players' rightful behaviors, sometimes without acknowledging how those visions differ from or contradict one another.

There is much value in recognizing the spectrum of play's manifesta-tions and meanings. By accommodating itself to this variety the academic study of play is thickened and made vigorous. Moreover, this strategy conforms to an emerging tradition in the academy, which is to acknowl-edge a multiplicity of perspectives and to show how those perspectives can be traced to various social, cultural, and psychological contexts. In that regard, play scholars and advocates offer accounts of play that cor-respond to their distinctive circumstances and interests.

Arguably, this diversity of viewpoint should be taken as a challenge to play scholars to explain why the different play theories, somewhat like Tolstoy's unhappy families, have developed each in their own way. However useful that project may be, my interest is less to comment on these different perspectives as self-supporting explanations, ideologies, or narratives (see Sutton-Smith 1997) than it is to discover what it is that transcends those different visions. That concern—in effect, to isolate and evaluate the qualities that make play different from similar activities— motivates the current undertaking. This uniformity, I stress, cannot be imposed. It must respond coherently to the disparate viewpoints that constitute the play studies community.

This chapter begins that process of creating a general account of play. With that end in mind, I offer first some examples of behavior that most people might consider play or, failing that, "almost play." Next comes a detailing of some different ways of thinking about this subject. That discussion leads to a number of definitions offered by contempo-rary scholars. This is followed by a discussion of Sutton-Smith's seven play rhetorics, essentially different explanatory schemes of play scholars. Most generally, the chapter's aim is to display some of the many ways of looking at this subject.

Examples of Play's Variation

Reflect momentarily on a few behaviors that most people would consider play or, at least, playlike. Start with a group of children cavorting at a swimming pool. They are laughing and shouting as they splash water in one another's faces and dunk unsuspecting comrades. Surely, this is play epitomized. One of the bigger children starts to dunk others repeatedly, however, and splashes water in their faces after they've asked him to stop. Our bully is clearly enjoying himself. Is this play?

Take another example. An artist is absorbed intensely in a painting she is making in her studio. Although the planning and execution of the painting have been difficult, she now finds that the project is going well indeed. She feels herself connected entirely to the canvas; each brush stroke seems effortless and true. This hard-won enjoyment could called play. Suddenly, her mind turns to a forthcoming show where she must display her work. She realizes that the event is only a few days away and the painting in front of her is far from finished. Her brow furrows. Is she still at play?

Consider another. An insult comedian is plying his trade in a crowded lounge. He picks his targets judiciously, makes his jibes, and pauses as the audience howls. Comedy is his profession and he plans on making many of the same jokes the following night. Is he playing with his audience? Are they playing when they laugh? Should we describe the person being ridiculed as playing or at least as being "in play"?

Shift the scene to an amusement park. Two friends are getting on a ride, perhaps a Ferris wheel. One of them is clearly pleased with the affair. As the ride moves to its highest point, she jiggles about in her seat, rocks the car, and shouts across the fairgrounds. Her companion, who does not care for heights, is in misery. Are both playing?

Still another case is the energetic teacher who wishes to incorporate active learning into her class and help her students have fun at the same time. She designs a role-playing exercise (perhaps the students are to be characters from a story they have read). She has her pupils select their roles, asks them to revisit the descriptions presented in the book, and establishes a problem that the characters must confront and solve. Then she encourages their interaction. Is all, or any of this, play?

Finally, think about the determined gambler, immersed in his favorite pastime at a casino. He makes his wager, speaks or performs some bodily movement to indicate his readiness for the next stage of the event, and pauses to see his fate revealed. Perhaps the cards, wheel, or dice will fall his way; perhaps they won't. Anxiously he waits. But is he playing?

As the reader will have gathered, such cases can be proliferated end-lessly. Are the sponsors of dog or cock fighting players? What about a group of friends watching their favorite sports team compete on tele-vision? Are they playing as they cheer and groan, or is it only the be-havior of the official performers that should be described in this way? Is taking a bubble bath on a lazy afternoon an act of play? Should yoga or some other meditative practice be described with this term? What about exercising on a treadmill? How about two politicians who are debating one another in a legislative chamber or, somewhat differently, two student debaters representing their colleges? Should any poten-tially pleasurable activity—associated perhaps with eating, drinking, sex, sport, music, literature, art, or even resting—be declared a species of play?

This list of ordinary behaviors has been presented to make clear two points that serve as counter-themes for this book. First, there is substan-tial variety in the activities that people call play. Play objects can include all manner of psychological, bodily, environmental, social, and cultural elements. The settings of play activities—and the roles of other people in those settings—may also vary dramatically. And players are able to draw different meanings from their play—and connect it to other activities in their lives—in ways that confound easy analysis. Although some forms of play are stationed firmly in the world, other playful moments are of the most subtle, fleeting character. Understanding play means coming to terms with this variety.

Second, this diversity of expression and interpretation should be seen as the empirical basis for discovering what is common to all forms of play. That attempt at synthesis is not, however, simply a taxonomic exercise. Instead, I want to show how play, understood in terms of these common traits, is important to the ways people live, both as individuals and as members of their societies. To understand the benefits and the limitations of play is to think about the dimensions of human possibil-ity and the role of every person in the determination of those prospects.

Ways of Thinking About Play

Anyone studying play must confront the question: what kind of occur-rence, pattern, or thing is play? In that regard, examining play is no dif-ferent than examining other forms of behavior, all of which can be looked at in many ways. The following section presents six different lenses for studying play and discusses some limitations of each.

PLAY AS ACTION

Perhaps the most common way to think about play is to see it as a distinctive pattern of behavior (see Rubin, Fein, and Vandenberg 1983). Typically, players express or enact their visions with movements that are visible to others. This is the approach of Jean Piaget (1962), who describes play as a kind of psychic imposition. Players try out preconceived strategies of thought and behavior, or schemas, on their surroundings. Play is said to occur when those acts of self-direction and control are done for the purpose of psychic pleasure, a condition he calls "assimilation."

Designating any occurrence as a behavior—or more narrowly, as a certain type of behavior—is not an uncomplicated affair, however. Consider some examples of what people do. Is tripping and falling down stairs behavior? What about belching accidentally? Are we behaving when we dream or, more expressively, when we toss and turn in our sleep? What if we get up and start to sleepwalk? Full-scale bodily movements are one thing. There are also the micro-adjustments of our bodies—fidgeting, twitching, wringing our hands, or making involuntary facial expressions.

Clearly, humans operate at many levels and employ different combinations of faculties at every moment. Some of our movements feature high levels of conscious control; others are involuntary. Most behavior occurs as a coordination of responses that vary in these ways. Play is an example of this coordination. It cannot be denied that some of the fun of play comes from finding ourselves moving forward with capabilities we did not know we possess or from the sudden reactions we produce to unanticipated circumstances. But just as certainly another source of pleasure is our ability to plan what we do, to reflect on the effectiveness of those strategies, and attempt something different in the next instant.

The tension between these two themes was emphasized by the philosopher Karl Groos (1898). In his view, play is the acting out of deep-seated, even instinctual forces. But play also reflects the efforts of creatures to control and refine these impulses and bring them to new levels of sophistication. For Groos, some of the joy of play comes from the "satisfaction of instinct" and from the pleasures inherent to "energetic action" (p. 298). Play also provides "joy in ability or power," however, especially when this results in success or victory over others (p. 290).

Although involuntary reactions and movements are important elements of play, they are central to all behavior. A book such as this one, which aspires to offer an integrative conception of play, must show how playful behaviors differ from the other things that people do. One approach to this problem is to conceptualize play as a distinctive pattern of *consciously guided* behavior, or "action."

However diverse theories of play may be, none of them presents play as a moment of lethargy, rest, or quiescence. Instead, play is said to be a pattern of involvement with the world. Players do not sit and regard passively what is occurring around them. Instead, they shift into modes of heightened attention. Players scrutinize; they fiddle and fidget. They lean forward, get up, and move. Heretofore stationary objects are picked up and turned into tools; others become barriers to action. Players itch to see what can be done with the world, or more to the point, to see what *they* can do with it. Even imaginary play, one subject of this book, features heightened mental activity, a restless sorting and arranging of life's possibilities. To repeat, players are not watchers; they are doers.

Players may be energized and stirred to action, but how should we describe the movements that follow? Sometimes we are able to decide that people or animals are playing even when we see their actions at a distance. We see them romping and cavorting, or, as one scholar (Miller 1973) describes it, "galumphing." That is, their behavior seems to have a bouncy, spirited quality. Moreover, it appears to be self-directed. Players control the pattern and pace of their own action, and even start and stop it, at will.

Although the player we are watching—let us say she is playing tennis—seems to be in control of what she's doing, her behavior is not entirely regimented or methodical. Instead, a quality of irregularity or even spontaneity prevails, so that the observer cannot anticipate precisely what she will do next. Still, the scene is not one of complete irregularity, as would be the case if she were frantically waving her arms to ward off an (unseen to us) swarm of bees. Instead, improbable occurrences seem to be mixed with or even flow out of the limited range of movements we see before us. Oddly—and this is what intrigues us as viewers—there is a curious tension between the predictable and the unpredictable. Our player seems to be trying to do something that she can almost, but not quite, do, or at least not do as well as she would like. Indeed, it appears that the player is willfully seeking a tipping point between being in and out of control. Once again, Huizinga's (1995, p. 10) comments are instructive, for he tells us that play is characterized by "tension, poise, balance, contrast, variation, and resolution."

This view of play as something individuals do is appealing to societies dominated by individualistic mythologies. Psychologists, as well as educators and recreation scholars who are interested in the personal development of their charges, tend to see play as a process of individual assertion, evaluation, and resolution. Creatures at play are directed by their own self-regulating frameworks. The purpose of play is to continually construct, support, and revise those frameworks. Some important statements of this viewpoint are discussed in Chapter 4.

PLAY AS INTERACTION

Who can deny the appeal of the viewpoint just presented? Surely, individual creatures direct their own behavior. They decide (by more or less conscious processes) to follow one line of action rather than another. They stop their behavior by withdrawing the physical and emotional energy they have committed to it. They start again by restoring those commitments. Arguably, play is one of the distinctive behavior patterns that creatures sponsor and sustain.

Yet there is something unsatisfying about this account. Play is not merely a process of moving oneself through the world; it is a pattern of *engagement* with that world. To be sure, players act. But they also react. They jump forward, but they also jump out of the way. When we play, we assume a distinctive stance toward the world's patterns and processes. We move forward and watch as the world responds to our movements. The world moves in its own ways and we respond in turn.

A different way of saying this is that players always play *at* or *with* something or someone. We learn about ourselves—that is, about our own qualities and character—by considering our ever-changing standings with regard to the world's objects, innumerable elements that include other people like ourselves. We discover those qualities by finding out what we can do to those others. So we test and tease the world in the spirit of players. We also learn about our own abilities to take what the world offers, that is, to resist or, more characteristically, to respond assertively to what is happening to us. To that degree, play is less an exercise or rehearsal of schemas (Piaget's view) than it is an attempt to discover resistance or difficulty.

Any self-knowledge arising from play arguably is attributable to this back-and-forth activity. We play to judge our own powers against the schemes of otherness. Those struggles lead us to new self-estimations. Those same movements necessarily produce new understandings of the world's forms and forces. That quality of confrontation, contradiction, isolation, realignment, and difference is central to some contemporary accounts of play presented in Chapter 8. Play is to be understood dialectically (Sutton-Smith 1978) or dialogically (Bakhtin 1981).

It may be useful here to recall a famous Buddhist quandary. Whatever other responses may be made to that ancient question, play is emphatically not "the sound of one hand clapping." It is a distinctive pattern of interchange. Remember the example of the tennis player described above. If we watch her actions with a broader lens, we see that she is not only acting, she is reacting—certainly to the ball that is moving toward her but also (and somewhat less directly) to the actions of her opponent across the net. In other words, creatures at play do not simply *express* themselves; they *communicate*. Any claim that players are constructive (or, by contrast, destructive) is based on the premise that they are responding to and often reassembling well-established (and quite real) elements of the world.

As might be anticipated, then, this view of play as interaction is central to thinking in the more truly social (rather than behavioral) sciences such as sociology and social anthropology or in the branches of education, recreation, and social psychology that emphasize the development of relationships, families, and communities (see Vygotsky 1976). Such approaches focus less on what solitary persons do than on what people produce collectively when they gather to play.

PLAY AS ACTIVITY

Return again to the tennis player. To this point, we have focused on her actions (in isolation) and on the to-and-fro exchanges of the game. But what she and her opponent are doing can also be seen with a view that incorporates even broader ideas of time and space. If we watch their behavior for a while, we see that they are not only competing but also cooperating. For example, they seem to take turns serving. They agree on a score. They chat amiably between points; they change sides after a certain number of games. In other words, the little moments we've focused on are part of some wider scenario that both players understand and that helps them begin their activity, move it through its various phases, and then end it in a mutually accepted way.

In this third viewpoint, play is a form *of* and *for* human conduct. That wider sense of eventfulness, or what I'm calling "activity," is something that exists as a publicly comprehensible description of what people individually and collectively do. When children are told, "Go out and play," they have a general understanding of what their parents or teachers expect of them. They know that they should participate in a range of loosely related pursuits, from moseying about and exploring to more active forms of interpersonal challenge and creation. It is not anticipated that they should fall asleep or simply relax under a tree. Instead they should expend energy. More prescriptively, they are expected to play only with familiar others of approximately the same age and social status. Some activities are understood to be forbidden—sexual explorations, vandalism, drug use, hurting other children or animals—however amusing these pursuits may be. Players also know that they should not stray too far from their neighborhood or be too difficult to locate when the authorities call them back.

In other words, to see play as activity is to comprehend it as a broadly developed scenario that includes shared understandings of playmates, locale, duration, behaviors, consequences, and even pertinent emotions. Furthermore, having some sense of what play is (in the rough way defined above) helps participants clarify that other activities are not play. And it helps us recognize when others are not playing in the proper way, that is, when they are refusing to go along with the necessary forms of pretense by cheating, being a spoilsport, or otherwise failing to perform their part as they should.

Of course, most forms of play are more sharply defined than those resulting from the general instruction "Go out and play." Children know that ice skating is different from roller skating and quite different from fishing, snowboarding, playing video games, or dancing. Each of these activities tends to be situated in its own scenario, one that is much more specific than the loosely defined playing spaces, equipment, skill sets, behaviors, companions, and so forth discussed above. Note that, as my examples indicate, many play activities are named. These publicly recognized designations help participants and bystanders organize their behaviors as they go through the event. Simply because those understandings *antedate the moment of play*, they help people anticipate what they are going to do when they agree to conduct an activity of this type. In much the same fashion, these scenarios allow people to reflect on what they've done (after the event is over) and then communicate their experiences to others. Once we've been told that our friends went backpacking or skiing or skydiving, we can much more easily participate in a conversation with them about their adventures. To summarize, designations of activity tie together the past, present, and future tenses of behavior.

As the tennis example reveals, this process of cultural designation is especially apparent in games. Such forms, in effect frameworks that transmute behaviors into carefully regulated contests, may themselves be *institutionalized* in societies. That is, those (named) forms become widely established and accepted, so that one can anticipate that other people will know the rules of the game, possess some of its skills and equipment, and even have shared ideas about the proper placement of the event in society's routines. Games also, as Roger Caillois (2001b, pp. 27–36) argues, draw out the affair and complicate its levels of challenge. When people play games (what he calls "ludus") they enter culturally articulated forms. Spontaneous, whimsical play (what he calls "paidia") becomes subordinated to these constraints. Far from apologizing for this quality of restriction, Caillois (p. 33) emphasizes that the "general function [of ludus] is to give the fundamental categories of play their purity and excellence."

One additional theme should be noted. When people participate in identified activities or events, it is presumed that at least most of the actions and interactions going on in that setting may be thought of as examples of that activity. Thus, going to a dance is considered to be an entry into a playful event, though some of the moments of that event—such as sitting out while others are having fun, having someone "cut in" on you, or spilling a drink down the front of your outfit—may not be enjoyable. In much the same fashion, the tennis player suffers through periods of disappointment, fatigue, boredom, and injury. All this is a consequence of playing the game.

Just as the first view of play (as individual action) is congruent with psychological and biological perspectives and the second (as interaction) is pertinent to social studies, so this last vision implies a cultural perspective. In that regard, the disciplines of anthropology, folklore, literature, and the more structural forms of sociology are pertinent. Human behaviors and inter-behaviors exist as manifestations of named, publicly established systems of meaning.

PLAY AS DISPOSITION

The three accounts presented to this point are unsatisfying. To see play only as a pattern of behaving or doing is to disregard internal or subjective qualities that make the activity enjoyable and that give events of this type their color and dynamism. To some extent play becomes play only when the participants declare it to be so. That spirit or zest may be the most identifiable cause of the event. More certainly, it guides and sustains the behaviors that follow.

A fourth way to think about play, then, is as a "disposition," some pattern of attentiveness, readiness, or psychological commitment that orients behavior (Rubin, Fein, and Vandenberg 1983). Considered from this perspective, play behaviors feature motivations different from those associated with the other things we do. Commonly, people start to play because they have a vision of what will happen in the moments ahead. To recall the example of the artist from the preceding section, she may be playing instead of working if she embraces her activity in a certain way. Our tennis player looks forward to a "good game."

As noted above, players frequently display a distinctive quality of curiosity and enthusiasm that is exhibited in their facial expressions and in the bounciness of their movements. That bright-eyed, engaged quality may precede their playing and, indeed, may energize the ideas that the participants accept to guide their behavior. That zest for playing may continue during the event and perhaps keeps the player engaged when others have grown tired or quit. This disposition may persist after the player has finished her activity. Not satisfied with her newfound quiescence, our player wants to try it again. A classic explanation of play, the "surplus energy" theory (discussed in Chapter 5), formalizes this view. Creatures play when they are high-spirited or have energy to burn.

This eagerness to play is also exhibited by animals, as when our pets make clear that they want to play with us or with one another. In an account that has influenced many scholars, Gregory Bateson (1972) explains how monkeys indicate to one another that they wish to move from one pattern of behavior to another. Real fighting for monkeys—or for humans—is dangerous. Play fighting, by contrast, achieves some of the objectives of real fighting, such as indicating strength or dominance, without exposing the participants to such dangers. So monkeys who wish to play engage in specific gestures and use "play faces" to communicate that what follows is not to be taken seriously, or at least is not to be pursued with the relentless ferocity of real fighting.

Another student of animal behavior, Marc Bekoff (1995), has shown how dogs engage in what in he calls "play bows," a stereotyped lowering of the shoulders and head to indicate to their playmate that they will not push matters to their most extreme conclusions. Indeed, participants willingly take turns at dominance and submission, at chasing and being chased. Small strips of behavior are started and stopped, started and stopped again. Such introductory procedures are sometimes described as "meta-communication" or "framing," signals that forthcoming behaviors are to be understood in a certain way. Humans commencing the play-battles of organized sports—think about boxing, wrestling, or football matches—also may meet at the center of the field of play to acknowledge each other in this way. Although we cannot know the feelings of animals, it does seem that in both humans and animals the chain of behavior is much the same. Creatures signify to one another that they wish to engage in a certain pattern of behavior and that they will recognize one another as worthy comrades in that endeavor. Behavior arises from mutual consent.

In psychology, perhaps the best-known discussion of play disposi-tions is that of Nina Leiberman (1977). Lieberman studied what she called "playfulness" or the "play element in play." Some children seem to pos-sess levels of curiosity, energy, enthusiasm, and wit that impel them to engage with otherness—that is, with other persons and objects—in creative, spontaneous ways. This "cognitive style" encourages them to see many situations as play opportunities when others might see those same settings as occasions for drudgery or routine. Even those of us who are not blessed with such effervescent confidence can acknowledge that there are times when we feel playful.

Others have referred to this desire for engagement as "optimism" (Sutton-Smith 1999) or "curiosity" (Henricks 2012). One of the best de-scriptions of such readiness is presented by Scott Eberle (2014), who em-phasizes that although the appetite for play may be the initial impetus for the event, that appetite is whetted or re-vivified by the spiraling pro-cess of playful involvement. Thus, play begins with feelings of "antici-pation." As the event continues, those anticipatory feelings deepen to include "interest," "openness," "readiness," "expectation," "curiosity," and "desire" (p. 221). All draw the player forward.

Such points having been made, note that only sometimes does this readiness for action lead to actual behavior. Impish pupils may be told to sit down and be quiet by their teachers; young children may find that their older siblings are too busy to play with them; monkeys and dogs may be rebuffed by their fellows. And to take the opposite case, some-times participants must be lured into the playground or even forced to play (like a teenager dragged onto the dance floor). Only later do they become energized and discover that they are having fun. In other words, psychological commitment (that is, playfulness) is not enough for play to happen. Other elements must also be present.

PLAY AS EXPERIENCE

A fifth way of looking at play is to see it as a distinctive quality of ex-perience. If the previous section focuses on players' preparations for ac-tion, this section describes the patterns of awareness and satisfaction that people have while they are playing. Of course, disposition and ex-perience are related matters. That is, if I am playing a game and having an enjoyable time, I will probably want to keep playing. That commit-ment Stuart Brown (2009, p. 18) describes as "continuation desire." In that sense, the experience is both a reward for what is occurring now (psychic satisfaction of some sort) as well as a motivation fueled by an-ticipated satisfaction to come.

Huizinga, who disavowed external or functional explanations of play, identifies experience as central to that activity. He (1955, p. 2) asks: "Why does the baby crow with pleasure? Why does the gambler lose himself in his passion? Why is a huge crowd roused to frenzy by a football match?" He answers his own question: "[I]n this intensity, this absorption, this power of maddening, lies the very essence, the primordial quality of play." That "fun of playing," he continues, "resists all analysis." Indeed, people play to reject the claims of the extrinsic and the instrumental and to luxuriate in the happenings of the moment.

Perhaps the best-known contemporary account of the satisfactions of play is offered by Mihaly Csikszentmihalyi. A leading proponent of "positive psychology," Csikszentmihalyi (1991, 2000) studies people's subjective involvement in a wide range of activities, including rock climbing, games of chess, and art making. He is interested especially in a quality of experience he calls "flow," a level of deep involvement where the player is committed entirely to the situation at hand. At such times, participants are able to focus on the task before them without being distracted by external matters. Indeed, they become so deeply entranced that they "merge action and awareness" (1991, p. 53). People in flow lose feelings of self-consciousness and abandon interest in what their actions may bring in times to come. Instead, they are embedded in the event with a level of concentration that carries them forward. This view of play as a deep, almost mystical involvement is also developed by the poet and essayist Diane Ackerman (1999).

Csikszentmihalyi (1991, pp. 48–67) connects flow to enjoyment, which he contrasts with pleasure. Pleasure, in his view, is a closing rather than an opening of experience (p. 45). Pleasure occurs when expectations created by biological or social conditions have been met; it is a moment of release or restoration. Enjoyment, on the other hand, is a much more complicated experience that requires an investment of insight and energy by the player. Enjoyment commonly features tension, difficulty, and surprise; feelings of accomplishment may be delayed until the event is completed. It addresses challenges and requires skills and concentration. Pleasure tends to be passive and selfish in character. Enjoyment expresses active, open engagement with the world.

Deep involvement of this sort (a middle ground, in Csikszentmihalyi's view, between "boredom" and "anxiety") is an often happy state of affairs. This quality of experience is found in other activities besides play, however. For example, people can be engaged without reservation in love, work, or ritual. Indeed, one of Csikszentmihalyi's (2000, pp. 123–39) principal case studies of flow is surgery, a practice few would see as play.

Furthermore, rapt attention is not always a theme of play. Sometimes players exhibit a distanced, critical perspective on their own activity. They may smile, laugh, or shout as they address the challenges before them. But they are also capable of smiling, laughing, and shouting *at themselves* in the act of playing. Similarly, they can reflect on what is going on outside the play setting. That is to say, they may smile at the thought that they are playing while others are working, that their playmate with the skinned knee may have some explaining to do when she gets home, that the day is still early, and so forth. That sense of difference or exclusion may constitute a major portion of the fun.

Perhaps the greatest of the play theorists to take the latter point of view is the sociologist Georg Simmel (1950, 1971). In Simmel's view, people are always in and out of situations, near and far, at the same time. Further, most of us believe that we have enduring traits of character and disposition that we bring to each moment of our lives. Moreover, we recognize ongoing connections to such established social formations as families, friendship groups, jobs, and societies and to the idea systems that govern those groups. Frequently our standings with regard to such forms become important parts of what we consider to be our stable *identities.* That is to say, we understand ourselves as exhibiting a continuity of character and purpose; we perceive ourselves to be much the same person as we move from one moment to the next. And we draw on some of those resources as we play.

When we play, then—or, indeed, participate in any momentary situation—we experience an intersection between the perceived necessities of the event at hand (Csikszentmihalyi's emphasis) and the claims of external identities and relationships (Simmel's emphasis). Seen from that expanded perspective, play can be described as engagement with many different relationships at the same time. Much of the satisfaction of play comes from seeing how those different levels of commitment mesh. Erving Goffman, a sociologist who extends Simmel's views, says this in a different way. As he puts it, "[W]hile it is as players that we can win, it is only as participants that we can get fun out of this winning" (1961, p. 37). In other words, play is not merely the activity of moving pieces—or ourselves—around a board. It involves a distinctive pattern of engagement between two versions of the self: the player and the person.

Taken together, the two perspectives suggest the complexity of subjective involvement in what we are doing. Some forms of play feature childlike entrancement; others feature a ransacking of psychological, social, and cultural themes that are brought in and out of the scene. Even the kinds and levels of enjoyment players experience are variable. Sometimes satisfaction is fairly undiluted (as when a thrower successfully skips a flat stone across a lake and smiles at the result). More frequently (as in sports and games) satisfaction comes and goes or is otherwise problematic. Indeed, who of us always skips a stone successfully? For such reasons, it is difficult to define play only as a distinctive quality of experience. It cannot be denied that fun, enjoyment, or other positive feelings are essential parts of the play equation, but there are many ways of being satisfied and other activities that promote related feelings.

PLAY AS CONTEXT

A sixth approach to play is to conceive of it as a set of conditions or arrangements that encourage behavior of this sort. In the view of Rubin, Fein, and Vandenberg (1983), play is facilitated by such circumstances as minimal adult intervention, free choice, familiarity with people and objects, and an absence of stress. This perspective can be extended to include many kinds of supporting conditions.

For example, play can be seen as a response to various forms of physical capability or readiness, that is, something that occurs when energy levels, urges to satisfy bodily needs, and other changes in neurophysiology are occurring. Those physiological themes will be explored in Chapter 5. Alternatively, play—or at least certain kinds of it—may be encouraged when the physical environment is of a certain character. Most of us do not play if the temperature is too hot or too cold, if it is too windy or rainy outside, if the spaces we are in are too confining, if the terrain is too steep, and so forth. Nor do we play easily if there are no objects present that we can climb, handle, and move. In other words, we seem to operate best when external challenges match our skill levels or, to return to Csikszentmihalyi's terminology, when we successfully avoid the extremes of boredom and anxiety. These environmental factors are analyzed in Chapter 6.

We have already looked at the issue of whether play happens when participants have a certain psychological readiness or disposition. This theme is developed in Chapter 4. Different again are cultural supports, the focus of Chapter 8. Do we play more easily if there are ready-made models for our pursuit, if our society values activity of this sort, if play is linked in strategic ways to other spheres (as a cultivation of "useful" skills, understandings, values, and norms)? Nor should we disregard cultural artifacts. Surely, a game of baseball proceeds more smoothly if we have a bat and ball, mitts, bases, a suitable field, foul lines, and the like.

Finally, play is supported by social conditions. As Rubin, Fein, and Vandenburg emphasize, we play more easily when there are others who reaffirm our behaviors by watching and applauding, by helping us develop pertinent skills, by challenging us to compete with them, or simply by joining with us in shared ventures. Such are themes are explored at several points in the book and especially in Chapter 7.

Although these matters are foci of chapters to come, it is difficult to argue that supporting conditions or "contexts," in and of themselves, are equivalent to play. Supporting contexts make play easier or, in extreme cases, possible. They are the patterns *within* which and sometimes *with* which we play; they shape the forms in which play emerges. But play itself is usually thought to be something that creatures do. It is not the settings in which they do it, the objects they use to express their impulses, or the "opportunity systems" that grant them permission to carry on in this way.

As the reader will have noted, each perspective has been criticized. One should not conclude, however, that those approaches, or any one of them, is an inappropriate way of thinking about play. No perspective by itself is sufficient, but each adds an important dimension to the understanding of this phenomenon. Play is minded behavior; it features challenge-based interaction; it extends itself as a coherent activity. Play also depends on a willingness to engage, on a stream of pleasant experiences that sustain the affair, and on a stimulating environment. Without these elements, would-be players find themselves with nothing to do.

Theorists' Conceptions of Play

Six ways of looking at play—as disposition, experience, context, action, interaction, and activity—have been discussed. Yet those same perspectives can be applied to any behavior that humans produce. Hence, the question remains: what characteristics of play make it different from the other things we do?

Although some theorists push forward singular ideas of play's nature and implications, several of which I discuss in this book, most contemporary commentators accommodate their visions to what others have said and, on that basis, position themselves within the wider community of researchers. Furthermore, most of these theorists are inclined less to offer a strict definition of their subject than they are to provide a list of essential qualities, characteristics, or traits. My own response to this question of play's key characteristics is presented in Chapter 2. For now, I give some of the different lists and suggest some commonalities among them.

Because Huizinga figures so prominently in this work, it is appropriate to begin with his description of play. As he sees it, play

> is a free activity standing quite consciously outside "ordinary" life as being "not serious," but at the same time absorbing the player intensely and utterly. It is activity connected with no material interest, and no profit can be gained by it. It proceeds within its own proper boundaries of time and space according to fixed rules and in an orderly manner. It guides the formation of social groupings which tend to surround themselves with secrecy and to stress their difference from the common world by disguise or other means. (1955, p. 13)

In other words, play features (1) voluntarism, (2) separation from material consequence, (3) seclusion and limitation, (4) creative tension between order and disorder, and (5) fascination with secrecy. As we've seen, Huizinga was committed to the idea that people should be allowed to step away from the obligations and material consequences common to the more regimented portions of their lives so that they can freely address the themes of their societies. Huizinga's players like to seclude themselves from others. Once separated, they engage in spirited wrangling.

Caillois (2001b, pp. 9–10) describes play as having six characteristics. Play is free, separate, uncertain, unproductive, governed by rules, and marked by make-believe. In the discussion that precedes this listing, he criticizes Huizinga for emphasizing the idea of secrecy. On the contrary, Caillois (p. 4) argues, play works to "the detriment of the secret and mysterious" to the extent that it "exposes, publishes, and somehow expends." He also believes that Huizinga erred by discounting the role of "material consequence" in play. For Caillois (p. 5), games of chance are key examples of play. He is also drawn to the idea that play is unproductive in the sense that no goods are produced. That the activity "creates no wealth or goods" is what distinguishes play "from work or art." Finally, he stresses the theme of make-believe. Play, or rather some forms of it, is hypothetical or fictive. Some forms, however, such as "chess, prisoner's base, polo, and baccarat are played *for real. As if* is not necessary" (italics in original). And only some forms of play are rule-bound.

Although these contradictions mar his definition, they support his view that there are different forms of play. Indeed, his book develops the thesis that it takes four fundamental, irreducible forms: *agon* (contest), *alea* (chance), *ilinx* (vertigo), and mimicry (imaginative role performance). Caillois's theory is further discussed in Chapter 9.

Most contemporary play scholars continue this process of defining play by aggregating its traits. For example, on the basis of her review of play research, Doris Fromberg (1992, p. 43) claims that play is symbolic, meaningful, active, pleasurable, voluntary, rule-governed, and episodic. In contrast to Huizinga and Caillois, Fromberg adds some themes: pleasure, meaningfulness, and symbolism. Added as well is an idea of how play proceeds. Play behaviors are "episodic." Strips of behavior are started and stopped, started and stopped.

Drawing inspiration from earlier accounts (Garvey 1977; Rubin, Fein, and Vandenberg 1983), James Johnson, James Christie, and Thomas Yawkey (1999, pp. 16–17) identify five traits. These are non-literality, intrinsic motivation, process (as opposed to product) orientation, free choice, and positive affect. Of these, the themes of non-literality and positive affect bear special mention. To treat the occurrences of the world in a non-literal way is to impose one's own imaginative interpretations on them and to claim that this new definition should be honored. By such standards a piece of wood is now a teacup; an empty teacup is claimed to be full. The theme of positive affect entails the idea that although the play event is not always pleasing for participants, there is something about the event that draws people onward. That satisfaction need not be extreme. Indeed, the sense of conquering one's own fears—as accomplished, for example, by going down a steep slide again and again—may be enough.

Elizabeth Wood (2009, p. 167) concludes that play features "intrinsic motivation, engagement, dependence on internal rather than external rules, control and autonomy, and attention to means rather than ends." Such an account puts emphasis on how players manage their own action and experience. Although participants are said to be engaged, that involvement takes a special focus: they concentrate on means rather than ends. In other words, players are preoccupied with processes more than with outputs or end states. Wood thus provides a definition that is more individualized (even psychological) than the social and cultural qualities expressed by Huizinga and Caillois.

Another play scholar, Gwen Gordon (2009, p. 8), provides her list of traits in the following sentence: "Play is the voluntary movement across boundaries, opening with total absorption into a highly flexible field, releasing tension in ways that are pleasurable, exposing players to the unexpected, and making transformation possible." This view, as the reader can see, is an especially dynamic one. Players do not seek to control the environments they enter; instead, they seek a series of pleasant surprises. Each moment should be different from the next.

Attention to the dynamic uncertainty of play is also paramount in the contributions of Scott Eberle (2014), who argues that play has a generally recognized set of characteristics. That is, play is understood to be voluntary, fun, set apart, an end in itself, and marked by rule-making (though this may also include rule-breaking). He is less interested in these structural qualities, however, than he is in the process of play itself and in the emotional and personal rewards that come to those who participate. With that commitment in mind, Eberle describes play as an emergent, spiraling process, much like a vortex, that participants enter and then find themselves being carried forward within. Personal experiences include (initially) "anticipation," which is followed by "surprise," which leads to "pleasure" and then (successively) to "understanding," "strength," and "poise." That end point (poise) is marked by conditions of body and mind such as grace, composure, and balance, which become the basis for new kinds of anticipation. So the activity continues.

To summarize Eberle's approach, play is an entry into many patterns of awareness that combine and deepen as one moves through the event. Play does not narrow but rather opens up possibility. This approach, is influenced by psychologist Robert Plutchik's (2003) noted "color wheel" theory of the emotions, which describes the way feelings shift, blend, and reemerge as qualitatively different experiences.

Stuart Brown resisted defining play for many years, in part because of its great variability and because he felt that it must be experienced to be appreciated. But it was also because for Brown (2009, p. 16), "play is a very primal activity. It is preconscious and preverbal—it arises out of ancient biological structures that existed before our consciousness or our ability to speak." Nevertheless, he defines play as "apparently purposeless" and "voluntary" and as featuring "inherent attraction," "freedom from time," "diminished consciousness of self," "improvisational potential," and "continuation desire." Such themes draw comparison to Csikszentmihalyi's and Ackerman's themes of flow or deep involvement. And they are reminiscent of Eberle's ideas about players' being led into situations by their own curiosity and then being carried forward by the momentum of what is occurring.

Still another account of play is presented by Terry Marks-Tarlow (2010, pp. 38–39), who emphasizes that activity's nonlinear or even "fractal" qualities. She argues that play is "recursive" (repeated time and again), "entraining" (featuring brain waves that become attuned to or resonate with oscillations in the environment), and "self-organizing" (emphasizing "bottom up" or creative activity by the brain as a response to changing conditions). To complete her list, play is "disequilibrious" (that is, in search of novelty and arousal), "attractor-driven" (focused on designated objects), "fractal" (creating microcosms that reproduce themes of more embracing patterns), and "sensitive to and dependent on initial conditions" (illustrating the ways in which responses to particular occurrences lead to often unanticipated chains of consequence). Marks-Tarlow's approach emphasizes how one play moment leads to the next and how playful behaviors emerge as responses to sudden, initiating conditions.

Animal behavior researcher Gordon Burghardt (2005) defines play differently. He argues that play is "1) incompletely functional in the context expressed; 2) voluntary, pleasurable, or self-rewarding; 3) different structurally or temporally from related serious behavior systems; 4) expressed repeatedly during at least some part of an animal's life span; and 5) initiated in relatively benign situations" (p. 382). Burghardt's view of play is discussed further in Chapter 6. For now, it is enough to say that animals—and humans—seem committed to reproducing behaviors that are not directly linked to immediate survival needs. The final theorist I discuss here combines various perspectives.

Sutton-Smith's Synthesis and Play Rhetorics

A fitting conclusion to this section is Sutton-Smith's (1999) attempt to identify a "consilience of play definitions." Sutton-Smith describes play as follows: "Play, as a unique form of adaptive variability, instigates an imagined but equilibrial reality within which disequilibrial exigencies can be paradoxically simulated and give rise to the pleasurable effects of excitement and optimism. The genres of such play are humor, skill, pretence, fantasy, risk, contest, and celebrations, all of which are selective simulations of paradoxical variability" (p. 253). The previously noted theme of paradox is here, as is the creative tension between equilibrium and disequilibrium. Play is adaptive because it expands the variability of behavioral possibilities, and, for that reason, it promotes the survival of both humans and animals. Play is optimistic and life-enhancing. And most conspicuously, it defies the attempts of those who would define it narrowly.

Sutton-Smith (1997) is also the author of what is perhaps the best book-length treatment of play's many qualities and implications. In contrast to theorists who concentrate on the perspectives of one or two academic disciplines, he analyzes contributions from across the natural sciences, social sciences, and humanities. His conclusion is that play theories, for the most part, fall into one of seven explanatory frameworks, or rhetorics. These include the previously mentioned theory that the play of young children (and young animals) can be understood as commitment to *build-ing knowledge and skills* that are (if only potentially) useful in contexts outside the playground. So understood, play both expresses and builds personal character. As noted, this "play as progress" ideology has special appeal within education, psychology, and animal behavior studies.

Quite different is the second rhetoric: play is a confrontation with *fate*. As we've seen, this was a special interest of Caillois, but that general emphasis—that players flirt with powers they cannot control—has been an ongoing interest of historians, classicists, scholars of religion, and anthropologists. People play to remind themselves that they are not alone in the universe, that otherness is deep and abiding. The quality portrayed here—that players are those who dive into thickly configured circumstances—has been resurrected in recent decades by postmodernism (see Hans 1981; Spariosu 1989).

Sutton-Smith's third rhetoric is *power*. This is the theme that Huizinga exploits in his view of play as rivalry, contest, and battle. Players try to impose their wills on one another. Even when they are playing alone they try to conquer environmental or cultural forces. However committed participants may be to ideals of "fair play," play is not, in the final analysis, a moral affair. Success and victory—indeed, the experience of power—is every player's ambition. Issues of strategy or persuasive argument take center stage.

The fourth—and seemingly opposite—rhetoric is *community identity*. People play in order to feel their connections with other people and with the customs that guide those interactions. At least in traditional societies, play is often found within what Huizinga (1955, p. 31) calls the "play-festival-rite" complex. That is, people frequently play in public settings that are highly charged with symbolic meanings. As we struggle to accomplish our playground goals, we learn more important lessons about the centrality of community, about the segments of that community to which we are most strongly attached, and about the critical significance of moral commandments in preserving those social formations. Play is one means to find our place in the social order.

Fifth is what Sutton-Smith calls the rhetoric of *the imaginary*. If play is an exploration of community-based forms and forces, it is perhaps even more an expression of subjectively maintained commitments. Play is an occasion to dream and improvise. Unfettered by customary social constraints, players create works of art, poetry, and literature. They make jokes and puns. They sing crazily in the shower. Always, they listen to themselves, to see what they do well and do poorly. Play of this sort is a process of construction, presentation, destruction, and repair. In our minds, we try out possibilities that other people might disapprove.

Sixth is the rhetoric of *self*. In contrast to the previous theme, which focuses on mental construction, this one emphasizes acts of experiencing. Play, in this viewpoint, is connected to our processes or desiring, attaining, and being satisfied with what we have attained. Play is "fun," "relaxation," "escape" (Sutton-Smith, 1997, p. 11). For his part, the author is critical of any view of play that dwells only on the positive emotions. Fairer, perhaps, is the idea that play affords people the chance to sort through a wide range of emotions, a process that reveals to them how these feelings are connected to experiences of security and danger, success and failure, recognition and disregard.

The last framework is *frivolity*. Much of the above has emphasized the energetic, purposive qualities of players. People play, or so it seems, to figure out where they stand in the world. Sometimes that means constructing things from that world (such as a child's sand castle) that we regard intently and then demolish. But those conscientious, appraising, character-building qualities are not pronounced in all forms of play. Sometimes, play is a form of retrogression or inversion, when participants mock other people's (and their own) pretensions. Players "move ahead" (by developing new skills and understandings) but they also retreat into foolishness and inanity. We enjoy carnivals, festivals, parties, and the like, where we do not have to be our "best" or even our ordinary selves. As anthropologists who study fools and tricksters know (see Radin 1987; Reder and Morra 2010), these silly, disreputable, and sometimes obscene exploits exhibit both personal and sociocultural meanings. They can be understood as privileged holidays that counterbalance more sober routines. Or they can be seen as forms of anti-structure that work through the possibilities of more effective resistance to the dominant patterns.

Sutton-Smith's thesis is that each of these approaches is connected to the cultural and, indeed, sociopolitical agenda of its makers. All of us have visions of what people—individually and collectively—*are* like and *should be* like. We want to honor these preferred visions of society and perhaps bring them into being. In that light, scholars focusing on the role of play in industrialized or "modern" societies have tended to concentrate on three play rhetorics: progress, the self, and the imaginary. All these approaches focus on the power of individuals to create, imagine, and otherwise turn the world to their own purposes. Scholars who embrace themes of older or tradition-based societies emphasize the other four rhetorics: fate, power, community identity, and frivolity. In that view, play is a fascination with the great forces of the world, a willing leap into vast and uncontrollable realms of order and disorder.

A fitting tribute to play's variety and to the restless spirit of players themselves is found in Sutton-Smith's account. Play and players can be many things. No culturally approved setting entirely contains play. Events can be organized in different ways, and different meanings can be applied to what occurs there. Still, and as the theorists' definitions reveal, there seems to be rough agreement about play's nature and implications. That theme is developed in Chapter 2.

2 Play Compared to Other Behaviors

The previous chapter celebrated play's various forms and meanings. This chapter pursues an opposite ambition: to develop a general understanding of play. In what follows, I try to identify play's defining qualities by contrasting play to three similar but rival patterns of willfully directed behavior. Those patterns are work, ritual, and the form of bonding and immersion termed communitas. These four behaviors are said to be distinctive "pathways of experience" (see Henricks 2012) featuring different acts of meaning-construction and self-expression. Each pathway is presented as an ideal type—first play, and then the other forms in comparison to play. Differences between the four forms are summarized and displayed in a chart. The chapter concludes by discussing how real-life events usually feature combinations of these four forms, as well as alternations in which one pattern leads to another.

Distinguishing Qualities of Play

Play is something people choose to do. Behaviors committed involuntarily, by accident, or under conditions of deceit are not play. But the three other forms to be discussed are also occasions when people run out lines of action and otherwise express themselves. In other words, all four patterns are extensions of people's desires, deliberations, and estimations of propriety. And all produce the private registrations of involvement we call experience.

So how is play different? In this section, the ideas presented in the play theorists' definitions are linked to the six perspectives for occurrences—that is, action, interaction, activity, disposition, experience, and context—introduced in Chapter 1. The same process is followed, though much more briefly, for work, ritual, and communitas.

PLAY AS ACTION

In my view, play as action is characterized by two key qualities: *transformation* and *consummation*. Play is not alone in its possession of these traits, but it is made different by the way these traits combine.

Transformation refers to the way in which personal understandings are linked to behavior. When people play, they try to impose their will on external circumstances. Again, this theme is central for Piaget (1962, pp. 87–212), who emphasizes that players render otherness according to their own orientations, strategies, or schemas. They do this in order to test, expand, and ultimately solidify their own powers. Although one effect of this assertive style is to change the world in some very modest way (for example, building a sand castle or marking a wall with graffiti), its primary consequence is to strengthen players' interpretive or behavioral frameworks. For such reasons, play is described as manipulative or *transformative* (see Schwartzman 1978; Henricks 2006; Wood 2009; Gordon 2009).

Work also changes the world by turning it to the actor's purposes. Play is different in that its participants focus primarily on products and actions in the moments of their making. The term *consummation* is employed here to denote that sense of commitment to happenings in the present. To repeat some of the theorists' comments, play is process-oriented (Johnson, Christie, and Yawkey); it gives attention to means rather than ends (Wood). Because play frequently invokes people's abilities to respond to fast-changing situations, it is often emotionally charged or expressive. As noted above, we can often tell that people and animals are at play by the vibrancy of their gestures, their facial expressions, and the distinctive noises they produce. Generating these emotions—as integrations of thought, feeling, and action—is play's ambition.

Similarly, consummation emphasizes processes of ingestion. We have seen that ideas of non-instrumental expenditure, waste, and even immolation are central for Caillois, who was influenced strongly by the surrealist Georges Bataille (see Hollier 1988). This theme is also critical for radical Freudians and postmodernists (see N. Brown 1966; Spariosu 1989). Another way of describing this is to say that players are "intrinsically motivated" (Gordon 2009, p 8). Even though the action is attractor-driven (Marks-Tarlow), those objects and end states have little currency outside the sphere of play. Viewed from an external perspective, play is apparently purposeless (S. Brown).

Feelings of consummation are commonly encouraged by self-imposed boundaries for the event and by designated limits for behavior. Objects and actions have specialized meanings in this framework. For such reasons, play is said to feature seclusion, limitation, and secrecy (Huizinga 1955) as well as commitment to make-believe (Caillois). It expresses freedom from time (S. Brown) and non-literality (Johnson, Christie, and Yawkey). When we play we effectively consume matters inside this specialized frame.

To summarize, in play people are oriented toward satisfactions arising from their performance in the event. They desire experiences of completion, which serve as the behavior's principal rationale. And they pursue those satisfactions by actively manipulating the circumstances before them.

PLAY AS INTERACTION

Play can also be seen as something that occurs when individuals encounter one another or engage with external elements of the world. In that context, play is a quality of exchange, relationship, or interaction. This section proposes that play as interaction is characterized by two traits that, in combination, distinguish it from the other three patterns. Play is *contestive* and *unpredictable*.

Although I agree with Caillois that Huizinga overemphasizes the agon (or social competition), I support Huizinga's general thesis that play represents an assertive, *contestive* stance toward the world. To be sure—and as Huizinga (1955, pp. 50–51) makes plain—play sometimes develops as a competition "for something" that is desired by groups of people (such as a prize) or as a display "of something" (such as character or skill) that is valued by those same competitors. Still, the *things* with which we play are not, at least directly, other people or their evaluations of us. Rather, we interact with material and symbolic elements. We sing songs, hit baseballs, recite tongue-twisters, and scale cliffs. At times, we try to do this better than others or at least better than we ourselves have done before. However, even our most directly social competitions, such as boxing and wrestling matches, are manifestly confrontations of bodies. And mental contests such as chess matches are movements of miniature "men" and their symbolic equivalents.

Players desire more than movement and manipulation, however. They wish to encounter patterns and processes that challenge them rather than simply yield to their efforts. Walking steadily (and on only two legs!) across a room is in many ways a wonderful accomplishment, but most of us do not think of this as play. Instead, players are fascinated by difficulties and obstacles. Indeed, if the challenges found in a backyard are too easy, children will heighten the difficulties artificially by building ramps and platforms, by walking precariously on a pile of rocks, and so forth. All of us want, or so it seems, playthings that can "give us a good game." In play we select forms that are *almost* too heavy, too slippery, too high, too rough, and too bouncy. As in video games, moving through these levels of difficulty is the process by which we develop and display our caliber as players and, by extension, as persons.

When play's objects are capable of responding to us directly (instead of merely resisting), the interaction acquires a back-and-forth character. We push; the plaything pushes back. Alternatively, the object confounds us by its failure to respond as we intend. The unwillingness of golf and tennis balls to go where we desire should cause us to quit those sports. Instead, that perplexity draws us in.

For such reasons, I maintain that play (as interaction) features optimal levels of *unpredictability*, especially as this affects the prospects of participants' attaining their declared goals. Play is tense (Huizinga), uncertain (Caillois), and unexpected (Gordon). Most of us do not want our playing companions to "give" us putts of every length in golf or to call tennis serves that are three feet out of bounds "in." Even Bekoff's dogs, it may be recalled, willfully alternate experiences of dominance and submission. In short, creatures want to inhabit contexts that make real the prospects of dissatisfaction. Only then do accomplishments give them pleasure. To summarize, play features contestive interactions, but those interactions must be unpredictable enough to sustain our interest.

PLAY AS ACTIVITY

Play was also described as a scenario, event, or activity that features sometimes complex understandings of how the process should begin, go through middle stages, and reach a conclusion. Places and times, materials, rules, and roles of participants are specified. Comprehensions of experience widen to include broad stretches of space and time. Consistent with this view, I believe two characteristics distinguish play—as activity—from its rivals. Play is *self-regulated* and *episodic.*

Both terms refer to the way the activity is organized. *Self-regulation* describes the source of event governance, the way in which action is developed, monitored, and sustained. Many of life's activities follow pre-established scripts and are administered by leaders whose authority derives from statuses external to the event. Although play commonly has its leaders and rules, ideally these arise as event-based agreements of the participants themselves. For these reasons, such theorists as Huizinga, Caillois, Fromberg, Gordon, Eberle, and Burghardt define play as "free" or "voluntary."

This condition is not problematic when someone is playing alone. But when many are playing, the group is challenged to make decisions that honor everyone's right to choose, act, and experience satisfying emotions. Because of that difficulty, collective play features a loose, if easily fractured, equality. This choice-making extends to rules. To recall Wood's phrase, play features "dependence on internal rather than external rules." In other words, players determine and enforce the standards for behavior.

A more complicated expression of this is Marks-Tarlow's assertion that play is self-organizing, in other words, that it displays creative or bottom-up activity by the brain in response to changing conditions. Play celebrates creativity or "improvisational potential" (S. Brown 2009, p. 16). Players are not content with the status quo. Instead, they disrupt, challenge, and pursue novelty. For Marks-Tarlow, this process is disequilibrious. For Huizinga, it is the strategic tension between order and disorder. For Sutton-Smith, it is the paradoxical relation of equilibrial and disequilibrial tendencies. Whatever the terms, players create and enforce restrictions (such as game rules), but their real fascination is with inventing interesting predicaments and discovering ways to respond to them. The event is organized, then, as a self-motivated quest for difficulty. Indeed, much of the satisfaction of having rules comes from the challenge of making and administering them and from the noisy disputes over people's misbehaviors.

Play as activity is *episodic*. Play events feature short, coherent passages that function as tiny chapters in the lives of individuals and societies. Such activities are episodes also in the sense they can be returned to and repeated, somewhat like favorite chapters in a book. To use Marks-Tarlow's (2010, p. 35) term, play is "recursive." However, and in a more pronounced way than rereading chapters in a favorite book, no revisiting is the same. Each play moment is an occasion of its own sort that features different strategies from the principals, shifts in the wind, odd bounces of the ball, lapses in attentiveness, and so forth. And once the activity begins, it builds on itself as a response to continually changing circumstances.

This episodic quality can be facilitated by the rules. Take the example of baseball. It is usually organized as a succession of pitches, at-bats, outs, innings, individual games, a series of games between two rivals, and a season. Each of these small units is comprehensible in its own terms and is repeated again and again. Larger units, such as a game or season, are understood to be completions and aggregations of smaller units. In that sense, play is fractal (Marks-Tarlow).

Of course, not all play is configured so precisely. But play activities often feature repetitions of narrowly defined actions—filling a sand pail, throwing a ball, or riding a surfboard. These are added together to organize the experience. For the most part, time spent playing is time spent performing small behaviors again and again. But it is players themselves who determine what these behaviors are, what rules apply and how those rules are to be enforced, how participants are selected, what success means, and when the experience is over.

PLAY AS DISPOSITION

Recalling Lieberman's theme, people vary in their readiness to play. Some children are especially playful, but others—because of ill health, mistreatment, or other factors—can be so depleted that that they lose their appetite for play. Setting aside such psychological and situational variability, most of us can get in the mood for play at least some of the time. What is that mood?

For the most part, the theorists mentioned in Chapter 1 do not emphasize this theme, at least directly, in their definitions of play. It appears most clearly in Eberle's (2014) discussions of the spiraling development of the play experience. That experience starts with anticipation. As the event continues that experience deepens to include interest, openness, readiness, expectation, curiosity, and desire (pp. 222–27). His point is that the process of playing rewards and strengthens the player's commitment. Recalling Brown's phrase, play features "continuation desire." For Sutton-Smith, one of play's consequences is also one of its causes: optimism.

My own emphasis is on *curiosity* as a prelude to actual experiences of playing (Henricks 2012, p. 198). People are drawn to play because they want to put their capabilities into action. Watching is not enough. In fact, watching is the opposite of "getting to play." Players want to get their hands on playing materials; they itch to see what they can do with them. And it is precisely because they do not know how this process will go—and what it will feel like—that they want to be involved.

PLAY AS EXPERIENCE

The theorists give more attention to the experience of playing than to disposition. Several accounts emphasize people's sense of being embedded or involved. Descriptions such as flow (Csikszentmihalyi), engagement (Wood), total absorption (Gordon), diminished consciousness of self

(Brown), and entraining (Marks-Tarlow) are employed. Others (Simmel and Goffman) emphasize the opposite point, namely, that experience centers on feelings of separation, that is, on the perception that one stands at an intersection between commitments required by the situation at hand and more general life commitments. One plays with the knowledge that different things, which one could be involved in, are going on elsewhere.

Yet others emphasize that it is not simply engagement—or strategic disengagement—that is critical but instead a certain feeling or tone. Play is pleasurable (Fromberg), fun (Eberle), and characterized by positive affect (Johnson, Christie, and Yawkey). Play "gives rise to the pleasurable effects of excitement and optimism" (Sutton-Smith, 1999, p. 253). It releases "tension in ways that are pleasurable" (Gordon, 2009, p. 8).

Once again, Eberle emphasizes that play experiences are transitions from one pattern of awareness to another. In his view (Eberle 2014, pp. 222–27), play leads from "anticipation" to "surprise" to "pleasure" to "strength" and "poise." Each of these five qualities deepens as the activity progresses through its various stages. Note that these comprehensions (also, forms of resolve) are understood in positive or beneficial terms. Play empowers people by expanding and consolidating their feelings about what they can be and do.

How might these somewhat different themes—focused engagement, disengagement, tension, pleasure, and transition—be integrated into a general view of the play experience? My attempt to do this emphasizes what I call "emotion-sequences," processes of preparation, engagement, and reflection that distinguish the four forms of activity (Henricks, 2012, pp. 197–203). Those sequences involve three stages: anticipation, feelings of the present, and feelings of remembrance. The sequence of play begins with the anticipation of *curiosity* (described above as the disposition for play). People play because they desire to know what it will feel like to be the executors of a newly constructed moment. Once the activity begins, it shifts between moments of *fun* (which are described here as feelings of excitement, exploration, and disorder) and those of *exhilaration* (feelings of pleasurable restoration and order). In other words, in-process feelings of stimulation and challenge alternate with feelings of completion (as when one finishes a move or makes a point in a game). Play's movements, then, are coherent surges, passages, or episodes during which participants may exert themselves quite energetically and then pause to consolidate and move forward again. At the conclusion of the activity, there is a feeling of *gratification*, the sense of being pleasurably spent or "played out." That moment of remembrance includes elements of self-congratulation, for it is the participants who pushed the activity forward and brought it to its end. As Eberle emphasizes, successful play leads to the conclusion that the participants can do more of this than they have done before.

Of course, all this assumes that events move forward in a consistently positive fashion. Opposite emotions such as frustration, anxiety, boredom, and feelings of failure and fatigue also challenge players. Too many of these negative feelings may flood the event and cause it to end prematurely. But smaller doses enhance the estimations of accomplishment and self-direction that keep the affair going.

PLAY AS CONTEXT

The final perspective concerns the relation of play to its supporting conditions or contexts. As we've seen, one can think of "context" as the bounded space-time configuration of the event itself. Within that intentionally contrived setting, players acknowledge limitations of the above-mentioned sorts and then (within those parameters) address other patterns of relationship. Recalling Caillois's theme, play in its simplest forms is paidia, behavior that expresses spontaneity, improvisation, and turbulence. Such play rebels against its own contexts. Other play, termed ludus, is more tightly regulated or artificially constrained. Even here, however, the purpose of rules is not to prevent the contestive and unpredictable but rather to encourage this pattern of inventiveness and struggle. Although there may be highly elaborated rules, the real play focuses on these transformations.

Another question is how any play event (as bounded reality) fits into the worldly context that surrounds it and from which it draws its themes. That is to say, there is a distinction to be made between the character of play *within* the event and *beyond* the event. Seen in that light, play events commonly function as rebellions or resistances against the wider world of officially recognized organizations, proprieties, and regimens. At such times, players escape routine responsibilities. They dally; they do things they shouldn't.

Among the theorists, Gordon (2009, p. 8) emphasizes this quality of openness and improbability. What play features is "absorption into a highly flexible field." That is, players seek and create conditions that do not confine them strictly but instead allow them to explore the implications of behavior. Similarly, Marks-Tarlow signals the extent to which play is bottom-up and nonlinear. It is "sensitive to and dependent on initial conditions" (2010, p. 39). Particular occurrences are the essential starting points, and these lead off in many different directions, with consequences that are hard to anticipate.

My own phrasing for this general relationship between play and its settings, both within the event and beyond the event, is that play exhibits *ascending meaning*. That is, play prizes a certain pattern of meaning creation, one that opens the possibilities of understanding and experience. Play centers on negotiations with the most particular aspects of the world and then uses those little moments to instigate new patterns of relationship. The inspirations of the participants—indeed, their most fleeting patterns of awareness—are crucial to this process, as are the equally sudden responses of play's objects and settings. And the behavioral scene that develops is understood to be a satisfying alternative to other life settings. This impetuous pattern of meaning-creation is contrasted with patterns of experience that emphasize conformity and submission to otherness (what I call *descending meaning*). The general theory of ascending and descending meaning is described in Chapter 3.

The above-stated themes can now be summarized. As action, play is *transformative* and *consummatory*. As interaction, it is *contestive* and *unpredictable*. As activity, it is *self-regulated* and *episodic*. As a pattern of disposition and experience, play features an emotion-sequence that leads from *curiosity* to alternations of *fun* and *exhilaration* to remembrances of *gratification*. In relation to its context, play reveals a pattern of *ascending meaning* both within the event and beyond the event. When we play, we address the implications of these themes and reflect on those experiences.

Work (and Play)

Of the different forms of behavior to be considered here, work is the easiest to contrast to play. In industrializing societies, much is made of the importance of separating work from the other things people do. People commonly go to work and return home, where they address other life commitments, including some (such as household chores) that are unpaid versions of the tasks they perform at their official workplace. Regardless of place and level of remuneration, people understand the expression "get to work." And young children and adolescents are very sure that work is somehow play's rival (see Wing 1995, Holmes 1999; Patte 2009).

To be sure, this opposition is historically situated, for traditional, community-based societies often mix (what we think of as) work and play. In those settings, work is not time purchased from the stream of life; it is also an opportunity to chat, sing, gossip, and otherwise build human relationships at the same time daily needs are met. At least, that is its idealized version. This broad interpretation of labor, including its social dimension, is central to the Marxian tradition (see Lefebvre 1969, pp. 25–58). Although some forms of activity arise from people's physical needs and express their connections to the natural world (*poiesis*), others reflect wide-ranging engagement with social, economic, and political realms that are humanly created and maintained (*praxis*). In short, humans are involved in many kinds of practical (and potentially creative) activity. Commodification, a special concern of Marxian analysis, is only one way of organizing these efforts. Indeed, advanced industrial societies, as noted in the introduction, display their own distinctive combinations of work and play.

Although work and play can be tightly paired—and perhaps should be paired in order to sustain a satisfying life (see S. Brown 2009, pp. 123–55)—few would say they are the same. Some behaviors feel very instrumental, task-like, or forced (such as cleaning a toilet or taking a multiple-choice exam). Others are understood to be more generous expressions of personal anticipation and desire. With that beginning, consider some differences between work and play using the framework of the six perspectives.

As action, play was described as *transformative* and *consummatory*. The other major example of transformative behavior is work. Like players, workers change the world by turning it to their purposes. Work is different from play, however, in that workers focus on the products they create and, more than that, on the usefulness of those products in settings outside the circumstances of their making. That is to say, their orientation is instrumental. Workers create in order to acquire things they do not currently possess; players create in order to know and feel.

As interaction, play is *contestive* and *unpredictable*. Work also is contestive, in that workers commonly take on the most difficult challenges presented by externality. Yet because work is focused more on end states, it tends to follow a more linear or predictable path. In contrast, players seek the unexpected; they are fascinated by novelty and surprise. Workers try to eliminate confusions and inconsistencies. Their finished product is essentially a declaration that these tensions have been resolved. Furthermore, the object they create is judged not by the quality of subjective experience that was pertinent to its making but by canons of effectiveness or efficiency (as an optimal expenditure of time, energy, and materials).

As activity, play is *self-regulated* and *episodic*. Work, in my view, is *self-regulated* and *interdependent*. The first of these designations may strike the reader as absurd. After all, we live in an age dominated by machines and by huge bureaucratic organizations. What control do most of us have over our working conditions? Indeed, this is the point that dominates Marx's (1964, pp. 167–77) discussions of expropriated or alienated labor. Ideally, labor is the process by which people realize themselves through self-directed activity in the world. In our era (as in Marx's) many jobs have lost this character.

Note that this is the same argument that Huizinga develops with regard to historical changes in play. People used to be in control of play; now they aren't. Doubtless, both work and play can be organized from above by large organizations but the vast majority of work and play activities are conducted as small-scale, informal affairs that feature self-regulation. Furthermore, much confusion results if one thinks of work only as the job we get paid for, or if play is considered to be only the highly organized, commercialized versions of that activity.

Taking this wider perspective, most acts of work feature self-managed routines such as going upstairs to get something one has forgotten, washing dishes, picking up a child after school, or sitting down to eat. As workers, we move through the world in order to accomplish preconceived ends. Even when obligated to perform the activity in question, we direct the course of events by a series of decisions and enactments.

Work also is *interdependent* rather than episodic. Play, as we've seen, is often a "doing over" (with variation) of small movements to explore the pleasures and pains associated with the activity. Experience is the activity's end product. By contrast, workers tend to follow steps or stages that lead to completion of their appointed task. Means are subordinated to ends. To be sure, play can be stretched out as a carefully regulated pursuit of some longer-term goal (such as running a marathon). Work is the more common example of such protracted instrumentality, however. Most of us claim we do not want to perform our daily tasks—to go upstairs to look for that lost object. But we acknowledge the place of this project in some broader life scheme to which we are committed. So we color our activity with such terms as *duty* and *need*.

Play's disposition was described as *curiosity*, the wish to enter a situation that is unusual or stimulating, and more precisely, to see if one can recast that situation to make it have those qualities. Workers also believe that they have the ability to turn situations in the direction they choose, and in the process to create, alter, or construct elements within those situations. They are preoccupied less with experiences, however, than they are with their ability to accomplish their ends. In that sense, the key disposition for workers is *self-confidence*. In order to work well, people must believe that they possess certain habits of mind and character, for such skills prevent the behavior from being bungled. Players enjoy creative disarray; workers seek control.

How does the experience of work differ from that of play? Play's emotional sequence is *fun, exhilaration,* and *gratification.* Sometimes, workers experience these emotionally charged states (as when a scientist makes a discovery), and workers sometimes appreciate new and exciting challenges. But workers' broader commitment to situational end states (and beyond that to the longer-term consequences) transmutes motivation into a pattern that is more steadfast, determined, and emotionally level. For such reasons, I believe *interest* is a better term to describe the initial stage of workers' engagement. The successful completion of some element of a project may be expressed in (the emotionally more neutral) feelings of *satisfaction.* At the event's end, feelings of accomplishment can be described as *pride.* The latter reflection is based on the conclusion that the worker has been the creator of something substantial, even if it is only a "good day's work." To summarize, this *interest-satisfaction-pride* sequence is consistent with an activity whose real goal is to improve circumstances that transcend the situation at hand.

Finally, there is the question of relation to context. Play was said to feature *ascending meaning,* both within the event and beyond the event. Work features a *mixed* pattern of ascending and descending meaning. Within the event, workers transform external elements; those acts of creation (expressions of ascending meaning) are impositions of human will. Beyond the event, workers subordinate themselves to established external patterns (descending meaning). They take seriously certain needs (providing for themselves and their families, maintaining their places within a group or organization, getting a reward, and so forth) that strictly bind their activity. In conclusion, work features themes of personal control within a framework of regimen and duty.

Ritual (and Play)

Perhaps the most striking contrast is that between play and ritual. This distinction is the challenge that Huizinga and Caillois confront directly. For his part, Huizinga was ambivalent about the relationship of the two forms. On one hand, he stresses that "the ritual act has all the formal and essential characteristics of play" (1955, p. 18) and that "all true ritual is sung, danced, and played" (p. 158). On the other, he recognizes that ritual and play are not the same, or at least have developed in ways that now separate them. As already noted, his identification of the "play-festival-rite" complex reflects both the past union of the three forms and the fact they are different matters.

In my view, Huizinga's motivation for linking ritual and play stems from his commitment to show that play is not trivial escapism or worse, a fiddling with the world. Quite the opposite, "play may rise to heights of beauty and sublimity that leave seriousness far beneath" (Huizinga 1955, p. 8). Important also is his understanding of ritual as a *dromenon*, a culturally safeguarded form of acting out or imaginative performance (p. 14). The purpose of rites is not to imitate or represent the sacred; instead, rites bring it into being. In that sense, rites are *methectic* rather than *mimetic* (pp. 14–15). Finally, his joining of the two behaviors reflects his view that both are often separated, rule-bound, and purposefully exotic settings for the development of human possibility. At their best, perhaps, ritual is played and play is ritualized.

This combinatorial view has been pushed forward by some contemporary scholars of ritual who stress ritual's role as a hypothetical, "as if" construction according to which people can act out the possibilities of living (Seligman et al. 2008; Schechner 1995; Bell 2009). By such lights, ritual is not an imposition of firmly fixed beliefs but rather a pattern of performing or doing that celebrates irreverence and ambiguity. That pattern contrasts with the "sincere" or serious modality of everyday life in which people pledge themselves to honor their personal commitments. Far from stabilizing society, ritual (or rather ritual joined to play) is a setting that disturbs and transforms its participants. It even foments lying and deceit (Seligman et al. 2008, pp. 62–64).

Such attempts to join ritual and play are rejected by Caillois, who in his book *Man and the Sacred* argues that play opposes the sacred and the ritual forms that serve as symbolic bridges to that realm (Caillois 2001a, pp. 152–62). Indeed, play and the sacred sit at opposite ends of what he (p. 160) calls the "sacred-profane-play" hierarchy. In Caillois's view, we accord the sacred a level of respect, obligation, and permanence that is entirely at odds with play's temporary, irreverent spirit. For Caillois (p. 157), "play is pure form, activity that is an end in itself, rules that are respected for their own sake." In that light, play's "content is secondary." By contrast, sacred rites exhibit "pure content," which functions as "an indivisible, equivocal, fugitive, and efficacious force."

In this section, the approach I'm taking is similar to that of Caillois, though I use the terms *rite* and *ritual* in a much more general, secular way than he does. In my view, people engage in rituals when they commit themselves to externally based forms and forces that are used to guide them into and through the various portions of their lives. Such rituals include the daily ablutions most of us go through almost unthinkingly to prepare ourselves for the day, the social "identity ceremonies" that are the centerpieces of interpersonal encounters (Goffman 1967), and the symbolic commitments to community that are stressed by Durkheim (1965). Rituals can be avenues to the sacred, as Huizinga and Caillois maintain, but they can also be formalized behaviors (some of them habits) that address the smallest concerns. In every instance, we engage in ritual practices in order to be empowered by patterns we do not control.

Play as action was defined as *transformative* and *consummatory* and work as action as *transformative* and *instrumental*. Ritual as action, as I see it, is *conformative* and *instrumental*. In other words, it is the form of action opposite to play.

Rituals—be they bodily, psychological, social, or cultural—rely on seemingly external formations. The ritual actor wishes to be guided by these formations, in part so that consciousness can be released to address other matters. Ritual is called conformative because this process involves accepting, adjusting, or conforming to these patterns. Furthermore, this acquiescent posture is not chosen simply for the pleasure of involvement. Rather, we engage in rites in order to feel ourselves being moved through the moments of life. Players (and workers) want to transform the world; ritualists wish to be transformed by otherness.

As a pattern of interaction, play was said to be *contestive* and *unpredictable*; work was the predictable version of this contestive format. By contrast, ritual (as interaction) is described as *integrative* and *predictable*. Once again, this is the opposite of play. The first of these terms implies that ritualists pursue (as their desired end state) a sense of connection with that which stands beyond them. That condition of connection, wholeness, or integration is essentially reconciliation with otherness. To be sure, rituals sometimes involve stages of test and struggle, and sometimes they make people confront conditions of cosmological openness and disorder (see Chapter 8 for both themes). Still, the general effect of rituals is to reaffirm belief in, and respect for, transcendent occurrences. Rituals remind us of the powers of psychological, biological, social, cultural, and environmental patterning. At the same time, they accentuate the inconstancies of life and then direct us through these oppositions and confusions.

Although people engage in rituals to help them discover what the world, including its more abstract, transcendent realms, has to offer, those participants are interested less in the excitement of those encounters than in finding a course through that situation and into the next. That is, assurance or *predictability* is fundamental. In that light, Claude Lévi-Strauss

(1969, p. 30) describes ritual as a "favored instance of a game." Rituals tend to have pre-established outcomes and rely on a sequence of most appropriate practices. Both means and ends, two crucial concerns for any actor, are regulated. Entry into (and exit from) the ritual ground may be strictly controlled. And although there is usually some latitude for how participants may respond during the event, officials are often present to see that things move forward as they should. According to Roy Rappaport (1979, pp. 174–78), rituals are "repetitive" and, in their extreme, "invariant" (see also C. Bell 2009, pp. 91–92).

As activity, ritual is *other-regulated* and *interdependent*. Play, it may be recalled, is self-regulated and episodic. Yet again, the two forms are opposites. The first of these terms refers to the degree to which external models organize the action. This general theme was just discussed, but there are additional elements to mention. In the first instance, ritualists are less likely than are players to control the choice and character of their activity. Sometimes participation is chosen for them as a public obligation. In more extreme instances, as in the case of the obsessive-compulsive rituals studied by psychologists, it seems to *choose them*, and subjects feel almost powerless to resist. Other decisions—when and where the event will occur, who will participate, how it will be directed, and why people should be involved—may be dictated by others. Although turn-taking exists, these turns are sometimes merely moments when the subject demonstrates or avows compliance. And respect for authority figures (or at least for the norms of honored traditions) is prominent.

It can be argued that this vision of ritual is authoritarian, formal, hierarchical, and otherwise "dead" and that the best rituals are those which energize, inspire, and creatively engage their participants. I do not disagree. But I'm making the more general point that all rituals—obsessive behaviors, physically based habits, religious services, social courtesies, and the like—are fundamentally acknowledgments of external patterns as appropriate supports for consciousness. We bring these forms to life by our willingness to participate in them and by our public displays of engagement and resolve.

Ritual's other distinguishing quality (as activity) is interdependence. As cordoned off (and sanctified) as some of these events may be, rituals are affairs that tie together the segments of life. We participate in rituals to ready ourselves, and sometimes to change ourselves, for what is to come. A religious ceremony or greeting ritual is not a moment to be regarded lightly. That is because occasions of this sort are times to define individual and group identity, to make public who people are and how they should be treated. Even the ritualized meetings between team leaders at the center of sports fields before an event begins are of this character. Vows made there—for example, to follow the canons of sportsmanship—are to be honored throughout the event.

Ritual also displays interdependence or linkage in the sense that the event occurs as a sequence of behaviors. If play is segmental or episodic (like baseball's at-bats and innings), ritual features stages or progressions. Acts completed in one portion of the event are preparations for what follows. Acts of penitence, humiliation, and self-sacrifice are sometimes necessary forms of personal cleansing. Only a person so readied is allowed to move forward. Victor Turner's (1969) classic work *The Ritual Process* details this carefully regulated transition. Separation, initiation, and return are the three stages by which current secular identity is dismantled, personal character is assessed through test and trial, and then new identity is bestowed on those who have demonstrated themselves worthy.

Is there a ritual disposition? Against play's curiosity and work's self-confidence, ritual is prepared by *faith.* Although this term has religious overtones, it is not used in that sense here. Rather, ritualists believe that they can deal with the challenges of life by relying on pre-established external patterns from many sources. In that sense, they operate on the basis of feelings of confidence. But this is different from the self-confidence of the worker who believes that she can impose her own visions on otherness; instead, rites feature the belief that otherness can take over and direct the self in productive ways.

The emotional sequence of play was described as fun-exhilaration-gratification, and that of work as interest-satisfaction-pride. Because ritual is organized differently from these patterns, the experience of the event is different, as well. In my view (Henricks 2012, p. 201), ritual leads from anticipations of faith to self-stirrings that can be called *enchantment.* Those sensations of exploration and disorder (in which the person feels herself challenged or reoriented by something powerful and compelling) are followed by moments of restoration and stability, designated here as *rapture.* Rapture expresses the comprehension that one has been transported to another place or level that provides new visions of the world and of the self. Finally, there are the feelings of remembrance that can be called respect or *reverence.*

Although I've emphasized positive emotions, I acknowledge that rituals also produce feelings of anxiety and dread (as people sense themselves being taken over and transported). Furthermore, rituals are frequently attended by a somber mood that contrasts dramatically with play's light-heartedness. All of this is consistent with the argument that rituals reinforce beliefs that there are well-established forms and forces that can be counted on. The "enchantment-rapture-reverence" terminology expresses the positive mode of such faith.

Finally, there is the relation of ritualized behaviors to their sponsoring contexts. If play celebrates ascending meaning (both within the event and beyond the event), ritual represents the most extensive expression of descending meaning. Within the event, ritualists accept the powers of pre-established forms to control personal actions, the statuses that are assumed, and meanings that are imposed on what is occurring. Looking beyond the event, there is acceptance of realities that are more important than what is occurring here. For Caillois, as we've seen, that means accepting the transcending and transformative power of the sacred. But this pattern of accommodation also applies to the more ordinary, secular rituals of everyday life. Although not exalted in the fashion of religion, fundamental matters of living are serious affairs that demand our attention. Our ritualized behaviors are both responses to and preparations for these. We ready ourselves for living through other-directed acts of recognition and adjustment.

Communitas (and Play)

Most difficult to distinguish from play is *communitas*, a term used here to summarize Huizinga's ideas of festival, festivity, and bonding. Most of us draw strength from being in the presence of other people, at least when those others support us and remind us of what we hold in common. In that sense, the contagious high spirits that lift everyone at a party, dance, wedding reception, rock concert, and sporting venue are critical to the event. At such times, we sense that there are occurrences more important or interesting than ourselves and even that a community is being established on the basis of these shared (if momentary) commitments.

Perhaps the best-known development of this term in the social sciences is provided by Victor Turner (1969). For Turner, *communitas* refers to feelings of common plight and egalitarian support that sometimes arise when people find themselves collectively sequestered, set apart from society's prevailing routines and statuses. These feelings are associated especially with one stage of his "ritual process," described above, specifically that intermediate stage of seclusion, test, and trial when initiates endure hardships and look to one another for support. The bonding created during difficult moments is very powerful, as is the appeal of values that seem fresh and inspired.

Turner (1982, pp. 47–51) extends this term to other group experiences in historic and contemporary societies. Some events feature "spontaneous" communitas, a special style of interaction that forges deep bonds quickly. Different is "ideological" communitas, which takes place when practitioners try to conceptualize that pattern of relating. Third and finally is "normative" communitas, in which groups take it upon themselves to perpetuate procedures that honor these intense feelings. In such ways, communitas escapes the ritual ground and incorporates some of the very structures it resists.

A similar view of social bonding is offered by Durkheim (1965, pp. 420–33), who describes this as collective "effervescence." Although most rites point to the sacred and follow clearly prescribed procedures, some events disregard this emphasis and focus instead on the thrill of public involvement. That shared exuberance may even lead to the formation of new ideals and alliances. As Durkheim (1972, pp. 228–29) argues in another context, it "is in fact at such moments of collective ferment that are born the great ideals upon which civilizations rest."

Although this theme of social bonding is very important, I am using *communitas* in a much more general sense to describe people's willful immersion into external forms, whether these forms be social and cultural (in the manner of Durkheim and Turner), psychological, bodily, or environmental. To be specific, appreciating the beauty of a summer's evening, taking a leisurely bath, being thrilled by an orchestra's performance, or engaging in a meditative practice such as yoga are all forms of communion. So also are more ebullient activities such as going to a rock concert, a football game, or crowded bar. To engage in communitas is to seek feelings of transcendence that expand and integrate the self. To be sure, the current book celebrates the quest of players to create and manage the terms of their own existence. But equally important is the quest of communitas, where people seek to experience the re-creative or regenerative power of otherness.

Play as action was described as transformative and consummatory. Communitas shares play's quality of consummation. In the various occasions of communitas—again, parties, wedding receptions, picnics, rock concerts, amusement park rides, fireworks displays, and the like—people want to feel energized, perhaps elevated, by what is going on around them. However, and in contrast to play, participants do not depend primarily on their own insights and actions to enliven those occasions. Instead, they understand themselves to be part of a setting which presents interesting occurrences—cultural artifacts, behaviors of other people, wonders of the natural world, or even the biochemical surges of the body—which they have opportunities to experience. Understood in that context, communitas features *conformative* behaviors, actions that adjust or fit into what is going on. As we've seen, ritual is the other pattern that emphasizes this type of accommodation. But ritual is geared to ends beyond the event, while communitas focuses on within-the-event experiences of immersion.

As interaction, communitas is *integrative* and *unpredictable*. The first quality, which communitas shares with ritual, means that these events display cooperative or mutually supportive practices. Participants feel themselves to exist in shared circumstances; ideas of "we" are prevalent. This emphasis is in contrast with play's feisty spirit, which dwells on tensions and oppositions. Communitas does, nonetheless, share with play the sense that the occurrence at hand has a relatively high level of unpredictability. Unlike attendance at a ritual (where people have a good sense of how the affair will end), all of us go to parties, concerts, and the like because we do not know how events will unfold. It is that (as yet unknown) procession of sights, sounds, smells, tastes, and touches that draws us in.

As activity, communitas is *other-regulated* and *episodic*. Once again, both terms address the way the event is organized. It is undeniable that communing people do contribute to the event in question or make it happen by their expressions of enthusiasm and support. But the major shape of the event is determined largely by the form itself and by the inputs of the collectivity as a whole. Even the enjoyment of a quiet walk through a meadow depends on the ever-changing circumstances of that setting. Usually, we do not disrupt that scene but instead appreciate what it is and encourage its continuation by our respect and attentiveness.

Like play, communitas is episodic. Just as the event is separated from other life spheres, so the action is organized as a series of self-contained moments or episodes. At a party, for example, the behavior typically centers on conversational circles, all much the same. These form and re-form as the evening wears on. Similarly, a concert features a sequence of individual songs; a baseball game has its innings; and a walk displays one scene after another. These occurrences are not related to one another in a specifically connected or sequential way. People move from one moment to the next, and the entire occasion is declared a success when those moments aggregate in a pleasing way.

If any disposition is to be singled out as pertinent to communitas, I would identify it as *hope*. Hope expresses the anticipation that something enriching or fascinating will occur in the moments to come. But unlike ritual (which depends on the anticipation of faith), communitas presents so much unpredictability that it is unclear just what will transpire. Most of us have had "high hopes" for an upcoming dance, party, or trip. In a similar way, we anticipate a reunion with a loved one who is coming back to us after a long absence. We live with an optimism that may or may not be rewarded.

As in the other forms of behavior, the experience of communitas may involve positive or negative emotions or the occasion may leave us flat. Nevertheless, I suggest that communitas follows its anticipatory stage (hope) with a positive emotion sequence of *delight-joy-blessedness*. The first of these terms refers to in-process feelings of challenge, disorder, and novelty. When we enter a great museum, park, or arena, our senses are highly stimulated. We may be stunned that such circumstances exist. Those feelings of excitement lead (ideally) to moments of restoration and order. The highest form of such consolidation is joy. Arguably, this is what we feel when we embrace our long-absent loved one or return to some unspoiled place that was important in our youth. At the end of the event, there is a feeling of appreciation for what occurred, or *blessedness*. If play features the gratification that comes from exercising our powers of creativity, communitas centers on the satisfaction that comes from receiving the recognition, support, and love of others.

Finally, there is the relation of communitas to its context. I've described play as the most extensive (or pure) form of ascending meaning and ritual as the extreme pattern of descending meaning. Work is a mixed form in which relationships within the event are ascending and those beyond the event are descending. Communitas is work's opposite. Within the event, participants are guided by the forms and forces prevailing in that situation. Personal standing and experience are understood to comprise a fitting into or accommodation to what is going on. However, that (descending) pattern of meaning-making can be contrasted to the event's relation to occurrences beyond the event. Activities involving communitas such as parties, reunions, and fairs are not organized to achieve changes in ongoing statuses and relationships. Rituals such as weddings and baptisms *are* preparations of this sort. In other words, communitas shares with play the project of opening the possibilities of meaning for participants. Each activity provides models of how things might be. But the event's implications are left entirely to the discretion of those involved.

Combinations and Refinements

The preceding accounts of play, work, ritual, and communitas are presented as four ideal types of behavior. In the academic world, an ideal type is a conceptual model used to identify and organize the qualities of the real behaviors that people produce. Such models are not ideal in any moral sense. Nor are they meant to deny the importance of the historical circumstances that shape what people do. Most important, they are not efforts to identify some Platonic essences or eternal qualities that prefigure the turnings of the world. For contemporary thinkers such as the play scholars described in Chapter 1, models are simply attempts to describe and explain and, at their best, to build communities of shared discourse.

Figure 1 summarizes the four forms. The upper section of the figure compares play, work, communitas, and ritual as patterns of behavior, identified more specifically as action, interaction, and activity. The lower section describes differences of disposition, experience, and context. These latter themes express the ways in which people invest themselves in the behavior and give it meaning.

As the figure reveals, some qualities are shared by the four patterns. Work and communitas each share three traits with play, though the traits they share are not the same. Ritual shares no traits with play. Work and communitas also are opposites (sharing no traits). Again, my concern is to show how the four forms differ and to show how each behavior becomes distinctive through its *combination* of sometimes shared traits. Because of these distinctive combinations of organizing principles, each form is marked by its own pattern of disposition, experience, and context.

The reader may object that the terms used by the author are not the best choices for the behaviors in question or, at least, that they are different from the words the reader would select. Well-chosen or not, those terms are extensions of the concepts of the play theorists introduced in Chapter 1. Figure 1 only names and organizes those ideas. It may also be objected that most events do not roll forward with the steady coherence and progression that the ideal types imply. To be sure, all behaviors feature hesitations, false directions, and latitudes of meaning. There is the ever-present prospect that an event may shift radically or even lose its character entirely. Negative rather than positive emotions may claim the day. The whole affair may falter for lack of coherence.

In that light, I emphasize that many events are organized (intentionally) so that they begin in one fashion and then move to subsequent

Figure 1. Play Compared to Three Other Patterns of Expression

	Play	**Work**	**Communitas**	**Ritual**
As action				
Stance toward object-world	transformative	transformative	conformative	conformative
Rationale for behavior	consummatory	instrumental	consummatory	instrumental
As interaction				
Directionality of engagement	unpredictable	predictable	unpredictable	predictable
Pattern of engagement	contestive	contestive	integrative	integrative
As activity				
Source of event governance	self-regulated	self-regulated	other-regulated	other-regulated
Organization of action sequences	episodic	interdependent	episodic	interdependent
As disposition				
Readiness for action	curiosity	self-confidence	hope	faith
As experience				
Feelings of exploration	fun	interest	delight	enchantment
Feelings of restoration	exhilaration	satisfaction	joy	rapture
Feelings of remembrance	gratification	pride	blessedness	reverence
As context				
Meanings within event	ascending	ascending	descending	descending
Meanings beyond event	ascending	descending	ascending	descending

stages that feature other kinds of activity. As we've seen, Turner's stage model of ritual, which displays communitas as an intermediary moment, is of this character. Sporting activities, it may be recalled, are often heavily ritualized at their beginnings and ends. Love-making may interpose acts of teasing on its moments of communion. Recognizing such alternations does not make events incomprehensible. Instead, it helps one identify the stages or movements of meaning in real-life activities. Finally, there is the point that very few real behaviors—at any moment of their production—occur as the analytically pure types described here. Quite the opposite, behaviors are typically mixed affairs. The following discusses briefly how play combines with the other three forms.

PLAY-WORK COMBINATIONS

Worklike play. Often we cannot tell if a person is working or playing, at least if we rely only on our observations. Think of a child building a castle with some blocks or making a drawing in the most fastidious way. Our player has a serious facial expression; the project is developed in a studied, sequential fashion; an end product is achieved; there may be feelings of dissatisfaction and frustration. Perhaps it is only we adults (who commonly dismiss the products of children as unimportant or of only developmental interest) who declare this to be play. The same could be said, however, of adult exercisers, long-distance runners, amateur painters, golfers, and workers of crossword puzzles.

As the figure suggests, play becomes worklike when it is colored by an instrumental rationale, when it is relatively predictable in its interaction, and when it features interdependent behavior sequences. When we play in a worklike way, usually we are trying to accomplish something. We understand our movements to constitute a progression toward that goal. And we recognize that what we are doing has implications for the other portions of our lives. We are not just having fun; we are trying to get fit, win a game, or display our skills. Although fun may be involved, that experience is overridden by satisfactions of accomplishment.

Playful work. Work and play share the qualities of transformation, a contestive relation to external elements, and a predominant role for self-regulation in the direction of the activity. Work becomes playful when it is colored by three of play's themes: a consummatory rationale, unpredictability, and an episodic organization of the sequence of actions. Under such conditions, tasks are converted into challenges or puzzles. Responsibilities beyond the work-moment (descending meaning) are forgotten. Like Csikszentmihalyi's surgeons or artists, we become preoccupied with tiny movements, some of which we do over and over again. We are lost—or better, found—in our commitment to intricacy.

PLAY-RITUAL COMBINATIONS

Ritualistic play. Although play is often high-spirited and fanciful, it can become heavy with rule, routine, and external direction. Some of Freud's examples of play (see Chapter 4) bear this character. That is, they seem to be little more than obsessive-compulsive rituals in which the player finds pleasure (or avoids un-pleasure) by performing one small act repeatedly. Many activities performed in the name of play—doing a crossword puzzle, going to a gym to exercise, and swimming laps—are established so deeply in our daily routines that we feel unsettled if we do not perform them. As we have seen, activities of this type are work-like. Yet they can also be acts of *self*-transformation and reaffirmation, declarations that we can still do familiar things well. That is because ritual and work share the qualities of instrumentalism, predictability, and interdependence.

Ritual differs from play in three other ways, each of which alters the course of behavior. Real play becomes conformative (rather than trans-formative) when it is rooted in well-established skills and routines. It becomes integrative (rather than contestive) when it features support for valued elements of the play setting (such as cherished companions or favorite possessions). Ritualized play also permits us feelings of "letting ourselves go," when we turn over conscious direction of the activity to reliable patterns and settings (other-regulation). In that light, a cherished family activity (such as a board game or picture puzzle) may have mean-ings that are much more important than momentary experiences of fun. Perhaps only one or two of these themes redirect the event in question. When all are prominent, the behavior should be described as ritual in-stead of play.

Playful ritual. As Huizinga stresses, rituals need not be somber, regimented affairs supervised by officials in quasi-sacred roles. Instead, communication with the sacred may be vibrant, joyful, personalized, and seemingly spontaneous. Rituals of this second sort are not steady marches ahead. They are moments when the connections between past, present, and future are performed or "danced."

Consistent with what has been presented, ritual becomes playful when the role of the participant becomes altered. By degrees, transformative orientations challenge, or replace, conformative postures; an experience-based (or consummatory) theme undermines longer-term (instrumental) purposes; and the course of action (like that of an exuberant, informal dance) becomes unpredictable, not only for observers but also for partici-pants. Playful rituals feature active challenges or trials (are contestive), emphasize the actors' responsibilities to move the action ahead (involve self-regulation), and become relatively "episodic" in character (by featur-ing small strips of behavior, such as chants or dance movements, again and again). The presence of too many of these themes changes the activity from ritual to play, or rather, it remains ritual only in the most profound sense in that participants are doing their all to propitiate some transcen-dent reality. By energetic personal improvisation, playful ritualists adore otherness and request its forbearance.

PLAY-COMMUNITAS COMBINATIONS

Communal play. Because play and communitas are closely related, they feature some of the most facile combinations. As noted, play and communitas share three basic themes; both are consummatory, unpredictable, and episodic. They part company over issues related to the stance of the actor toward the object world, the pattern of engagement, and the manner in which the event is governed.

Most of the examples of play in this book are of the feisty, feuding sort. Play is described as a chance to take on a variety of challenges and to assert oneself in response to them. Themes of constructing and destroying, succeeding and failing, winning and losing prevail. I do not reverse that viewpoint here. But think about the (playful) examples of collective dancing, sexual expression, performing in a theatrical play, choral singing, building a playhouse with other children, or even being on a team in a competitive activity. At such times, emphasis shifts to what people can do together. Each element in the play setting (like an actor in a troupe) is asked to make its proper contribution. If the action is to move forward, it must do so in this collective manner. When we perform a dance together or compete as a team, we complete small acts (or episodes), deal with unpredictable interaction patterns, and achieve momentary satisfactions (consummation). I emphasize that the pleasure we experience is not ours alone: it is something we share with our co-creators. Indeed, our enjoyment is magnified by their enthusiasm. Play of this type shifts questions of transformation and accomplishment from "I" to "we."

Playful communitas. In this combination, play is dominated by the major themes of communitas: experiencing integration with otherness, conforming to its needs, and allowing external patterns to regulate what occurs (other-regulation). Ritualists follow these principles because they believe it is in their longer-term interest to do so. Participants in communitas do so in order to experience feelings of common commitment and shared circumstance.

If communal play features spirited collective assertion, then playful communitas features acts of bonding that are animated by play's feisty spirit. So acts of love, however light and teasing they may be, are understood better as expressions of communitas than as playful indulgence. Similarly, other forms of festivity—parties, reunions, banquets, and the like—may be infused with jokes and antics that draw attention to the jokester. Still, and like ill-considered remarks at a wedding banquet, not all improvisations are welcome, for the overall goal of playful communitas is to bond all participants through effusive expressions of support.

The reader may feel that this listing of combinations makes clear the opposite of the author's thesis: that play's qualities cannot be abstracted from the real behaviors that people produce. Real life is pregnant with named and unnamed possibilities. Many events combine all four types of behavior at once! Again, my point is that using the above perspectives helps one analyze the way real events are constructed. Human behavior can be seen as being more or less playful, ritualistic, worklike, or communitarian in spirit. Play may forever remain ambiguous or paradoxical, but elucidating its guiding themes is the first step to understanding its possibilities.

3   Play as Sense-Making

Why do we play, and how is that behavior connected to the other portions of our lives? To be sure, one might simply accept Huizinga's thesis that play activities express some primal urge that is our animal heritage. We play because we feel impelled to do so—and because it's fun. Still, this explanation, what one critic calls the "jargon of primordiality" (Nagel 1998, p. 19), doesn't account for play's wonderful variety. Nor does it make clear why some categories of people (young children, for example) play more frequently and choose activities different from those of other people. Similarly, societies and groups within those societies encourage certain kinds of play and censure others. Play may well be a manifestation of some very fundamental yearning of human beings, but play also is sensitive to the contexts in which it occurs.

This chapter addresses that double theme. The first part develops the point that play (and indeed, all behavior) is shaped by different kinds of worldly occurrences. The play behaviors we produce and feel express the intersection of those factors. The second part describes play as a special strategy for addressing and making sense of those occurrences. That sense-making operation is said to have one primary goal: to help players realize their capabilities and limitations in widely varying situations. That continually changing awareness of who we are and what we can do is discussed as the project of self-realization.

A Model of the Contexts of Action and Experience

One way to start a discussion of play's different contexts is to recall the examples from Chapter 1 of behavior that most people think of as play or almost-play. The first of these was some children cavorting at a swimming pool. Water is being splashed, people are being dunked. Play in this particular setting focuses on the movement of bodies in a physical environment and on the ability of those bodies to wreak havoc on what they find there. A land-based species has entered a watery environment presenting real dangers. But members of this particular species, or at least its youthful representatives, have done this voluntarily and, more intrepidly yet, have committed themselves to having fun while doing so.

Similar issues are confronted by the Ferris wheel riders. Human ancestors, at least for the past several million years, have been ground dwellers. Why should flightless creatures willfully subject themselves to the gradually attained heights of the Ferris wheel or to the even more dreadful whirling contraptions of the fairgrounds? Instead of avoiding ilinx, to use Caillois's term, these players have actively sought out that sense of vertigo and confusion.

Play often focuses on physical encounters like the ones just described. Things—blocks, sand, water, toy cars, or checkers—are captured and moved about. Our own bodies can be counted among these things. To some degree, the example of the painter fits this account. That painter is involved in a process of moving material elements from palette to canvas. However, that activity is not simply sensuous, physical exploration of the sort displayed in children's finger-painting. Instead, her art is an intensely willful construction that expresses her own judgments about what is before her (and within her). Her brush strokes are controlled precisely. Some strokes are deemed to be effective; others (just as carefully produced) are deemed unworthy and are wiped away. Arguably, the observable portions of the painting are avenues to the artist's (and subsequently, to the viewer's) comprehension of what it means to be situated in the world. In other words, this sort of play is mindful of a wide range of cultural traditions about art and experience and is judged to be creative (or not) in those terms.

The idea that people play with understandings, both their own and other people's is also central in the example of the insult comedian. Our performer is in a social setting, a club. To be sure, he could do his stand-up act just by offering a string of jokes, each of them the strategic puncturing of what people expect from their fellow humans. Comedy celebrates social and cultural incongruity; it identifies inconsistencies in patterns of belief and behavior. To choose to laugh at the human condition (and especially at one's own predicament) is to rob the world of its powers over us. Like players throwing and catching balls, participants in comedy make and "get" jokes.

The insult comedian, however, prefers an audience that is rowdy, edgy, and otherwise alive. He must have his flesh-and-blood examples of inebriation, baldness, and obesity. The late-arriving couple finds that they are suddenly the center of attention; the overly coiffed woman grimaces as she waits her turn. The comedian wants to be challenged by that audience, accepting their jibes as he offers his. This contesting of real people is social play. That agon, to repeat Huizinga's (and Caillois's) descriptor, is one of the fundamental arenas of play. Arguably, we cannot know who we are until we measure our abilities against those of the creatures most like ourselves. So we fight, play sports, trade jibes, and relish pointless arguments.

Return to our role-playing students, who were asked to inhabit characters from a story. Caillois called such imaginative investigation mimicry. The schoolchildren must bring their characters to life, a process that involves not only moving and speaking in a convincing way but also reacting to the speeches and movements of others. This would be hard enough if they had a script to memorize, but they have been asked to *invent* the words and actions of their characters. Such activity involves several levels of understanding. As Gary Alan Fine (1983) states, players must know how other people are likely to understand their own character (including its qualities, biography, and limitations); they must also apply those understandings to shared conventions about social interaction specific to each particular situation and role. And they must interpret how the characters they play would think about and react to challenges presented to them by the other performers. In other words, mimicry of this sort involves the most probing kinds of cultural, social, and psychological inquiry.

The chapter's final example was the gambler. That player readies himself as he can, shows his bravado with a stunning wager, and waits for a reaction he cannot control. Caillois called this tempting of fate *alea*. On one hand, our gamester can do nothing to determine his destiny. On the other, he tries energetically to beat the system. When he plays the slot machine or roulette wheel and wins, what is it that he beats? Is it the clinking tumblers of a machine, the random concourse of materiality, or some more supernaturally endowed version of fatefulness?

These examples make a simple point: humans understand themselves through their encounters with many kinds of patterns that are external to them. Sometimes those patterns take firm shape and are considered to be objects or things (such as rocks, trees, spoken words, material inventions, fixed ideas, and social organizations). Other occurrences are more fluid and must be identified instead as movements, forces, or processes (such as the wind, waves, a fast-moving pitch, a conversation, and a drop in temperature). Firmly fashioned or not, such forms and forces constitute the circumstances of existence. Some, though always an extremely small portion, of these occurrences are selected as foci of conscious attention. Aided by our capacities for sensation, perception, and conception, we *recognize* that we are in the presence of such matters and ponder how we will *respond* to them. Play, as I will show, is one specific strategy of recognition and response.

In the examples given, five different kinds of occurrences or patterns were described: the physical environment, the body or organism (itself a specialized version of the physical environment), the mind or psyche, the social or society (as the patterning of human relationships), and culture (as the patterning of humanly created resources). These "fields of relationships" are critical contexts for thought, feeling, and action.

Most willfully controlled behaviors feature intersections of all these contexts at every moment. Return a final time to the painter. Her putting brush to canvas is, in the first instance, a *bodily* movement that is informed by long-developed skills of hand and eye. It is at the same time *environmental* engagement, a collision of brush, paint, and canvas. Her brushwork is also *cultural* engagement, a commentary on the cognitive, aesthetic, and moral values of her society. So is it a *social* matter. Whether or not she communicates directly with others as she works, her painting, in effect, speaks to those who are present at the moment of its creation and to audiences who see it later. Ideally, its images insinuate themselves into their ways of seeing. Finally, her painting is a profoundly *psychological* occurrence. It is she who thinks hard to determine the painting's future and she who will brood most about what has (and has not) been done.

Framing Behavior

In an example like the one just provided, where so many things are going on, how does behavior find a clear and steady course? After all, every moment of our lives has seemingly unlimited opportunities to develop behavior in one direction or another. What keeps us on the course that we've established and carries us from one moment to the next coherently? Why are we not overwhelmed by fitfulness of attention, confusion, and depletion of life energies?

In the social sciences, it has become common to use the term *framing* to describe the ways in which people impute coherence to events. One of the key proponents of this metaphor was Bateson (1972) who, it may be recalled from Chapter 1, explained how monkeys (and by extension, humans) erect publicly recognized guidelines for what is to occur. Like monkeys adopting play faces, we declare that the next few moments are to be organized in a certain way. That commitment means that specialized rules, roles, and relationships are to be observed. Erving Goffman also emphasized this theme in his book *Frame Analysis* (1974). Most human encounters, as he saw it, are socially and culturally framed. That is, we rely on ready-made public definitions that tell us what kind of situation we are in and how we should proceed in a setting so defined. Cognitive psychologists also have been sensitive to this general theme (see Sternberg 2008). In that discipline, people are said to approach and organize the world by the use of internally maintained perceptual filters, patterns of orientation, or "gestalts." Although we are not consciously aware of most of the perspectives we rely on, there are others we are able to bring to consciousness and to communicate to fellow humans. And these ways of seeing are also influenced profoundly by processes of socialization, as the internalization of socially shared values, beliefs, and norms.

As a social scientist, I support this view that cultural, social, and psychological directives give shape and purpose to what occurs. Surely, people define (and name) the situations they confront. Once defined, those situations become "symbolic realities," conceptually bounded worlds whose principles the participants accept, if only for the moments of that encounter. Indeed, the preceding description of play as a distinctive kind of *action, interaction, activity, disposition, experience,* and *context* is consistent with this viewpoint. In every case, people want to know the circumstances they are getting into, including the different behaviors and experiences that are pertinent to those settings and that are essential to moving the activity forward.

Still, this conceptual, or cognitive, approach is not a complete description of how behavior is given direction or of how people make sense of what is going on. Environmental and biological patterns are also tremendously important. Humans operate as they do (in large part) because of their bodily capacities, needs, and dispositions. And they are able to move through the world only to the extent that the physical environment

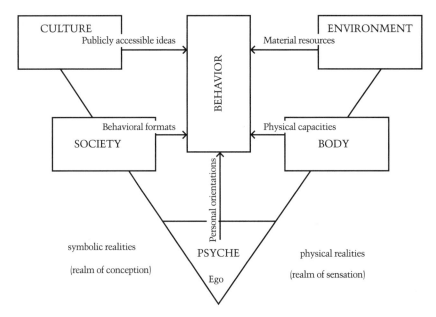

Figure 2. Fields-of-Relationships as Frames for Behavior

allows them to do so. It is appropriate, therefore, to think of framing—in an expanded meaning of this term—as including physical supports, resources, and "affordances" (see Burghardt 2005) as well as the psychological, social, and cultural patterns that were emphasized above.

So understood, occurrences that are erected and sustained in the world—behaviors, words, ideas and images, emotions, and interactions with others—depend on different kinds of resources or "inputs" that give those occurrences stability and direction. A list of such resources, preceded by their pertinent context or "field of relationships," follows: *culture* (publicly accessible ideas), *society* (shared behavioral formats), *environment* (material resources), *body* (physical capacities), and *psyche* (personal orientations). These resources serve a double function. On one hand, they are constraints or restrictions on what can happen. On the other, they are forms of enablement, which create the possibilities of happening. A graphic representation of these ideas is presented in figure 2.

As the reader can see, the model arranges the different kinds of contexts or fields-of relationships described above. Behavior, in the center of the diagram, is pictured as being supported by resources of the five types named in the figure. Different versions of this model, accompanied by more elaborate rationales, are presented elsewhere (see Henricks 1999, 2012). This chapter offers only brief comments about the model's triangular shape and the positioning of the five fields of relationships.

The psyche, the context that organizes people's recognitions and responses, is presented at the bottom of the triangle as a field of relationships that receives and evaluates information from the other four fields. Those patterns and processes—body, society, environment, and culture—are the settings for action in the world. Again, only specific elements from these settings become objects of conscious attention. The rest, indeed, most of the world's occurrences, affect us in ways that escape our noticing.

Fields of relationships on the right-hand side of the triangle (that is, environment and body) are presented as predominantly physical realities where processes of sensation are critical forms of recognition. In animals those recognition systems include sight, hearing, smell, touch, and taste. Fields of relationships on the left-hand side of the triangle feature primarily symbolic realities, that is, patterns dominated by idea systems. These social and cultural processes, as the figure denotes, emphasize recognition systems based on conception. The psyche is the context that features both symbolic and physical forms of recognition and, for that reason, is placed at the center of the diagram. Finally, the term *ego* is used to designate a point of convergence of these matters, where human subjectivity reconciles different influences and monitors the willful behaviors called actions.

Why does the model present some fields of relationships as being closer to the psyche (and ultimately to consciousness) than others? In my view, fields of relationships at the middle of the triangle (that is, body and society) are *mediating* contexts. In that sense, the body is both the physical setting within which the mind operates and the vehicle by which forays into the environment are made. Any thoughts that the psyche develops are made possible by bodies and brains. In much the same way, the body is stationed in the broader physical environment. That is, although our bodies may find themselves in opposition to goings-on in the (external) physical world, they also exist in interpenetrating relationships with that environment and indeed are constituted by it. It is very difficult to conceive of the body outside of this physical surround.

On the left-hand side of the figure, the context closest to the psyche is society. Human mentality is developed through our relationships with other people; our thoughts and actions are made possible by socially proffered behavioral directives. And fellow humans are the principal sounding boards for that communication. But this social world is only one small (and behaviorally specified) portion of the set of informational relationships we term culture. Society restricts this vast range of cultural possibilities and guides us in their use. To summarize, people operate in environmental and cultural contexts, but their capabilities in those contexts are biologically and socially mediated.

Play as a Distinctive Way of Constructing Reality

This chapter has developed a simple theme. Behaviors, including play behaviors, occur as they do because factors of several types make possible their occurring. In order for people to control behavior (that is, to convert it into action) it is helpful to have models of what is happening. Once we've decided what kind of reality we are dealing with, we can focus attention on certain aspects of that setting and plan behaviors appropriate to them. Patterns of *expectation*—both symbolic and physical—are useful guides in this process. Still, this description fits any activity that people engage in. What makes play different?

Elsewhere, I've argued that play is perhaps the greatest exemplar of ascending meaning, a process people follow to determine the character of what is occurring and then to assess the significance of those occurrences (Henricks 1999, 2006). In Chapter 2 I suggested that play behaviors encourage people to open up the possibilities of meaning both *within events* and *beyond events*. This section of the chapter develops that approach and connects it to the imagery of figure 2.

At the outset, the reader should know that I use the term *meaning* here in an expanded way. Meaning (or meaningfulness) denotes a relationship that exists when one element is *able to recognize and respond* to some other element. Usually, we think of things being meaningful in a cognitive or symbolic way; that is, something makes sense to us when we can fit it into idea systems we possess. To use the vernacular, we get our minds around it.

Things also make sense, however, when they can be recognized and responded to by bodily processes that are largely unconscious. We do not "learn" how to recognize our child's face or how to blink our eyelid in response to a gnat (see LeDoux 1996; Damasio 1999). Just as some recognition systems are symbolically organized, so others are physically organized. Those processes of sense-making are much older (and more deeply centered in our brains) than is the regime of ideas. Symbolic and physical recognition systems are often linked, as when we (unconsciously) form an image of some worldly occurrence in our minds and then consciously reflect on its possible meanings.

To see play as a project of ascending meaning is to focus on how people construct the character of situations. In instances of ascending meaning, we impose our own action schemes on environments. We try to find out what we can do *in* and *to* the world. Once again, this general viewpoint conforms to Piaget's thesis that players are guided by their own preoccupations. Playful action is judged not only by how well players are able to assert themselves but also by how pleased they feel as a result of those assertions.

This strategy stands in contrast to the project of descending meaning, exemplified in its purest form by ritual. Descending meaning emphasizes the importance of external forms as guides for action and interpretation. Oriented in this way, people willfully cede control of the direction of action to patterns beyond themselves. Behavior develops as a strategy of self-adjustment, realignment, or what Piaget calls "accommodation."

In my view, play is a rebellion against the forms and forces of the world. Players confront and challenge "claims" coming from their own bodies, the environment, the social world, and culture. In those confrontations, they try to manage behavior *their* way. They may even take this confrontational stance toward privately held ideas and desires, that is, toward their own psychological formations. In this intra-psychic style of play, players summon up heretofore latent mental commitments, bring them to consciousness, and control how they are manifested. So all of us dream, muse, fantasize, and otherwise explore the possibilities of ideas, images, and feelings. Much of the pleasure of play arises from this sense of personal efficacy.

This central role of the psyche—for action and experience—is expressed by its placement in figure 2. In acts of play, the psyche (as a field of relationships) extends its own claims by addressing challenges from the other fields of relationships represented in the model. On the basis of the positioning of fields in the model, this process can be envisioned as an *upward* or ascending movement, hence the name of this theory. Psychologically emboldened, players willfully destabilize bodies, environments, societies, and cultures. Within the psyche, playful consciousness (represented by the ego) seeks to destabilize selected psychobiological and psychocultural formations, patterns that stand *above* it in the figure.

Of course, notions of "upward" and "downward" are merely figments of the model. The more important point is that play can be described as a quest by subjectivity to forestall the claims of otherness and to subvert them for its own purposes. That creative, disruptive project is said to arise from the psyche's desire to impose itself on circumstances. Note, however, that the figure also displays other intersections of playful encounter. In physical play (like that of the cavorting swimmers), it is bodies that rebel against the constraints of environments. In symbolic play (like the insult comedian and his responsive audience) it is sociality that rebels against cultural proprieties. Although the psyche is involved in both these types of play, the real focus of action is the way these mediating contexts—bodies and social groupings—can discover new ways of confronting the broader settings that limit them. According to the figure, these acts of resistance and disturbance can be pictured as ascending processes.

The ascending metaphor also describes two levels of event construction: meanings *within events* and meanings *beyond events*. Within events, play's assertive style expresses itself in three ways. As action, play is *transformative* (in effect, a quest to manipulate or render otherness). As interaction, play is *contestive* (a pattern of engagement that depends on mutual assertion and resistance). As activity, play is *self-regulating* (a style of event creation that relies on participants to conceive and execute what occurs). Although these represent increasingly expansive (and abstract) ways of thinking about behavior, they are otherwise the same. Play depends on the inspirations of persons, individually and collectively. Those inspirations reflect sudden responses to shifting predicaments, quickly invented strategies, and emotion-based judgments about what just occurred. These assessments are the basis for what happens next.

Finally, play displays ascending meaning beyond the event. As noted above, play activities are disconnected intentionally from external, longer-range purposes. Within events, players may pursue end states, but meanings outside the event are not emphasized. More generally, ascribing ascending meaning to play suggests that creative, exciting, or disruptive events are stored only as memories by the participants. Those lived experiences can be brought forward as resources (involving skills, understandings, and forms of emotional resolve) for other times and places. In that sense, we lift out and apply meanings generated by these particular encounters. However, the passing affair may be forgotten or the skills never applied. That openness of meaning at the beyond-event level is the theme that play shares with communitas.

Is Play Functional?

To recall Huizinga's argument, we play because we feel some urge to enter situations that present us with challenges and that offer us the chance to respond to those challenges in relatively safe and inconsequential ways. Having entered the playground, our initial curiosity deepens.

What fascinates us is our own ability (and inability) to do something in a particular setting. For a few minutes or hours we are captured in little dramas in which we are the central actors. Then the spell is broken, and we walk away with only memories of what was done.

However satisfying this view may be, most play scholars wish to connect play to patterns outside those play settings. Things going on in the various fields of relationships—body, environment, society, culture, and psyche—are thought to influence our choices of when and how to play. Rarely are those precipitating conditions said to be the *causes* of play, at least in any strict or necessitous way. Instead, external circumstances are said to facilitate, encourage, sponsor, enable, or otherwise make possible our flights of fancy. Alternatively, conditions in the five fields of relationships may be claimed as outcomes of participation in play. Again, most scholars are disinclined to see these outcomes as direct *consequences* that follow necessarily from what was done. But softer (and more distant) versions of consequence such as benefits, contributions, by-products, and implications may be expressed. Even Huizinga was seduced by the idea that play has beneficial effects for the societies that sponsor that activity in free and spirited ways.

Scholars in the field of play studies commonly claim that play is "functional" or "adaptive" (see Smith 1982; Sutton-Smith 1997, pp. 18–51). That is, play activities—and, of course, other recurrent behaviors—are thought to be patterns of expression that are structurally supported by elements of the five fields of relationships. Play exists because it effectively responds to some insistence or need of that element and, in a longer time frame, promotes the survival of that element. This explanatory approach is prevalent in biology where bodies are sometimes seen as integrated wholes or "systems" that feature boundaries, interdependent parts with specialized roles, and processes that keep the body (and its constituent organs) in dynamic equilibrium. Usually, activities are considered functional when they support the survival, development, and reproductive ability of organisms.

Ideas of function are not restricted to biology. Play may also be psychologically functional; that is, it may promote flexible coherence in systems of mental orientation and analysis. Play may be socially functional; that is, it may aid the abilities of groups and organizations to clarify their identities and to coordinate the activities of their members. And, although this is less commonly said, play may serve certain cultural functions. That is, it may be activity that helps public informational systems display the implications of their own logics and introduce new themes to those patterns. Finally, play may be pertinent to the survival of communities of organisms or even to the sustenance of the broader ecosystem of which these creatures are one part. I deal with claims of this sort in the chapters that follow.

One of the best treatments of function in the social sciences is provided by Talcott Parsons. In an extension of his earlier views, Parsons (1971) argued that all systems feature four fundamental requisites that must be addressed and honored if those systems are to maintain themselves coherently. These four requisites (designated in his theories by the letters A, G, I, and L) are adaptation, goal-attainment, integration, and (latent) pattern maintenance. *Adaptation* refers to a system's ability to adjust to (and use) its surrounding environment in ways that meet that system's basic needs (such as nourishment or reproduction in the case of organisms). *Goal-attainment* describes a system's ability to formulate and then achieve goals in a coordinated way. *Integration* is the extent to which systems broker relationships among their constituent parts to promote cohesion within the system as a whole. Finally, *latency* or *pattern-maintenance* describes the processes by which systems make clear their broad operating principles and motivate their members to accept those principles.

Parsons's approach (like functionalism more generally) can be criticized for overemphasizing stability and coherence in the units he calls "systems" or, indeed, for excessively applying the concept of systems to describe the tenuous, conflict-ridden, and ever-changing relationships of human affairs. However, his attempt to differentiate four fundamental kinds of functions and his recognition that different parts of systems (much like organs in the body) may have special responsibilities with regard to these functions remains valuable. For my purposes, the theme to be emphasized is the prospect that different patterns of activity may be understood as focused responses to these four requirements of human functioning. All this begets a question. Does play address a specific set of human concerns, and is this the larger reason for play's existence? I offer my response to this question below.

It is one thing to spell out possible implications, consequences, or functions of play within the different fields of relationships. It is quite another to provide evidence that play in fact performs the functions claimed or, indeed, that it fulfills those functions better than other activities do. After all, some theorists have defined play precisely on the basis that it is "non-functional" or "incompletely functional" (Fagen 1981; Burghardt 2005).

Play as Self-Realization

Is there some overriding benefit, contribution, or function that play has for human existence? I believe play is an activity that helps people recognize their general character and capabilities. Such recognitions cannot be developed effectively by abstract pondering. Instead, people must discover their capabilities through *interaction* with a wide range of forms of forces. Only in that way can they comprehend how they are situated.

What does it mean to be "situated" or "in a situation"? All of us are deeply situated in the five fields of relationships described above, whether we choose those predicaments or not. We live *in* bodies, environments, cultures, psyches, and societies. Patterns of those types frame and direct us at every moment; many of those influences occur without our noticing. A somewhat different issue is how we notice and analyze some of those goings-on and decide that they are pertinent to *us*. Moreover, we do not simply frame *events*, the theme emphasized by Bateson and Goffman; we also make judgments about *ourselves* and about our standings in those events.

That sense of being (personally) in a predicament is one meaning of the concept of being situated. It is also the meaning that connects us directly with the experiences of other animal species. All creatures live in a concrete, sensuous present. They feel themselves moving through the world; they react to occurrences around them including the stirrings of their own bodies. Possessed of specialized (and genetically programmed) behavioral arrays, they address their own (and, by extension, their species') survival needs. Higher creatures are said to have more flexible (and partly learned) behavioral arrays. They have the capabilities of memory and of planning behavioral strategies. In other words, they live in a psychological realm that transcends moment-to-moment existence. They not only recognize the character of the situation they are in, but they also recognize that it is *they*—as a special point of reference in the world—that are in the situation (see Damasio 1994, 1999).

Humans are interesting, and perhaps unique, in their ability to extend the meaning of being situated. People recognize that they are not merely participants in scenes or encounters; they are also members of relationships (such as family and friendship circles) that transcend the co-presence of those individuals. More abstractly yet, people understand themselves to be committed to symbolically wrought patterns or structures (such as ideas, values, organizations, and personal orientations) that stabilize and give direction to their lives. To be human is to recognize wide varieties of attachments. Our minds are preoccupied with things beyond momentary doings.

Stated simply, people operate with "smaller" and "larger" meanings of being situated. In the first case, we acknowledge ourselves to be elements of events. We understand that we have a particular standing in that event (how we are doing at any one time). Like our animal relatives, we can restrict our focus to elements within our range of sensory perception. We are able to commit ourselves to actions that are pertinent to those narrowly defined circumstances. To use an example, two people playing table tennis understand their circumstance to be the challenge of returning a bouncing ball that is headed toward them.

As we have seen, there are wider ideas of context, such as the event as a whole. While playing table tennis, we may decide that our situation consists not of instantaneous occurrences but of our (more abstract) standing in a particular point that is being played, in a game, or (more widely and abstractly) in the match that is developing. In that latter sense, we understand ourselves to be ahead or behind, making a comeback, playing well, and so forth.

The larger meaning of the event refers to its implications for other occurrences and patterns beyond the boundaries of that event. This beyond-the-event sensibility commonly entails ideas of time and space. That is, we may decide that we are playing better than we were in previous matches. Looking ahead, we comprehend our current efforts to be a stepping stone; if we win, we may advance in a tournament. In the alternative, events can be connected to matters that are coterminous but outside the boundaries of the game. Perhaps we are trying to impress a group of friends who are watching us play. Perhaps we are playing in a large arena surrounded by fans, teammates, reporters, and television crews. At such times, our situation seems to be more important or serious. At least it is more widely drawn.

I believe that ritual and work (as interdependent and instrumental activities) emphasize this broader meaning of being situated. Ritual and work encourage people to think about the long-term implications of what they are doing, including the effects of their activity on their relationships with others. By contrast, communitas and play focus on narrower meanings of being situated. At such times, we are encouraged to be involved, to think only of what is happening immediately around us. The success of such events depends on the spirit or zest that we bring to them; a demurring word or period of distraction ruins the reality that has been constructed. To be more precise, it is ruined because outside issues flood over the boundaries of the event and reveal that our little occasion is not so special or protected after all.

Situated Selves

People are concerned with events and what they can do in those events. But they are also involved in another kind of situation: their own estimations of who they are. Recalling Goffman's phrase, we are not simply players, we are persons who play. Any fun we get from a situation—and any benefit that accrues to us from that activity—occurs as a reaction between these two levels of being. On one hand (as players), we are deeply involved in the action possibilities of situations, what we can get our game pieces (or ourselves) to do. On the other (as persons), we are concerned with our more general standing as individuals possessed of a certain character and capability. Our play is not merely interaction with the external objects; it is interaction with our own sometimes deeply cherished visions. In brief, our play with objects is inevitably self-play.

My thesis is that the overriding function of all forms of play (however various these may be) is to help people refine their *general* understandings of who they are and what they can do. On the face of it, such a claim seems ill founded, for play events focus on very narrow actions (hitting that ping-pong ball with a paddle) in extremely limited, artificial situations (such as a game that makes actions of this sort reasonable and, more curiously, important). Surely play is only an escape from our regular identities into a little world where we can be someone else, if only for a few moments.

That prospect of becoming something else—a baseball player, card shark, hungry bear about to devour some other children, or swashbuckling pirate—undeniably is fundamental to the play equation. To play means to take on alternative, and artificially defined, personas and to perform the implications of those identities in specialized events. Even a boy jumping back and forth across a stream becomes for a few minutes simply a jumper, a very narrow version of all the things a boy can be.

This opportunity to step into an alternative reality is part of play's appeal. Still, this explanation, that play is essentially a pleasurable escape into a carefully defined micro-world, doesn't account for why we should want to do this in the first place or, more important, why we should invest ourselves in these moments with such purpose and enthusiasm. Putting the matter bluntly, what do we get out of play? If it is felt to be pleasing or enjoyable, how are these judgments about the character of the experience constructed?

As suggested, my view is that play features interactions between narrow "situational" versions of ourselves (for example, our pirate self) and our more general understandings of who we are (as persons who transcend all situations). Play is fun for us because those activities speak to our general standards for experience, standards that are both physical and symbolic. We like play *not* because it allows us to leave our regular selves behind but because it "calls out" (and transforms) those regular selves. Play does not allow us to sit back and operate as passive observers. It makes us bring our qualities of character and resolve to the occurrence. *People* make play happen, and the result is different from that which any other person (or groups of persons) could produce. To be sure, when the leading lady becomes ill, the play must go on with the understudy in that role. Whether the resulting performance is better or worse, we as audience members know it is not the same. People animate their roles as players—from jumping across streams to playing Lady Macbeth—in their own, thoroughly personalized ways.

So how are particular play events connected to one another—and to the wider sphere of operations that is the person? A classic response to this question is provided in Simmel's essay "The Adventurer" (1971, pp. 187–98), about a social type who seemingly experiences his life as play. As Simmel explains, adventures are moments cut off from the regular stream of life. Such escapades—be they exhilarating travels to a foreign place, fascinating trials of strength and daring, love affairs, or perhaps only drug-based encounters—are occasions that are complete in themselves. To have an adventure is to voluntarily commit oneself to a strange (but personally stimulating) predicament. That situation has a recognized beginning and end. While we are in it, we are allowed to do extraordinary things. Then the adventure ends and we go home to rest, reflect, and plan for the days ahead.

As the title of his essay indicates, Simmel is especially interested in the adventurer, the *person* who chooses to live in such a fashion. Most of us, or so I believe, enjoy putting down roots. We cultivate long-standing relationships with people; we prefer to have a regular job and other continuing commitments. In contrast, the adventurer understands life to be a series of interludes, each (like love affairs) to be kept separate from the others. If anything is built by such activities, it is simply a fascinating collection of experience-based memories.

One might claim that the adventurer lives an entirely segmented, or pointedly disconnected, life. Simmel's point is the opposite. He argues that there is one place where these experiences are integrated. That place is the sphere of the person, or what I'm calling the self. However exotic our adventures may be, it is we ourselves who inevitably make each of them the same. We can only undertake these challenges in the ways that we are able. It is we who savor those experiences and remember what was done. And it is we who decide to go off again in this way. Adventurers may not acquire stable families, houses, cars, and jobs. What they do acquire is an understanding of themselves as people who can enter (and thrive in) wide varieties of challenging situations. Some life stories are written as narratives in which each chapter leads to the next. The life history of the adventurer is a series of intentionally compartmentalized experiences. All that connects them is the character of the writer.

Expanding the Concept of the Self

Since so much attention is being given to the self as a gathering place of involvements, it is important to clarify that term (see Baumeister 1999; Seiger 2005). To begin, self is not equivalent to psyche, the reference point of so many studies of play. *Psyche*, as discussed above, refers to the field of relationships within the person that processes both conceptual and sensual information and organizes willful behavior. That is, *psyche* describes our mental faculties and dispositions.

Self differs somewhat in that it denotes our connections to the world around us or at least the connections that we recognize as our own. A classic definition was offered by William James (1952, p. 188): *"In its widest possible sense*, however, *a man's Self is the sum total of all that he CAN call his*, not only his body and his psychic powers, but his clothes and his house, his wife and children, his ancestors and friends, his reputation and works, his lands and horses, and yacht and bank-account" (italics in original).

James's definition makes clear that the self is a commitment of *persons* and not simply a conclusion of *mind*. We are attached to our bodies and see them as extensions of ourselves. We recognize ourselves to have a certain age and appearance and to possess distinctive physical abilities. But we are also attached to other elements of the material world (such as houses, clothes, and bank accounts). In that light, we see the theft of a valued possession or the destruction of our house as a violation of who we are. Furthermore, people have important social connections. We are attached strongly to our loved ones and feel injuries to them as deeply as we do our own ailments. More generally, we understand ourselves to be people who have a certain set of friends, work for a certain organization, or attend a certain church. Finally, James describes self as a set of psychic connections. That is, we think of ourselves as possessing the mental faculties, memories, and personal dispositions that psychologists emphasize.

James's point was that people comprehend their standings in the world as connections to their bodies, to elements of the physical environment, to social groups, and to their own psyches. To his list I add a fifth field of relationships: culture. We understand ourselves to possess certain publicly recognized beliefs, values, norms, and skills. We hold certain political and religious beliefs, are good at skills such as guitar playing or ballroom dancing, and speak the language of our country of residence. We locate ourselves in the world by claiming some cultural resources as our own and by rejecting (or ignoring) others. To summarize, self is the aggregation of our qualities and capabilities. That assessment includes not only our present-time connections but also the envisioned attachments that represent our biographical past and (most interesting, perhaps) our ideas and images of who we can be in the days ahead.

I also stress, departing somewhat from James, that self is not the same as identity. *Identity* refers to our locations in the world as they are viewed with a more objective or external lens. Most of us have publicly recognized, or cultural, forms of identity (such as a driver's license, Social Security card, and distinctive signature). We also, as James emphasizes, exist in the minds of other people. That is, people who know us are usually able to identify us at sight and have ideas about our life history, connections, character, and demeanor. By contrast, *self* refers to people's *subjective involvement* in who they are. All of us have certain ideas about our connections and capabilities that differ from the way others think of us. As is sometimes said, a dead body has an identity (and indeed, may need to be identified by someone who knew that person well); only living persons have selves.

James, and his sociological counterparts Charles Cooley (1964) and George Herbert Mead (1964), argued that the self has two aspects, one relatively passive and the other more dynamic. In the first instance, we understand ourselves to be a fairly stable empirical presence in the world (what those authors call a "me"). We recognize that other people have ideas about who we are, that we have established connections to family and friends, that we have "done" certain things in the past, and so forth. We regard ourselves as having a certain standing in the world (a standing that is unique if all our attachments are taken into account) and as deserving to be treated in a fashion consistent with that standing. We operate in society as effectively as we do because we are relatively confident about what others expect of us.

The self also has a more active component, however: what James, Cooley, and Mead call the "I." We are not only objects; we are persons who direct our own activity and who experience subjectively what happens to us. Though it cannot be denied that much of our behavior is influenced, structured, or framed by bodily, social, cultural, environmental, and psychic patterns, we also manage our participation in these fields of relationships through processes of choice-making. That capacity to mentally arrange and then respond to external occurrences with lines of action is the foundation for our visions as prosecutors or agents of our own destinies.

James and Mead emphasized self-realization as an individual—even egoistic—pursuit, a preoccupation with "I" and "me." Cooley (1962, 1964) had a more expansive view of the possibilities of personhood. He wished to know how persons embrace (what are still quite subjective) understandings of "we" and "us." When we care about others, we include them in our ideas of who we are. Things that affect them (such as a life-threatening illness, a promotion at work, or a marriage proposal) also affect us, not in some narrowly egoistic way but in the sense that we see ourselves as being connected to their welfare. Frequently, humans do not act alone; they plan and develop lines of action jointly. On such occasions, it is not we as individuals who succeed and fail; it is our group that does so.

Once again, this process of noticing, judging, and responding is not merely a psychological affair (that is, purely mental consideration). Instead, the self features the *interaction* of a person with various (and quite real) elements of the world. People do not decide who they are simply by thinking about things; they make those judgments by engaging actively with otherness. Thus the self is also a "you," that is, someone presumed to have a (subjective) capacity to understand and act and who can call out that same pattern of sympathetic awareness in others (see Wiley 1994). Martin Buber (1996) offered one of the most important treatments of this theme. People bring selves—their own and others'—into being by acts of recognition and respect. Each of us can honor the subjectivity of others, but we can also dishonor and abuse. Different versions of the "you" can be called out, and people can also be treated as "them" or 'it."

Buber's theory makes necessary a final point. Because selfhood is interactional, people experience "standings" as well as "statuses." Although some patterns of treatment are fairly stable (statuses), others shift from moment to moment (standings). We can be ahead in a game and suddenly find ourselves behind. Elsewhere, I've discussed four different kinds of self-standings (Henricks 2012). Those standings are pictured as a balance of claims (in effect, abilities to influence behavior) between selves and others. The first of these is the condition of "privilege," in which the self is able to manipulate the other with little regard for its subjectivity. In the second, "subordination," otherness is able to make strong claims on the self without substantive repercussions. Third is "engagement," which features a balance or reciprocity between strong claims from each participant. Fourth is "marginality," a distanced relationship in which neither self nor other is able to make strong claims. In such terms, selfhood is shifting and relational. Experiencing self means positioning oneself in the world, but those positions reflect the changing capabilities and intentions of the otherness as well as one's own powers and desires.

Playful Selves

Selves are projections of personhood, ways people put themselves forward in situations. Those versions of the self are often very narrow (the hitter of a ping-pong ball). They are also broader and more abstract (a participant in a game of table tennis). And they widen to much more general views (a good table-tennis player or good athlete). When we interact in situations, these broader and narrower versions of the self intersect. Those involvements (and estimations) vary from moment to moment. During any period of play, we win and lose points, games, and matches. If we play badly enough, we may have to find new playmates or revise our view that we are a good player.

Interactions also bring into play issues of identity, or what others think of us. Others can subordinate us as "it," call on us as "you," and exalt our possibilities as "I." They can recognize our mutuality as a "we" and "us." To be sure, some persons—and some relationships and events—are much more important than others, but the general point is that our interpretations of who we are and what we can do are confirmed (and disconfirmed) by our encounters with otherness.

The theory presented here is that play represents a special process of self-construction and evaluation, one that celebrates the role of agency in human affairs. Momentary successes and failures of players are essentially forms of knowledge-building, conclusions reached about what we can do in different sort of events. So are patterns of affiliation and disaffiliation, joining with others or opposing them. Some of the conclusions we reach are idea-based (in terms we can communicate to others); others are sense-based (that is, judgments about what feels comfortable or right). Although it is impossible to know with certainty if any particular event leads to powerful conclusions that we will remember for future encounters, I claim that this process of "existential testing" creates the possibility for favored strategies, schemas, or life lessons.

I emphasize that play is not the only way of learning such routes. Work is also a strategy that celebrates agency or ascending meaning. Although work commonly lacks the qualities of pleasurable self-stimulation found in play, it makes up for this motivational deficiency with its emphases on routine, steady improvement, and felt necessity. Through repetitive activity, workers perfect or learn pertinent skills. And the kinds of things those workers (sometimes feel forced to) learn can expand their sense of self.

Ritual and communitas are other fundamental strategies of sense-making. In both of these we rely on the directives of otherness to move us along. In order to participate fully in these events, we must accept those external commitments as our own (even if they are initially unpleasant or otherwise contradict our preferred ways of being). Of the two, ritual—wherein the participant follows other-directed standards to reach instrumental ends—is the more extreme form of subservience. Communitas, its softer and more genial relative, is the pattern of knowledge-making in which we allow momentary personal satisfaction (consummation) and the stimulation of unpredictability to help us stay focused.

Of the four forms, play is the one that most conspicuously emphasizes self-teaching. When we play, we do what *we* want on our own terms and time. Activities projected to be too boring or too stressful are excluded in advance or are discovered through processes of doing. Some circumstances are judged to be pleasant or fun; others are deemed painful. Some require skills we don't possess but which seem possible to develop if we keep at the activity (as in playing a musical instrument). Some are too well learned (like walking across a room) to be of interest. Still other skills we risk losing if we do not revisit them from time to time (like playing certain card games, swimming, or dancing). In these examples—and indeed in all examples of play—what is reaffirmed is the ability of persons to envision the boundaries for their own lives.

Developing those general orientations—and the skills sets to put those orientations into action—is, in my view, the general function of play. It is also, to use Parsons's functionalist language, the theme of "goal attainment" (as a basic requirement of action systems). When people play, as individuals and as groups, they learn what they can reasonably or safely do (in both the symbolic and the physical meanings of those terms).

By contrast, the behavioral strategy of work seems central to the satisfaction of basic humans needs (that is, to "adaptation"). Work helps people narrow the range of behavioral possibilities. When we work, we get better and better at sharply defined tasks. If play teaches us effectiveness (what we can do well), work teaches us efficiency (what we can do well with the best expenditure of resources). The behavioral strategy of ritual, by contrast, is an exercise in values affirmation or "pattern maintenance." When we act ritualistically, we trust the orderliness of the world that surrounds us. When those external formations guide us well, we develop confidence that we can move through life's situations in secure, stable, and predictable ways. Once those basic frameworks have been embraced, we can turn our attention to smaller matters. Finally, the strategy of communitas centers on Parsons's theme of "integration." On such occasions, we join with the other elements of world (including other people) to prove that people can reconcile their disparities and disagreements. Communitas (successfully realized) makes us feel connected and whole.

Each pathway offers important lessons. Of the four, play best teaches people how to conceive self-directed lines of action and to mobilize varieties of resources to realize those ambitions. All play is the same is its cultivation of assertiveness, but play's strategies of resistance vary depending on the worldly elements it encounters (Henricks 2012). Some play, like that emphasized by Piaget, is manipulative. Activity of this type (associated with the self-standing of privilege) treats external forms and forces as passive or inert. By contrast, rebellious play confronts elements that are too enduring and powerful to be disabled. So players (confronted with subordination) taunt, deface, and run way. Different again is dialogical play, in which participants find themselves in relatively balanced relationships (engagement). Here, it is easiest to honor mutual subjectivity. Finally, there is exploratory play, where participants stand at a distance (exhibiting marginality) from the objects of their attention. Relatively unfettered, such play celebrates imagination. Chapter 4 provides examples of all these different patterns. This chapter has stressed the opposite theme: that all play forms unite as opportunities to develop capability, stripped of its specific applications.

4   The Psychology of Play

This chapter begins the examination of five contexts that support play and provide the terms for its explorations. The first of these contexts, the psyche, has received the most attention from scholars. That emphasis is not unwarranted, for play always expresses "personal orientations" (see figure 2), subjectively maintained strategies for dealing with the world. Experiences of play—essentially assessments of the implications of these strategies for self-standing—are largely psychological matters. And the psyche itself is often the central theater for play's ambitions, as we project one scenario after another, always with a sense for what may happen if dreams are made real.

Because the scholarly literature concerning psychological aspects of play is so extensive, I make no attempt to summarize it here (see Millar 1968; Ellis 1973; Levy 1978; Rubin, Fein, and Vandenberg 1983; Sutton-Smith 1997; Power 2005). Instead the chapter emphasizes key themes that are pertinent to psychological interpretations of play. Initially, the discussion focuses on three classic descriptions of how play is "minded." Those descriptions are provided by Jean Piaget, Sigmund Freud, and Lev Vygotsky. I describe each theory and note some standard criticisms. The middle portion of the chapter describes perspectives of some contemporary scholars who advance the theories presented above by offering their own integrative visions of play. The final section addresses the therapeutic implications of this scholarship.

Piaget's Theory of Play as Cognitive-Moral Behavior

Piaget offers perhaps the best-known theory of how play exemplifies—and contributes to—personal development. His theory of play is part of his broader commitment to understand how people make sense of the world and, as a consequence of those investigations, fortify their own abilities and character. In his view, individuals develop conceptually based action plans, strategies, or schemas that assign characteristics to occurrences and serve as frameworks for their attempts to control them. So understood, the task of the developing person is to establish mental patterns that comprehend occurrences in increasingly effective—that is, logically correct, comprehensive, and abstract—ways.

As the reader may note, this general approach is indebted to Kant's (2008) view that people construct reality through privately maintained perceptual filters. Piaget's concern is to demonstrate that these conceptual abilities are not static but rather, develop in an orderly transition from infancy to adulthood. Children are not miniature adults who become filled with experiences and knowledge. Instead, the capacities of children to think about the world move through qualitatively distinct stages, each dependent on both biological and socio-environmental factors.

For Piaget, developing effective schemas is a process of trial and error. Some approaches seem not to work very well (either as guides for action or as explanations for what is happening around us). Others are better approximations. In that sense, children—and the rest of us—operate as little scientists who are intent on developing strategies that improve the ones currently being used. As noted in Chapter 3, Piaget's approach to the process of knowledge-making features two complementary styles of adaptation to the object-world (Piaget 1962, 1966b). *Assimilation* refers to the person's attempt to fit (and thereby control) the external world by placing it into currently established ideas, strategies, or approaches. For example, a baby may try to understand what something is—perhaps a rattle—by placing it into his mouth. But using the mouth to assess reality may not be effective for comprehending other objects such as a large ball. Perhaps a better strategy in the latter case might be to grasp the object with both hands. The development of this second strategy, in effect to modify thoughts and movements in response to external conditions, Piaget calls *accommodation*. Note that assimilation and accommodation exist in a dialectical or back-and-forth relationship. We impose ourselves on the world by using established strategies. When those strategies fail, we modify or reinvent them.

Piaget (1955; Piaget and Inhelder 1972) identifies four principal stages of cognitive development. From birth to two years, child awareness is dominated by the *sensorimotor* stage, itself composed of several substages. Piaget argues that young children comprehend or quite literally grasp reality through combinations of bodily movement and sensory recognition. During this period, they develop awareness that self and object-world are different matters; each has its own (ongoing) existence and can influence the other. From age two to age seven, children exhibit the *preoperational* stage. Preschool children use language, ideas, and images to process the world, but these are mostly devices to move themselves (and objects) about. Egotism is prominent in the early years of this stage, and children have little capacity for abstraction.

The ability to comprehend and use abstract codes and principles develops in years seven to eleven, a period termed the *concrete operational* stage. Children at this age still have difficulty thinking of abstract matters without concrete examples, and logical errors continue. For example, in order to understand the concept of death a child may need to think about a favorite pet that is no longer with the family. The fourth and final stage develops during years eleven to sixteen and is termed the *formal operational.* At this point, people establish and maintain their own abstract classificatory schemes and logic-driven processes, which allow them to consider the world in a reflective, dispassionate way.

This general viewpoint—basically an expression of Enlightenment ideals that societies should be guided by individually sponsored, reason-based, universalistic principles—is featured also in Piaget's theory of moral development. Relying on his interrogations of children playing games, Piaget (1966a, pp. 26–29) argues that they initially have little sense of moral rules. Rather, their behavior is governed by their own "desires and motor habits." During years two to five, children accept codified rules and follow these in an imitative way. Still, they are fundamentally egocentric in the way they play. Each plays "on his own (everyone can win at once)." In years seven and eight they display *incipient cooperation*, which has its basis in the fact that children now understand clearly the concept of winning (a status attained through social competition and comparison) and conclude that rules are necessary to facilitate this process. By ages eleven and twelve, players emphasize the *codification* of rules. Older children can recite rules in detail and understand their function as devices to define and control any particular instance of a game.

Piaget famously argued that children's attitudes toward rules move from relative egocentrism (rules are just constraints to be dealt with) to severe "moral realism" (belief in the sanctity and permanence of rules) to a view of rules as expressions of "mutual consent" (p. 28). This last stage acknowledges that rules are abstractions that have been created by people and can be modified by people. Because Piaget is committed to principles of rationality and mutual consent, his explanation opposes the theory of morality presented by Emile Durkheim in his influential book *Moral Education*. Durkheim (1961) emphasizes that schoolchildren must learn morality by subjecting themselves to the rituals of schools and their authority figures (as representatives of society). Piaget argues that moral lessons are better learned from games with peers, where negotiations about rules give people the opportunities (and the skill sets) to free themselves from moral realism.

Piaget's ideas about play and its importance to the developing person are consistent with his general theory of development. Play is said to be an example of extreme or pure assimilation, when behavioral strategies are repeated "purely for functional pleasure" (1962, p. 89). This is especially the case in the earliest (sensorimotor) stage. The small child "looks for the sake of looking, handles for the sake of handling" (p. 90). These actions are essentially ends in themselves. Through acts of calling up and commanding bodily actions, the child gains confidence in his capacity to move himself through the world. Those abilities may arise initially as acts of creative accommodation to the demands of daily living or (less intentionally) as unplanned reactions to sudden happenings. In play, those responses are practiced and refined.

Later stages of play feature more complicated styles of bodily control and relationships with the object-world. Some movements become ritualized, practiced to the point at which they require little conscious attention (for example, grabbing a rattle). At that point, the pleasure of self-control is combined with the pleasure of being able to control the external world. Children also acquire pleasure from their ability to apply the same schema to different objects (for example, to grab a stuffed animal instead of a rattle), to move from one schema to another (as from grabbing to shaking), and to combine these action strategies in more complicated ways. In summary, simple pleasures derived from bodily movement are refocused as interest in wider fields of mastery.

Ultimately, this ability to call up and command action patterns is recognized to be an expression of personal intent or will, and the actions themselves acquire a more distanced or objective quality. At that point, children know that they are participating in a distinctive style of behavior (a game, perhaps) and that this game is "just pretend." To use one of Piaget's examples, his daughter would pretend to eat a piece of paper and comment that it tasted "very nice" (1962, p. 96). Clearly, this ability to create action scenarios populated with symbolically charged objects (paper as food) and to move those events forward by appropriate words and gestures is a tremendous intellectual step. Even more impressive in this symbolic play is the knowledge that one is "only playing," that is, that such behaviors are not to be confused with real eating. To conclude, play of this symbolic type (characterized by a sense of pretense or make-believe) is qualitatively different from the simple motor activities of earlier years.

Perhaps most important among these differences is the child's growing recognition that her playful behaviors have socially conventional or arbitrary meanings. When our player sees a pillow and puts her head down and pretends to sleep (1962, p. 98), she has no intention of completing that activity in the usual way (that is, of actually going to sleep). Instead, she wants her audience—and, indeed, wants herself—to imagine the act of sleeping without going through all the rigmarole of such an affair. Sleeping emerges as an idea, format, or frame—something that people can hold lightly, ponder, and otherwise play at. The great lesson of play, then, is that human beings are not trapped by fixed or stereotypical behavior patterns. They can choose their actions (by lying down to sleep), interrupt those actions at will (by popping up suddenly to show that they are "not tired"), and even control the idea systems that interpret that behavior (by placing the drama of sleeping into a meta-narrative of make-believe).

Such behaviors can become ritualized as games. Under such conditions, they stop being inspired, one-of-a-kind improvisations and appear instead as repeated (and repeatable) actions. Piaget uses the example of a boy jumping across a stream. The first time, perhaps, this was done to get across the stream, but the act of jumping was such fun that the boy starts jumping back and forth across the same current. Now only the jumping matters.

In that context, Piaget distinguishes three kinds of games. The first (exemplified by the jumping boy) he calls *practice games*, controlled repetitions of physical movements. The second type (exemplified by the sleeping girl) he calls *symbolic games*. A child pushing a box about while pretending that box is a car is engaged in a make-believe world that contains all manner of conventionalized ideas about what cars are, what they do, how they sound, and so forth. Third, and finally, are *games with rules.* Activities with abstract communicable directives facilitate social play. Furthermore, they allow activities to be prolonged by moving them through stages toward potential end states.

Commitment to these forms of play varies with age (Piaget 1962, p. 142). Practice play starts in the first months of life; symbolic play emerges in the second year. Games with rules begin before age seven but are especially prominent during years seven to eleven. Adults may participate in all these forms, but they tend to focus on games with rules. Such activities honor the cognitive complexity that adults are expected to possess. But their popularity also suggests a sadder conclusion: that adult have subordinated their creative impulses to regulating frameworks.

Piaget's research is one of the great contributions to the social and behavioral sciences. It continues to be a major part of the study of human development and has influenced important work in other disciplines. That having been said, his account of play can be criticized for its heavily cognitive or rationalist emphasis. As other scholars discussed in this chapter explain, play also centers on feelings. Piaget's descriptions focus on the ways in which individuals develop and operate with relatively firm action strategies. Those commitments are challenged by psychologists presenting more fluid, interactional visions of play. His stage model of human development, with its commitments to rationalism, abstraction, and sphere of control, springs from a specific, historically situated European context. Other societies and other categories of people experience cognitive-moral development and pursue play in different ways (Whiting and Edwards 1988; Göncü and Gaskins 2007).

Finally, his view of play as pure assimilation has been criticized (Sutton-Smith 1966). To be sure, there are styles of play that feature the practicing and refinement of abilities the player already possesses (as in the stream-jumping boy). But is play a refinement of what one knows already, or is it understood better as a search for what one does *not* know? Play activities often are patterned, repetitive, ritualized, and otherwise order-seeking, but play also expresses people's desires for novelty, excitement, and change. Perhaps accommodation is just as important to play as assimilation.

Freud's Theory of Play as Expressive Behavior

As different as Piaget's and Freud's intellectual projects are, the two scholars exhibit some common commitments. Both were interested in processes of the natural world (Freud was a medical doctor and Piaget completed a doctorate in science). Both shifted their inquiry from a search for the physiological foundations of thought and behavior to an increasing appreciation of cognition and symbolism. Both were committed to understanding psychological development and offered stage models of those changes. Each posited the presence of psychic formations that guide moment-to-moment activity. And both relied on the interrogation of subjects to reveal those formations. These similarities are not coincidental, for Piaget studied Freud's work (under Carl Jung) and early in his career was interested in becoming a clinician.

Piaget, however, was much more influenced by academic philosophy. And although his later work does include image-based thinking (Piaget and Inhelder 1972), he was a determined rationalist. Like Piaget, Freud analyzed people's reasoning processes (in part to expose their slips, errors, and inconsistencies), but Freud also used this information to uncover deeper psycho-biological processes. In the Freudian tradition, humans are not thinking machines but rather psycho-physical creatures influenced powerfully by impulses, anxieties, and desires. Whatever our desires for reason-based consistency, applications of logic—even when presented as the most carefully devised interpretations, stories, mythologies, or rationalizations—cannot control behavior entirely. For Freud, psychological conflict can never be eliminated; it can only be managed. That is because the claims on consciousness are too various and too strongly established for that to happen. Expressions of the tensions arising from these contradictory claims flare up at the least opportune times. Things slip out.

Such differences in viewpoint influence the two scholars' understandings of development—and of play. As we have seen, Piaget's vision of development features qualitative advances in reasoning capability. Freud shared Piaget's interest in reasoning and moral regulation, but he was not concerned with these as exhibitions of *skill* (that is, as more or less logical understandings of how the world operates). Rather, he was interested in *will*, the processes that lead (often mysteriously) to the behaviors we actually produce. Because of Piaget's emphasis on thinking skills, his model of development is a more straight-ahead affair (for why would a person abandon "better" thinking procedures after these have been obtained?). Freud's stages also build on one another, but they are understood as confrontations with distinctive life challenges (and bodily challenges) that are of special significance to the child at different ages. One does not simply get better at the process of thought management; he moves to new, more complicated challenges. Moreover, and as Erik Erikson's more reason-based extension of Freud indicates (see below), these stages should be seen as times of life when certain tensions about self-direction in thought and behavior are prominent. Ideally, perhaps, we reconcile these tensions and transition to new life issues with confidence and resolve. Often, however, we do not. We become stuck or "fixated" on early life tensions. In that context, psychoanalysis is a strategy for revisiting our earlier life dilemmas (from a week ago or from the first stages of life), to help us identify unresolved but still operative issues, and to fashion new narratives that effectively overcome those tensions. Moving forward in life frequently means moving backward and beginning again.

Freud's understandings of play should be seen in this context. Play is one way in which people express themselves. It is of special interest to the clinician because it features people satisfying themselves in restricted settings that are understood to be departures from socially consequential routines. Self-directed behavior takes center stage. Prominent also are emotionality and "primary process" thinking (in which less heavily censored ideas and images become envisioned, stated, and acted out). The same qualities are prominent in dreams and daydreams (where people work out the implications of their wishes and fears) and in the related matters of wit and humor.

In all these cases, Freud's interest was the psychic wishes behind people's expressions (often the result of multiple hidden factors) and the ways in which the subject channels those intentions into conscious (and typically more socially acceptable) formulations. Humor, in particular, is a device people use to rob situations (including other people as elements of those situations) of their powers over us. To quote Freud (1963, p. 265): "Humour is not resigned; it is rebellious. It signifies the triumph not only of the ego, but also of the pleasure principle, which is strong enough to assert itself here in the face of adverse real circumstances." This capacity to resist, rebel, and construct is displayed as well by creative activity in literature and the arts (two areas of special interest for Freud). It is also prominent in play.

The perceived connection between imaginative activity in literature and play led Freud to make perhaps his clearest statement on the latter concept: "Perhaps we may say that every child at play behaves like an imaginative writer, in that he creates a world of his own, or more truly, he rearranges the things of his world and orders it in a new way that pleases him better" (S. Freud 1958, p. 45). Freud states further that the child takes his play "very seriously and expends a great deal of emotion in it" and notes pointedly that "the opposite of play is not serious occupation but—reality." The child is aware of that difference, for he brings things from the real world into his games and redefines them as play objects.

Thus play typically has a materiality that sheer fantasy or daydreaming does not.

Freud goes on to state that the child at play is motivated by one fundamental desire, "which is to be grown-up, the wish that helps to 'bring him up'" (1958, p. 47). Play, or so he argued, is activity that anticipates or imitates what the child knows of adult life. For grown-ups, the urge to play diminishes. Freud (p. 46) states this flatly: "As they grow up, people cease to play, and appear to give up the pleasure they derived from play." Said in a more complicated way, the adults of Freud's social milieu felt pressure to behave in upright, respectable ways. Their play impulses—for who can forget entirely a pleasure once experienced?—were expressed in less direct or sublimated ways, that is, in humor and fantasy.

His theory of play displays his commitment to the role of the "pleasure principle" (the satisfying discharge of build-ups of psychic tension) and to the importance of the ego (as conscious director) in creating and officiating settings where this discharge can occur. In the latter stages of his career, however, he came to doubt his own theory. This criticism of his earlier view is made plain in the title of his book *Beyond the Pleasure Principle* (S. Freud 1967). His quandary was essentially this: If pleasure is what occurs when people try to eliminate nervous excitation or "unpleasure," why should people actively seek out tension or difficulty as they obviously do in all sorts of games and challenges?

Freud's famous example of this issue was a child's game with a "reel," a wooden object tied to a string that the boy would throw repeatedly over the edge of his crib and then pull back into view. As he (S. Freud 1967, pp. 33–34) describes it: "What he did was to hold the reel by the string and very skillfully throw it over the edge of his curtained cot, so that it disappeared into it, at the same time uttering his expressive 'o-o-o-o.' He then pulled the reel out of the cot again by the string and hailed its reappearance with a joyful 'da' ['there']. This then was the complete game—disappearance and return." What puzzled Freud was the child's focus on the first part of the game, in which he caused the reel (for Freud, a symbol of the child's mother) to disappear.

He concluded that the boy was not engaged in simple pleasure-seeking. Instead, he was pursuing a strategy of instinctual renunciation, an effort by the ego to demonstrate its control over the desire for the mother. The continual re-doing of the game was described as a pattern of "repetition-compulsion," a persistent re-creation of a scene filled with psychic tension in order to translate that tension into manageable, consciously accessible forms. Perhaps, Freud argued against his previous theory, there are principles beyond the pleasure principle. Thus, patterns of the ego were opposed by Freud to libidinal drives; desires for tranquility and return were set against desires for increased stimulation and growth; and a mysterious "death instinct" was raised against the instinct for life. Said plainly, feelings of conscious control or ego mastery may be satisfactions of a quite different type than feelings of pleasurable release.

Freud's interpretation of the reel game is consistent with his rather dark view of personality as a battleground between potentially antisocial instinctual urges, socially guided (but now internalized) moral directives, and the efforts of the ego to direct and coordinate these matters amid the demands of external reality. In that light, consciousness struggles to assert itself against dimly perceived forms of resistance and compulsion, both internal and external. In a dramatic formulation, Freud associated certain ego patterns with the "death instinct" because the ego (like the impulse to death) seeks to narrow the field of stimulation, to frame experience, and to repeat previously established forms of behavior. Play is essentially an exercise in ego mastery in which the psyche draws pleasure from its ability to instigate and control its own patterns of stimulation.

Others have criticized Freud's theories, in part for their being rooted in a distinctive sociohistorical context. His commentaries are especially sensitive to the life patterns of a predominantly middle-class, industrial European populace at the turning of the twentieth century. Although he was also fascinated by the themes of classical societies (as distant anticipations of modernity), his speculations about fundamental psychic processes arise from his bourgeois world. His imagery of physical drives, energy, and forces (as a sort of hydraulic system) conforms to ideas prevalent in the physical sciences of his day. So does his interest in deeply seated "instincts" such as sex and aggression. His wonderful reflections on the importance of conscience (or "superego") as a moral censor are also consistent with the social pressures felt by his clients (many of them high-minded bourgeois women). Psychoanalysis focuses on forbidden acts and unfulfilled expectations. Guilt, shame, and anxiety take center stage. His ideas about the universal meanings of symbols, female envy of male physicality, oedipal concerns, and the like must be interpreted in this context.

Freud's claim that people effectively think "through" their bodies (and center those understandings on bodily orifices) is an important thesis, but his famous model of the five stages of psychosexual development seems overly focused on this theme. Similarly, his insistence that the fundamental framework of personality is laid down in the first years of childhood is difficult to prove scientifically or to accept intuitively by those who feel that they have continued to change throughout their lifetimes. Freudian psychology reminds us of the powerful influence of past events (and of the curious narratives that maintain those events as elements of our lives). But present and future matters are just as important. Consistent with this, his theory of play is an explanation of how we work through issues that have been bothering us via solitary repetition-compulsions, socially protected performances, and enacted fantasy. But play is not merely a looking backward; it is also a willful move ahead or a clever step sideways.

Finally, Freud's vision of play as self-direction and mastery can be questioned. Some contemporary scholars argue that his original emphasis on psycho-biological forces (such as sexual and aggressive instincts) should not be subsumed or sanitized by rationalist explanations (Deleuze and Guattari 1984). Quite the opposite, an important aspect of being human is the sensation that one rides through life on currents of desire. Whatever guilt Freud and his patients may have attached to their urges, it is apparent that many contemporary people—and many in pre-modern societies—do not share these moral qualms. Not only do people crave what they do not have, but they actually enjoy feelings of anticipation. In other words, tension, uncertainty, and change are not unpleasant psychic conditions; they are the natural concomitants of Eros and Thanatos, the urges of life and death. One does not play to stop the world but to feel its movements.

Vygotsky's Theory of Play as Imaginative Performance

Although both Piaget and Freud describe the role of external situations (including other people) in psychic development, their theories focus on the ways in which individuals manage these influences and encounters. A more truly social psychology is offered by Vygotsky, who argued that human development is the result of complicated interactions between people and situations. Learning arises *in* experiences of rule-making, performance, and collective affirmation.

Vygotsky was familiar with some of Freud's and Piaget's writings, and his work represents a self-conscious departure from their views of development and of play. Perhaps the chief difference is that Vygotsky, like Marx, focused on action in the world and on thought as psychological participation in the processes involved in that action. This emphasis on interaction as a *process* made him oppose conceptions of knowledge as a fixed set of contents in the mind (ideas that are "in there," ready to jump out) and of language as some public spilling out of existing thought. Instead, his is a more dialectical view of human existence, a moving back and forth between thought and behavior as people negotiate the particular conditions of daily life. For such reasons, Vygotsky's writing is a source for contemporary scholars drawn to post-structuralist, non-objectivist interpretations (see Holzman 2008; Connery, John-Steiner, and Marjanovic-Shane 2010).

Vygotsky's theory of play is presented clearly in an essay first published in 1933. In that work, he rejects Freud's initial thesis that play is an honoring of the pleasure principle. After all, many other kinds of activities also give pleasure. And some games, which we think of as play, afford little pleasure (or at least grant it only at the end to those who have achieved their goals). Yet he is also critical of what he (Vygotsky 1976, p. 537) calls the "intellectualization of play," in effect, Piaget's view. Instead, play is behavior that responds to the "child's needs, inclinations, incentives, and motives to act." In other words, Vygotsky is concerned with combinations of thinking and feeling as these lead to (and arise within) actions.

This theory is developmental. That is, he associates the rise of play with a distinctive stage of child development, and he emphasizes the ways in which play preferences change as the child matures. Play styles and interests of any age are abandoned as children move on to new challenges. Indeed, this is Vygotsky's theory. As he (p. 538) puts it, "play is invented at the point unrealizable tendencies appear in development." Stated differently, as children all of us want things we cannot possess. We want to go to bed at a time of our choosing, eat sweets, and have a parent stay in our room until we go to sleep. Failure to achieve these desires is frustrating and may produce emotional outbursts.

Play, which Vygotsky (p. 540) describes as "essentially wish fulfillment," represents a new way of dealing with desires and frustrations. Although children cannot name the reasons they play ("only an adolescent can clearly determine for himself the reason he does this"), they do feel urges to redress general frustrations. In play, then, children create an "imaginary situation"; that is, they turn, transform, and rename available objects and activities in ways that help them control those newly conceived circumstances. Vygotsky is adamant that this is "never symbolic action," that is, a working out in some "algebraic" fashion the implications of ideas (surely a reference to Piaget). Instead, play involves the intersection of thinking, feeling, acting, and physical circumstances. Even more emphatically, he declares that imaginative play is not just one type of play among other types. Quite the opposite, imagination is central to all forms of play.

Furthermore, "every imaginary situation contains rules" (p. 543). This is clear in the case of games, of course, but Vygotsky means this in a deeper sense. When preschool children play, they impose new terms on their actions; that is, they choose to see (and in effect construct) a situation in a distinctive way and agree to operate by that definition of it. Players decide what objects are to be picked up and redefined, how they should be treated, what roles participants should occupy, and so forth. Even solitary play—as in Piaget's example of the boy who practices jumping across a stream—involves self-imposed restrictions, that is, expectations for what is to occur in the moments ahead. When people play, then, they engage in acts of pretense. Chief among these is the understanding that the player can determine the terms of his own action. This is not the same as freedom, which Vygotsky claims is illusory. Rather, people agree to follow self-imposed formats and adjust their actions to these constraints. Following Piaget, he argues that young children cannot distinguish clearly either the source or the potential flexibility of these rules; the ability to negotiate and alter rules comes later.

Vygotsky's theory of play is connected to his general view of the way people develop. Infants, as he sees it, can only react to conditions that are occurring around them and within them. To that degree, they demonstrate a "union of affect and perception." Something occurs that affects the baby and the baby responds; indeed, she cannot keep from responding. For toddlers, however, "things lose their motivating force" (p. 545). When three-year-olds play, they demonstrate to themselves and others that a rock need not stay in its current place or that it need not remain a rock. This process of readministering the terms of existence is a tremendous personal advance, for what it signifies is that objects (such as a rock) can be separated from their accepted meanings (what we have understood rocks to be).

This shift in awareness does not occur all at once. Indeed, play "is a transitional stage in this direction." Here (p. 546) he introduces his famous idea of the pivot. A pivot is a device (such as a broomstick) that helps the child move to a new "reality" (as when she supposedly rides a horse by straddling the broomstick). In contrast, adults have highly developed symbolic capabilities; they can decide to let a postcard (or any other object) stand for a horse. The young child requires an object that is closer to the idea it represents (a stick of a certain size). To summarize, play is "intermediary between the purely situational constraints of early childhood and thought that is totally free of real situations."

One of Vygotsky's most important ideas is that rules help the child develop impulse control. Rules force us to delay the gratification process; in that regard self-imposed rules are better than those enforced by others.

Moreover, when we accept the pretense of rules (as when we pretend to be a baby who is crying), we effectively separate ourselves from our own actions. That is, although we are making the sounds and gestures of crying, we are not really crying. Once again, play teaches us that we can impose our own meanings on the objects of the world and on our own actions.

Is all childhood activity, or the substantial portion of it, play? Vygotsky firmly says it is not (p. 551). Most of childhood is dominated by terms and requirements the child does not control. Child life, like that of adults, is difficult and demanding. Another question concerns the extent to which children imagine and perform: Is anything possible in play? Here Vygotsky (p. 552) introduces another of his most important concepts, the "zone of proximal development." As indicated above, children seem to tire quickly of activities once they have them under control. Instead, they prefer to address issues that are almost but not quite within their grasp. Play is one of the activities in which they extend and refine their grasp. Players always try to out-do themselves. As he puts it, "In play it is as though the child were trying to jump above the level of his normal behavior."

Although Vygotsky does not develop this theme in the essay discussed here, elsewhere (Vygotsky 1978) he states that other people play key roles in helping children expand their abilities. Teachers, parents, older children, and peers commonly define the terms of action in the more social forms of play. Adjusting one's behavior to those standards is the way in which new behaviors become established. Those standards must be set at levels that the child (with effort) can reach; once achieved, the standards may be set higher again. That "scaffolding," to use Bruner's (1978) term, is the mechanism by which new possibilities are shaped. Ideally, these strictures should be self-acknowledged and cooperatively maintained. We climb best when we want to climb and when the object of our quest is close enough that we forget the dangers of falling.

Because play is action-based and purposive, it is connected to development. Players, and this is particularly the case in games, have end states in mind. They push themselves forward. It is this process of movement and change, of doing, that can be called development. As people grow older, they become surer about the elements of games, including their own purposes for participating and the framework of rules that directs their activity. Settings and activities people are more able to control and to invest with their own meanings tend to be labeled as play; similar but more constrained activities are understood to be work.

To summarize, Vygotsky offered what may be called a performative view of play, one that focuses on the ways in which people use their imaginations to collectively reinvent situations and then act out their newfound responsibilities in those settings (Lobman and O'Neill 2011). These self-imposed restrictions—"rules" in their broadest meaning—are most satisfying and effective when they incrementally challenge what the child is currently able to do. Implicit in this theory is the view that children find satisfaction in self-advancement.

Vygotsky's stress on the role of imagination and pretense is important. By claiming that it is an ingredient necessary to all play, however, he discounted the possibility of infant play (sensorimotor activity). Likewise, his approach suggests that many other animal species, which presumably have less developed capacities than our own for consciously recognized pretense, do not play. Finally, and although this concern could be raised about most developmental theories, he does not emphasize adult play and development. All this raises the question of whether play leads in other directions besides self-advancement. People enjoy incremental challenges but they also enjoy simple dallying and worse (from a moralistic viewpoint), regressing to childish, forbidden, or dangerous exploits. People can climb down and across scaffolds as easily as they go up.

Some scholars have found in Vygotsky's work a model of the ways people engage with one another in activities that are creative, imaginative, and mutually supportive (see Newman and Holzman 2006; Edmiston 2008). Others argue that Vygotsky's theories of play and development are more authoritarian in spirit, a case of older people leading younger ones ahead through strategically fashioned challenges (Lambert and Clyde 2003). What is not debated is the importance of Vygotsky's central theme, which is that players engage in patterns of mutual pretense that reflect not only self-imposed restrictions but also the standards of their co-participants. From these jointly inhabited situations rise new directions for thought and behavior.

Selected Contemporary Contributions

The classic statements presented above continue to be important sources for studies of play. In that light, the current section describes selected contributions of modern psychologists. Typically, those works seek to integrate themes from the three traditions, introduce modifications to address theoretical deficiencies, or test the utility of the explanations by empirical investigation.

ERIK ERIKSON

Freud's focus on ego activity was carried forward by one of his most prominent interpreters, Erik Erikson, best known for his expansion of Freud's developmental model. Erikson turned this into a lifelong process (with eight stages) while recasting Freud's sexual focus as a treatment of more general "emotional" issues confronting the self. Erikson's theory of play is perhaps most clearly expressed in an influential essay, "Toys and Reasons." In it he argues that play "is a function of the ego, an attempt to synchronize the bodily and the social processes with the self" (Erikson 1963, p. 211). Young children, he argues, have "gangling" bodies and minds. They have not acquired the ability or the self-discipline to comprehend and regulate matters that are going on around them and within them. The "purpose of play," in his view, is to "hallucinate ego mastery and yet also to practice it in an intermediate reality between phantasy and actuality."

What issues do children wish to comprehend and control? Erikson (pp. 213–14) lists such fundamental forms and forces as "gravity" (reconsidered in games of jumping), "time" (defied by trifling and dallying), "fate and causality" (confronted in games of chance), "social reality" (addressed in imaginative performance), "bodily drives" (toying with our own urges), and even "love life" (exemplified in acts of exploration and sexual foreplay). To capitulate to any of these forces would be to experience life as subservience or compulsion. Play keeps alive a vision of people as agents of their own destiny. When we play, we turn "passivity into activity" (p. 217).

For Erikson, play is always minded. For this reason, he rejects the classic "surplus energy" theory of Herbert Spencer (1896) and the "cathartic theory" of early Freudianism. Play is not simply release of pent-up energy; it is an attempt to envision and re-enact situations charged with emotion. These situations are re-created as little fantasies, scenarios, or dramas wherein the child plays a more assertive (often heroic) role than the one in which other people usually see her.

Some play settings, however, are easier to control than others. Erikson therefore establishes three stages of playful development. *Autocosmic* play centers on the body. As small children, we explore and repeat our own "sensual perceptions," "kinesthetic sensations," and "vocalizations" (p. 220). Our sounds and movements (for example, crying) may be used to see if we can move objects in the environment (getting our mother to come).

The second and more complicated stage centers on the *microsphere*. This is "the small world of manageable toys," in effect, familiar objects the child can gather around her to do her bidding. If these objects resist the child's will (as when a block tower falls unexpectedly), she may return to autocosmic activity (such as thumb sucking). The third stage for play is the *macrosphere*. This is "the world shared with others." Initially, people are treated as things to be controlled. Soon enough, the child learns that playmates have wills comparable to her own.

Erikson was firm in his belief that children's play differs from the play of adults. The "playing child advances forward to new stages of mastery"; the "playing adult steps sideward into another reality" (p. 222). Children, it seems, are more exploratory and creative in their attempts to work out the possibilities of life. Adults seek "re-creation," a revisitation of or regression to earlier life issues. Whatever the time orientation of the playful project—as progression, regression, or digression—participants use imaginative reason to construct situations and manage behaviors and emotions within them.

JEROME BRUNER

The psychologist and educator Jerome Bruner argued that play is less a process of imposing oneself on the world (as Piaget contended) than it is an activity that explores and organizes that world. When people play, they permit themselves to use looser or even intuitive processes (rather than formal logic) to determine the character of situations. In that context, Bruner (1986a) identifies two versions of thought-making, the "paradigmatic" and the "narrative." Paradigmatic thought is mental activity of the orderly, logical sort that Piaget extols; understandings of this type are often formalized as verbal statements. Narrative thought, while still sequential, is more image-based and receptive to multiple layers of interpretation. Both skills are necessary for successful development. Narrative play helps people remember, cast up, and anticipate images of what may come. Paradigmatic play helps with orderly transitions and communication processes.

In a lecture on the connections between play, language, and thought, Bruner (1986b) described five themes of children's play. First, because play features reduced consequences for activity, it is "a superb medium for exploration. Play provides a courage all its own." Second, play softens the usual connections between means and ends. Players may abandon goals as the spirit moves them; they are fascinated more by procedures (or forms of doing) than by results. For such reasons, play "provides not only a medium for exploration, but also for invention."

The third point is that play is "very rarely random or by chance." Children decide what course of action is to be followed; they frame behavior with their own visions. To illustrate this, he re-presents a well-known example from psychology of twin sisters who declare to each other, "Let's play sisters!" Drama and pretense (Vygotsky's themes) are critical; relationships move into a new key. Fourth, "play is a projection of interior life onto the world in opposition to learning through which we interiorize the external world and make it part of ourselves." To that degree, Bruner supports the views of the previous theorists: play features an unusually assertive role for the self. Players imagine and try out scenarios. Fifth and finally, play offers pleasure. Without this understanding, he argues, "we are really missing the point of what it is about."

This account of play is consistent with Bruner's general approach to development and education. Abilities do not arise in a strict, age-related sequence. Rather, they come from familiarity with the materials one is to think about. Play is the process of creative handling wherein people get their minds (and bodies) around these materials. Children who have handled materials in their own imaginative ways are able to move more quickly to new styles of thinking. However, education is not simply a process of learning something and advancing to new challenges. It is a spiral path, a process of continually returning to life experiences and re-examining them with the knowledge of later years.

GRETA FEIN

Another integrative vision of play is provided by Greta Fein. Although Fein shared Vygotsky's interest in the sociodramatic aspects of play, she was committed also to understanding this process (essentially, an extension of pretense) in children younger than three years old and in doing this in a carefully observed, scientific manner (see Fein 1981, 1989). Moreover, her scholarship focuses on two additional variables that are crucial elements of play and learning: communication and emotion (or "affect").

Fein argues that childhood pretense (in which players use decontextualized knowledge, distinguish self from others, make object substitutions, and take roles) is the beginning of "storytelling" forms of play that become increasingly complicated and abstract as people move to adulthood. Participation in these narrative forms, she emphasizes, is less a ritualistic pattern of learning already existing forms than it is a free-floating, interpretive activity in which players improvise meanings in response to circumstances. When children play together, much of their effort is spent developing these flexible communicative frameworks.

Why do children play? Fein claims that that one of the major functions of narrative play is to help children bring to the surface deep feelings and anxieties. When we engage in socio-dramas, we create scenarios that place our general life concerns into altered formats where we can confront the issues involved and turn them into positive experiences. In that sense, she returns to Freud's emphasis on play as a response to fears and wishes, but she reconsiders these concerns as elements of public (that is, social and cultural) settings.

Fein also was interested in the interaction between structural factors (dispositions of the child) and situational factors (characteristics of the environment), especially as they influence the quality of activity in day-care centers and schools. In addition to arguing for improvements in such organizations, she was drawn to the question of why some children seem to be what she (1989) terms "master players," those who have special capacities for inventiveness and the energy to turn many settings into play (see also Lieberman 1977). The reverse of this condition—the existence of a "play deficit" in some socially and developmentally challenged children—is a prominent theme in the work of another scholar, Sara Smilansky (1968), and in the contributions of many contemporary play advocates (see F. Brown and Taylor 2008).

DOROTHY AND JEROME SINGER

The development of imagination is also central to the research of Dorothy and Jerome L. Singer. Like Fein, the Singers focus their work on the cultivation of pretense and narrative in children. Although they are conversant with all the theories described above, the Singers are especially sensitive to the Freudian tradition with its emphasis on daydreams, fantasy, nursery stories, and other imaginative exploits. For his part, Jerome Singer (see J. A. Singer and Salovey 1999) has established an integrating role as an experimental psychoanalyst who studies Freudian claims in scientifically controlled ways. Whereas Freud emphasizes play as an expression of people's long-standing concerns, the Singers are committed to seeing play as a creative opportunity, a chance to move development and learning ahead (see J. L. Singer, 1980). Furthermore, although Freud tended to emphasize past experiences as influences on psychic functioning, the Singers focus much more on current social and cultural influences. In that regard, they explore the social and psychological effects of media, especially such electronic media as television, video games, and the Internet (D. Singer and J. L. Singer 1990, 2005).

In an important work, *The House of Make-Believe*, the Singers (1990) amend Erikson's stage model of human development. As part of that reconceptualization, they identify twin themes of selfhood: individuation (learning to value one's own qualities and capabilities) and attachment (developing worthy connections to others). Note that concerns about attachment and individuation are not confined to any one stage of life. The Singers recognize that both processes can be developed to extremes (and thus exist in tension with one another). Their more general concern, however, is to supplement Erikson's focus on self-control, autonomy, and mastery (in some of the early periods of life) with more persistently social themes. Human beings need support and comradeship at every age in order to fully realize their abilities.

The Singers' view of play exemplifies this thesis. Although play is especially important to early development, people play throughout their lives. Imaginary play, their focus in *The House of Make-Believe,* addresses different life challenges. It is critically important that play is not merely a case of strategic assertion (a testing and refinement of children's powers); it is also a pattern of engagement involving touching, comforting, smiles of support, bonding, and respecting. In other words, the Singers argue that (what I call) communitas is a fundamental aspect of the best forms of play.

That interest in otherness as a source of personal support leads them to evaluate the roles of other people and of culturally supplied play formats as promoters of human development. Parents and teachers should not abandon their responsibilities (by letting children play in whatever ways they choose); they should guide that play in unobtrusive but supportive ways. Similarly, caregivers should monitor the television and computer habits of their charges. If parents choose not to play this supervisory role, they must recognize that other adults (as the makers and distributors of this material) will do so. Imaginary play (including television and video game participation) is not simply an expression of the players' psychic concerns; it is an intersection between biological development, personality, culturally produced formats, and social relationships. Not all play contexts are equal; some support human development better than others.

The work of the Singers is very wide-ranging in its examination of the many factors that sustain the play context, and they have become champions of adult-supported play. Their approach is still based on the dominant view in psychology that people thrive best when they are guided by orderly structures, patterns, or frameworks. Even the more daring feats of people—expressed by imagination, creativity, and play—should be bounded.

BRIAN SUTTON-SMITH

A different approach is taken by the folklorist and comparative psychologist Brian Sutton-Smith. He acknowledges that play is commonly a form of order-seeking, but he also stresses that players relish improbability, disorder, and destruction (see Sutton-Smith and Kelly-Byrne, 1984b). However well-intentioned authority figures may be in their efforts to guide children, they should recognize that children—and the rest of us—may try to evade those controls. This search for the untried and unapproved is not time wasted; it is the process by which creatures expand the range of their capabilities.

Probably more than any other major scholar, Sutton-Smith has concentrated his long career on the character and implications of play. Although his writing focuses on children's play, his interest is much more wide-ranging than this. His background as a folklorist has made him especially sensitive to the cross-cultural meanings of play. Furthermore, he incorporates animal behavior studies and neuroscience into his theories. His gathering of play research and theory, *The Ambiguity of Play* (Sutton-Smith 1997), brings together accounts from many disciplines. The seven rhetorics of play scholarship that he develops in that book were discussed in Chapter 1.

In an important essay, "The Idealization of Play," Sutton-Smith and Diana Kelly-Byrne (1984a) state a concern that is central to much of Sutton-Smith's writing. Because of many factors (including the widespread commitment to individual development and the humanistic values of play scholars themselves), the field of play studies has promoted the idea that play is an unmitigated good. To be sure, play often provides wholesome experiences for everyone involved, but it can take other guises such as physical attack, cruel teasing, and destruction of property. On the surface, activities of this sort may not seem especially functional as preparation for adult life; nor are they approved—at least in their rawer forms—by adult caretakers. Although some scholars see these rambunctious, deviant forms of play as problematic, Sutton-Smith and Kelly-Byrne argue that play should be recognized as an occasion when children defy social conventions.

In his memoir, Sutton-Smith (2008) identifies three stages of his theories. The first is that play is a "viability variable" (p. 90). On the basis of his experiences growing up in New Zealand and of his studies of children's playground games and jokes, he claims that play often exhibits a "labile, intentionally contrary" quality (p. 91). These acts of rebellion are fun, for they reflect a release from parental restriction and showcase personal will. Sutton-Smith argues that play of this sort may be functional. For animals as well as for humans, play operates as a "genetically based technique that allows us to triumph over regular, ordinary distress and disasters, or more simply, to feel good about life in general" (p. 95). He adds that play supports a "lively viability" that assists survival.

His second theoretical stage focuses on "culturally relative play forms" (p. 99). In examining accounts of play and especially teasing in other studies, Sutton-Smith emphasizes the different ways in which societies encourage joking. When young children are teased (and when they tease older relatives), they are freed from static patterns of relationship. They also learn that love is founded in "free and familiar" relations. The larger point is that play must be understood in its social context. Intragroup conflict, if channeled in certain ways, may produce social solidarity. At any rate, knowledge of traditional societies helps us counter "the modern notion of play as a realm of solitary imaginative freedom, autonomy, and non-functionality" (p. 108).

Sutton-Smith's third theoretical stage is "play as a co-evolutionary multiplex of functions" (p. 111). On the basis of his studies of play research from many disciplines, he concludes that no academic perspective—not even psychology—is adequate to identify play's variable expressions and multiple meanings. Play is caused by many different factors and assists relationships between the player and the wide range of circumstances that are the conditions of existence.

In that context, the first pattern of "adaptation" is what he calls the "evolutionary conflict origins of play" (p. 113). To state this briefly, play is initially an evolutionarily based response pattern that allows creatures to engage in faux conflict with their chief competitors (typically members of their own species) so as to establish placement in ongoing social relationships. The second adaptive layer is play as "reflexive and reflective" (ibid.). To paraphrase, the brains of creatures such as mammals develop processes that allow them to think before they act. Play becomes associated with imitation and learning.

The third adaptive layer features "the duality of primary and secondary emotions" (p. 114). Arguably, play is a mechanism that helps participants mediate between feelings that are biologically based (such as surprise, anger, and fear) and those which arise from participation in cultural and social forms (such as guilt, remorse, and humor). Play activities occur in settings where we awaken and then manage these feelings. Indeed, play helps us keep some of these feelings (presumably aids to survival) alive.

The fourth adaptive layer is "duality of play performances" (p. 115). Play is frequently a form of acting before others; it has social meanings. We tease and compete. But we also recognize that our place in the group depends on recognition from others. The fifth and final layer of adaptation he calls "dualistic, cultural scripts" (ibid.). Play is a form of cultural adaptation. It occurs (at least in human societies) as a response to patterns of opportunity and constraint created by social structure.

As may be apparent, Sutton-Smith's restless investigations of play signify his desire to discover the many contexts that are pertinent to human functioning. Different forms of play reflect different layers of adaptation; any play event can be meaningful at different layers. For such reasons play is usually "ambiguous." Still, I should note that his approach is largely an account of individual adaptation. Play exists as an ongoing feature of human and animal life because it helps creatures survive. For this reason, Sutton-Smith's interpretations stay close to the psychological camp.

Play as Therapy

Many psychologists and educators emphasize the connections between play and two aspects of cognition: knowledge of the world (that is, understandings of the world's forms and processes) and skills for creating and administering those understandings. They present evidence to show that play performs such functions as lengthening attention spans, cultivating creativity, achieving emotion control, and heightening social skills pertinent to other life settings (see D. Singer, Golinkoff, and Hirsch-Pasek 2009; Fromberg and Bergen 2006). A related issue is whether play promotes knowledge of the self. That is, does play help people come to terms with their own placement in the world and with the feelings that attend those circumstances?

As discussed above, the Freudian tradition has been a rich source of insights about our desires and emotions. People feel themselves carried along by sensations and feelings they have difficulty controlling or even naming. As a result, all of us say and do things we come to regret. Sometimes those unfortunate behaviors become habits or compulsions. Psychoanalysis creates safe spaces where people talk about those actions and experiences. Making these declarations (confessions of a sort) and interpreting them with a new meaning system is difficult for most of us. We cling to explanations we have lived with; we resist changes that make us uncomfortable. Furthermore, most of us do not have the social skills, cognitive acumen, or linguistic ability to easily re-create these frameworks. Children, in particular, have Erikson's "gangling" bodies and minds. Thus, expressions of less censored or formalized thought—in the guise of dreams, daydreams, memories of distant events, fantasies, art, angry outbursts, jokes, and play—may be revelations of deeper concerns.

Freud focused his therapy on older patients. His daughter Anna (A. Freud 1965) extended the fundamental approaches of psychoanalysis to young children. Play and toys were understood to be resources for the therapist, actions and objects that could substitute for verbal accounts. In opposition to her famous father, she argued that therapeutic interpretation (what words, objects, and actions "mean") must reflect the child's developmental stage and cognitive abilities.

Play's role in child therapy is also central to a rival Freudian tradition led by Melanie Klein. In contrast to Anna Freud's focus on ego development (as the emerging ability to make sense of internal and external reality), Klein (1955) emphasized deep-seated feelings (sexual and aggressive urges) as qualities of children. Recalling Freud's speculations about life and death instincts, Klein argued that young children are animated by contrary desires: to reach out, attach, and develop relationships with others and oppositely, to withdraw, resist, and destroy. These propensities to attach and oppose are fundamental human themes and not simply moral issues generated by some cognitively conceived conscience (or superego) that arises later in childhood.

Klein's focus on object relations, especially the connections between young children and their primary caregivers (as examples of human objects), influenced her approach to play therapy. She participated actively in play with her patients, willingly following their commands to be the shaggy dog or scolding parent. Her interpretations of these events consistently reflect her view that children in play explore feelings of hatred, envy, and libidinal desire toward parents, concerns that are usually thought to require greater physical and mental maturity than young children possess.

An intermediate position was advanced by D. W. Winnicott. Like Klein, Winnicott saw psychic development in the context of object relations (especially interpersonal relations). Some of these interactions express the deep, quasi-instinctual urges to attach and oppose (as Klein describes them), but others involve ego-dominated interpretations of challenges from the external environment (following Anna Freud). Winnicott understood play to be an activity that resides in the *space between* players (typically, mother and child in the earliest years). When people play—even when their actions are simply physical movements and responses to movement—they are exploring the character of their relationships and their own standing in those relationships. What elements of the world can be trusted? What must be feared?

As part of that learning process, Winnicott emphasized the importance of what he called the "transitional object," such as a favored blanket or teddy bear. Reminiscent of Vygotsky's pivots, such objects are devices that help us become aware of object relationships and of possible stances toward those objects (clinging to them, loving them, being mean to them, or leaving them behind). Furthermore, those objects help children make the transition from being deeply embedded in relationships (especially the mother-child dyad) to examining relationships in a more distanced, ego-controlled way.

In a striking argument, Winnicott states that therapy itself should be seen as play. As he (1971, p. 38) puts it: "Psychotherapy takes place in the overlap of two areas of play, that of the patient and that of the therapist. Psychotherapy has to do with two people playing together. The corollary of this is that where playing is not possible then the work done by the therapist is directed towards bringing the patient from a state of not being able to play into a state of being able to play." Several conclusions derive from this proposition. Therapists themselves must be willing to play, that is, to step down from their authoritative position to enter the world of the child. Furthermore, therapy must be reconceived as an *interactive, creative event* that draws energy from both participants. In that sense, play is different from fantasy, in which the child's imagination is given free rein. Play features real objects and real people. If the adult player's role is too strong, the activity becomes a pattern of conformity that causes the child to construct a "false self." For Winnicott, then, childhood play—and therapy as a special instance of this—is essential for developing reality-management skills. Self-confidence developed at this level may lead to artistic and professional creativity later in life.

Play therapists draw inspiration from other traditions besides the Freudian approach (see Schaefer 1992; Homeyer and Morrison 2008; Holzman 2008). Therapists use play both as an occasion to notice and identity pertinent issues and as a social theater, where participants act out new possibilities. Because play and toys are the language of children, concerns can be expressed with reduced fear of rebuke or censorship. Attachment issues, anxiety, anger, depression, attention deficit–hyperactivity disorder, and other issues can be addressed. More pointedly, and as Russell Meares (2005) emphasizes, play of this type builds the self. Players negotiate the relation of aloneness to togetherness. Paralleling the judgments of teachers, practitioners recognize that beneficial development depends on patterns of trust and open communication.

All this supports the general view taken in this book that play helps people explore the implications of self, in its individual and collective dimensions. Following Piaget, some play takes the form of manipulation or psychic imposition. Other forms, as Sutton-Smith emphasizes, are rebellion against powerful people and conventions. Still others are imaginative exploration, as the Singers, Fein, and Bruner maintain. Finally, following Vygotsky and Winnicott, there is the play of dialogue, in which participants honor one another through intersubjective exchanges, and by those processes, build relationships.

5 Play's Nature

This chapter explores another context or theater of play: the body. Play is always a biomechanical affair. This is obvious in the case of physically based games and sports. Yet even in such narrowly cognitive activities as solving puzzles and writing lines of poetry, we rely on physical capacities. Sometimes we can bring to consciousness the particular word we want to insert in our poem or crossword box; sometimes, however hard we try to remember, we cannot.

Our feats of thinking, feeling, and acting depend profoundly on structures of the body and the brain. Decisions to play are conditioned by our physical forms. Feelings about what we are doing—registered as sensations and emotions—arise from long-established physical processes. And we move through the world only as our bodies permit. Understanding play means understanding these physical processes. With that resolve, the current chapter focuses on studies of bodily movement, brain activity, consciousness, and affect in both humans and animals. Those descriptions are guided by a deeper concern: Is there some biological fundament of playfulness that motivates that activity and profits from its occurrence?

Animal Play

One of the most important ways to learn about the character and implications of play is to study other species. Play is widespread among mammals (90 percent of mammal species exhibiting that behavior) and among birds (Fagen 1981). Arguably, other types of creatures including fish, lizards, and turtles also produce playlike behavior (Burghardt 2005).

For the most part, animal play is studied for the same reasons human play is studied, that is, to understand what creatures are capable of and how they organize those behaviors. But the study of animals also provides insights into the evolutionary origins of our own species and into the ways in which the older (subcortical) regions of the brain operate. Researchers can observe animal behavior in both natural and artificial environments with an invasive scrutiny that is impermissible for human subjects (see Bekoff and Byers 1998). In addition, experiments are done on animals (such as separation of infants from mothers, surgical excisions, electrical stimulation, and chemical dosing) that cannot be done with people. The result of this research is that scientists now have much better understandings of how brains and bodies work (see Panksepp 2010).

Is animal play similar to human play? As the ethologist Niko Tinbergen (1963, p. 413) observed, assessments that animals are playing (and learning) inevitably have "subjectivist, anthropomorphic undertones." Who has not watched a kitten or puppy at play and been struck by how much that activity resembles the romping of a human toddler? Clearly, our pets orient themselves to us and try to engage us with their high spirits. We watch them explore behavior patterns. We see their desire to play decline as they age. Any trip to the zoo will show young animals interacting with their fellow inmates in much the same way. Is this the self-determined, creative type of play we identify with humans, or is it simply the exercising of deeply established compulsions?

This, perhaps, is the wrong question. According to the perspectives presented in preceding chapters, humans themselves operate at different levels. We are (at the same time) sensorimotor *creatures* as well as *creators* who accomplish fabulous symbolic exploits. Our play expresses this duality. When young children engage in rough-and-tumble play or when adults participate in vigorous sports they explore the assertive and responsive capabilities of their bodies. One learns quickly who is fast or slow, strong or weak, agile or clumsy; those abilities rank each boy and girl in the community of their fellows. Creative activity—building things via the arrangement of material objects or via symbolic expression—is simply another mode of assertion wherein people discover where they stand *within* (and what they can do *with*) the elements of the world. As Piaget's theory makes plain, play activities reflect a gradient between physical engagement and symbolic engagement. Between these extremes lie all manner of interesting combinations.

I have examined the question of whether play is the inspired creation of an unfettered ego. Although play is less restricted than most other activities, it is not ungrounded. Players need real-world elements to guide and measure their efforts. Nor can they bypass their own psychological orientations, the patterns of symbolic and sensory commitment that shape thought and behavior. Frequently, the choice to play is preceded by feelings of internal disturbance or compulsion. We feel bored or restless, and self-sponsored activity is one response to such complaints. Where these urges come from, as the Freudian tradition maintains, is difficult to discern. Yet most people, I think, would acknowledge that creatures need appropriate levels of stimulation or stress and counterbalancing tension release or relaxation. As discussed below, play may be a behavior that evolved to help creatures develop and monitor processes of physical equilibration.

Like humans, animals exhibit a range of play behaviors. Three types are commonly identified (Burghardt 2005). These are locomotor-rotational play (manipulations of the body, often performed alone), object play (explorations of non-utilitarian elements from the material world), and social play (interactive behaviors, especially chasing and fighting). There are other models as well. Mitchell (1990) suggests four levels, the last being seemingly intentional acts of pretense and communication. Fagen (1995) offers five levels, each featuring successively more complex social interaction and bonding. Whatever the number of levels, these approaches are based on the view that play types lower in the scheme are simpler and evolutionarily prior patterns. In that light, highly sophisticated creatures such as monkeys and dogs exhibit all these patterns.

If these evolutionary typologies of play are accepted, it follows that some species are capable of only the lowest levels of physical manipulation and perform them in such a (meandering, unspirited) way that many researchers have difficulty acknowledging that the term *play* should be applied. The contrasting claim that great numbers of species in the animal kingdom play has been advanced by Burghardt (2005, 2010). He argues, for example, that an octopus manipulating a foreign object (perhaps a bottle or Lego block) in varied, inventive ways for several minutes is an incidence of play. So is the activity of fishes that leap, juggle objects, and tease other inhabitants of their setting. As he (2010, p. 346) summarizes, "Current data strongly suggest that some animals from many other groups, including fishes, insects, mollusks, and reptiles, can and do play." Whether one agrees that the actions of smaller-brained creatures are at all equivalent to those of bigger-brained (and more behaviorally flexible) species, this question is intriguing. *At some point* behavioral flexibility—including the ability to engage the world in consciously directed but seemingly non-utilitarian ways—developed in species. Arguably, these simple manipulations foreshadow later, more complex forms.

More generally, researchers of other species have shown how interesting and complicated the lives of their subjects are and how that complexity includes the behaviors described above (see Smith 1984). This does not mean that defining play in animals is any easier than it is in humans. Indeed, the problem is more difficult because there are so many species (each with its own capabilities), because there is no uniformly accepted typology of animal behavior, and because researchers cannot talk to the animals to know what they are experiencing. Motives, intentions, and rewards must be surmised from observations of behavior, researcher-directed interactions, and measurements of physiological processes. This difficulty led the sociobiologist E. O. Wilson (1975, p. 114) to proclaim that "no behavioral concept has proved more ill-defined, elusive, controversial, and even unfashionable than play."

In the face of such complexities, Fagen (1981, p. 52) acknowledges that "though no molar category of behavior is easily defined, play does appear to be especially difficult." Nevertheless his classic book *Animal Play Behavior* is directed toward establishing a working definition of play, primarily so researchers can focus their observations more effectively and communicate their findings coherently to others. In his view, "play research needs better theory" (p. 37). With that end in mind, he states that play is "behavior that functions to develop, practice, or maintain physical or cognitive abilities and social relationships, including both tactics and strategies, by varying, repeating, and/or recombining already functional sequences of behavior outside their primary context. It is a matter of taste whether behaviors that do not simultaneously satisfy the structural, causal-contextual, functional, and developmental criteria of this definition are to be called play" (p. 65). As Fagen makes clear, there are several elements of play (structural, functional, developmental, and causal-contextual), and few real-life behaviors meet all the criteria he lists. His general approach is important, however, not only because he attempts a trans-species definition but also because he recognizes that play needs to be seen in relation to other kinds of behavior such as aggression, predator avoidance, sexual expression, and feeding patterns. Sometimes, segments of behavior pertinent to these themes are brought into the play context and become parts of it. Sometimes play turns into something more serious such as real aggression. But even when these intersections of behavior do not occur, it is critical to see play in the wider context of what creatures do. In its own way, the present book follows Fagen's "definition by contrast" approach.

Burghardt's (2005, pp. 69–82; 2010) five essential criteria for play, as noted in Chapter 1, include an activity's having a "limited immediate function" (that is, not clearly related to the creature's ongoing survival needs) and an "endogenous component" (it is pleasurable, intrinsically reinforcing, or otherwise done for its own sake). Play also exhibits "structural or temporal difference" (especially, incomplete and exaggerated strips of behavior), "repeated performance" (behaviors carried out again and again as if the creature is trying to get better at them), and a "relaxed field" (permitting the creature to be "adequately fed, healthy, and free from stress"). Burghardt (2005, p. 82) summarizes his view as follows: "*Play is repeated, incompletely functional behavior differing from more serious versions structurally, contextually, or ontogenetically, and initiated voluntarily when the animal is in a relaxed or low-stress setting*" (italics in original).

Although no definition is accepted universally, there is agreement among animal researchers that play is an important part of the maturation process. Some play seems to be an expression of young creatures seeking to get better at life skills, but other examples display what Fagen calls "post-mastery" activity—exploration, romping, and embellishment by individuals who already have established skill sets. Within species, older individuals are less inclined to play. The complexity of play is related to the species' brain size (as a percentage of body size), and play's prevalence is associated with periods when the brain is developing most rapidly. Other factors, as described below, are also important.

Classic Theories of Play

It is remarkable that the first influential book about animal play was written by a philosopher of aesthetics. Karl Groos's *Play of Animals* (1898) is an attempt to integrate the animal research of his time and, on that basis, to offer a theory of the origins of animal play and the extent to which that activity provides an ancient foundation for human art-making and aesthetic experience. Groos, like many academics of his time, was influenced strongly by Darwin's ideas of physical evolution and the role of natural selection in that process. Groos's concern was to show how behavior patterns are established in species and how those instincts become loosened in creatures that become dependent on learning or imitation. His theory, at least as it is usually described, is that play is a practicing of the instincts. As he (1898, p. xx) argues, young animals have instinctual inclinations and capabilities before they are ready to use them in adult ways. In that sense, play is preparation for adult life.

Equally important, however, is the idea that biological capacities for play (in which creatures refine skills and learn from experience) are associated with a softening of firmly established behavior patterns. Animals that develop through play do not require rigid, immediately useful, or "perfect" instincts. As Gross (p. xx) famously states, *"the very existence of youth is due to the necessity for play;* the animal does not play because he is young, he has a period of youth because he must play" (italics in original). Furthermore, the pleasure that creatures feel when they play is part of a motivational package that is there to ensure that play happens. Ultimately, these capacities expand further as cognitive complexity (and imitative learning) increasingly confer a survival advantage over animals with more limited behavioral repertoires. In humans, as Groos (1901) stated in a subsequent book, play is dominated by imitative impulses rather than by instincts. Seen in that light, Groos's theory is as much about supplementing and replacing instincts as it is about practicing them.

The Play of Animals was a response to the then-popular "surplus energy" theory of play. That approach owed much to the poet Schiller's 1795 postulation of a "play drive" that mediates between the two extremes of rationality and sensuality in human experience. For Schiller (1965), play comes from the welling up of an exuberant, sensual spirit that expresses itself ultimately in cultural or aesthetic form. Play reflects our important (and for the Romantics, essential) status as natural creatures. In such ways, play integrates symbolic and sensory meaning, the twin themes of the present book's account of play as a pattern of sense-making.

Schiller's theory was given an interesting refurbishing by the nineteenth-century social philosopher Herbert Spencer. Spencer was preoccupied with the application of Darwin's theory to the evolution of societies. In Spencer's (1896) view, simpler creatures tend to use all their energy meeting their daily needs—finding food, avoiding predators, staying warm, and procreating. Higher creatures are able to satisfy these needs and still have additional stores of energy to spend. This excess of energy is especially valuable (in terms of survival) for species that live in complicated environments and that exhibit diversified behaviors. Although these higher life forms also use energy to meet specific needs, they have reserves left for other purposes. When these reserves are overbuilt, the animal spills some of this excess in acts of tension release, or play.

Spencer tended to see imitation as key to play; creatures do what their comrades are doing. With regard to animals, at least, Groos argued against this view. As Groos pointed out, individual creatures of the same species (think of a kitten playing with a ball of yarn) behave in much the same way and require no models to follow. As he saw it, that similarity across isolated individuals must derive from some instinctual basis, which becomes elaborated through practice. Likewise, he opposed the Schiller-Spencer thesis that play should be understood primarily as a spending of energy. The process of energy buildup, release, and expenditure is not enough to explain why play takes the specific forms it does.

A variant of the above theory—indeed, in some ways its opposite—is the recreation perspective. According to this account (see Lazarus 1883), players do not expend energy. Rather, they build or create energy in their pursuits. This rejuvenation is to be contrasted with the wearying, stressful nature of work. In other words, boredom and fatigue are play's instigators. Different again is the relaxation theory (see Patrick 1916), which focuses primarily on human play in industrial societies. "Civilized" people, or so the thinking goes, are subject to physically confining jobs, long periods of sustained attention to narrow tasks, intensive cognitive activity, and the use of small muscle groups. Play is a counterbalancing maneuver whereby people try to free themselves from these unnatural conditions. As people play they recuperate or restore themselves. To use a modern example, hardworking schoolchildren—and the rest of us—need recess.

Still another theory was advanced by G. Stanley Hall, who (1931) argued that play is a recapitulation of previous stages of evolutionary development, a re-expression of behavior patterns that once were crucial to survival but are no longer needed. In several of the theories presented above, play is presented as a pleasing break from routine, doing what has not been done before. In Hall's theory, play is an act of evolutionary remembrance or exhumation. When we play, we rediscover capabilities buried deep within us.

Hall's theory expresses the once-popular doctrine that ontogeny recapitulates phylogeny. That is, individual creatures in the early periods of life go through stages of evolution that are necessary to the development of their species. This is illustrated by the fact that different species look similar at certain points in their embryonic stage or even (for closely related species) during their infancy. To cite a commonly used example, human fetuses at one stage in their development exhibit vestigial gill slits. As individuals mature, differentiation of the species occurs. The heads of human and chimpanzee infants look similar, but those of adult humans and chimpanzees are different. Play, which is preeminently an activity of youthful (and by definition, not developed) creatures, is the outward manifestation of these ancient formations and commitments.

These classical theories of play, like theories of every era, reflect the intellectual currents of their times. Nineteenth- and early twentieth-century ideas regarding physical evolution, species development, natural selection, and instincts abound. There is a fascination with energy and the mechanics of behavior. Also central are concerns about the relation of humans to animals (in which humans are presumed superior) and about the differences between "civilized" peoples and those who live in more traditional ways. In such a context, play is portrayed as a biologically supported behavior that allows creatures both to communicate with their evolutionary past and to prepare themselves for future life responsibilities. For most of the theorists, play is connected to ideas about individual and social development as "progress."

It is easy enough to dismiss these theories because of their partial (and taken as a whole, somewhat contradictory) claims and because of the absence at that time of a strong research tradition to evaluate their adequacy. Still, those general approaches, which flourished during a time when many people lived on fairly intimate terms with animals and had profound knowledge of them, remain pertinent. Interest in the evolution of species and the distinctive behaviors associated with each persists (although the notion of evolution as straight-line progress has been dropped). Important also are questions about the connection of creatures to their distant ancestors and to other present-day creatures that are genetically similar. The relation between inherited physical endowment and imitation or learning as factors in individual expression continues to be studied. And the rhetoric of play's performing some role in the adaptation of individuals and species lives on.

Rethinking the Role of the Organism in Play

Just as the concept of instinct has been replaced by more complicated understandings of the way animals operate, so the industrial era's commitment to the concept of energy has lost its steam (see Collins 2004, for an exception). It tends to be presumed now that creatures will find the resources to be active; the question is how they direct that activity. In that light, a somewhat different image of the way creatures become engaged with the world developed from the behaviorist tradition. That process—of becoming attracted to something and then responding to it—is described by Ellis (1973) as "stimulus-seeking."

As a distinctive approach to human and animal studies, behaviorism focuses on creatures' observable actions with regard to observable objects (see Skinner 1974). Occurrences or conditions in the external world are said to present themselves to consciousness as stimuli. Reactions of creatures to stimuli are termed *responses*. Behavior patterns are understood to be stimulus-response sequences. Some of these behaviors seem to be biologically programmed in more or less fixed ways; others are the result of experience or conditioning. As the name implies, behaviorists try to refrain from making inferences about what cannot be observed by researchers, most specifically the "black box" of the mind. Yet there is a presumption that creatures are either satisfied or dissatisfied by their encounters with stimuli. Rewarding experiences are thought to reinforce responses positively (and thus encourage their continuity); negative experiences discourage future associations of that type. The absence of stimulation—and thereby the deprivation of both reward and punishment—is a middle case, and problematic in its own way. So understood, behaviorism is a scientifically garbed utilitarianism, a theory that individual creatures establish life commitments based on their perceptions of self-interest (and more nakedly, on calculations of pleasure and pain).

Because studies of play typically involve speculations about the subjective experiences of players and focus on behavioral creativity and novelty, behaviorist accounts have not been prominent in this field. However, there is a version of behaviorism called S-O-R, or stimulus-organism-response, that provides insights into why creatures actively pursue novelty or otherwise break routine (Ellis 1973). As the name implies, this modified form of behaviorism grants the organism a more independent role as something that seeks stimuli, participates in the processing of that information, and selectively manages responses.

One of the most prominent of these researchers, Daniel Berlyne (1960, 1966), argued that animals and humans do not desire well-worn routines; they have a tendency—indeed, a biological predisposition—to discover new sources of stimulation and through those contacts to experience "arousal." The implication of this idea is important, because the concept of arousal suggests that creatures not only evaluate their relationships with stimuli as positive or negative but also judge the *intensity* of those satisfactions.

Most of us would acknowledge that too much of the same thing—even a thing we like very much—can become tiresome. Pleasant routines can become boring, or rather, can become so taken for granted that they fail to be experienced as pleasant. This inflationary effect, resulting in an absence of positive or negative stimulation, is problematic. Too little stimulation is undesirable; so is too much. It is easy enough to see that too much *negative* stimulation (such as extremely loud noises or threats from other people) is anxiety-producing, but it may also be the case that profusions of the pleasant—gifts, compliments, job offers, and the like—may also produce feelings of disorientation and uncertainty. In Berlyne's view, creatures seek optimal levels of arousal; that is, they prefer to operate between the latitudes of anxiety and boredom. That theme, it may be recalled, is also central to Csikszentmihalyi's depictions of flow, described in Chapter 2.

One might conclude that animals and humans depend (ultimately) on good fortune to find themselves in rich, complicated environments that stimulate them at the appropriate levels. Such is many people's view of paradise. Berlyne's theory is more complicated. He emphasizes the development of what behaviorists call a proactive "orienting reflex" (Ellis 1973, p. 84) in animals that helps them selectively attend to stimuli, create expectations about stimuli of that type, and determine whether future interaction with such elements is warranted. In other words, higher creatures do not wait passively for life opportunities to parade in front of them; they seek them out. Creatures that are even more cognitively complicated have acquired the ability to provide their own internal stimulation, experienced as the casting up of image-based memories and (at some point) conceptualized thought.

This ability of mind to seek out and process stimulation from external sources and then perform these same processes on an entirely internal basis is associated with the development of new areas of the brain. The older regions of the brain surrounding the end of the spinal cord are especially important for regulating sensorimotor activity, including such largely unconscious activities as breathing and digesting. The brain's newer (and more peripheral) regions play special roles in making mental associations, coordinating internal neural traffic, and expressing this interaction through deliberately controlled behaviors and vocalizations. As the ratio between (the sizes of) these new and old brain regions shifts in the direction of the new, so does the ability of species to consciously regulate their own stimulation.

To be sure, activities involved in the seeking of food and water, mates, predator avoidance, and protection from heat and cold are important sources of stimulation. Arousal of that sort is the natural concomitant of need-satisfaction (what I've described as "adaptation" or "work"). There also seems to be desire for non-utilitarian arousal, however. Creatures need to keep their internal processing systems sharp. This may mean seeking out new sources of external stimulation (during times when creatures are freed from their customary urgencies), exploring familiar stimuli in unfamiliar ways (to reconsider the possibilities they present and the variety of responses that can be made to them) or, in the case of the most mentally complicated creatures, to arouse themselves through imaginary exploit. At the individual level, creatures may experience this stimulus-seeking as pleasantly arousing and be motivated to continue it on those terms. But its unrecognized effect may be its development and expansion of experience-based knowledge and skill sets that are pertinent to life's unforeseen challenges. Such themes are elements of Sutton-Smith's theories of play, described in Chapter 4.

Arguably, then, play is one way in which creatures explore and express curiosity. Play features the interaction of internal and external realities. Players do not simply contemplate or observe the world; they ask that world to stimulate them in ways that arouse and please. Having worked through the possibilities of things (including their prospects for injury or gratification), players declare the event *consummated* and move on to something else. All this seems non-utilitarian, unless—as Chapter 3 insists—there is utility in refurbishing the self.

One way to think about this issue is to see play as a building and maintenance of expectation systems. If simple creatures have the orienting reflex that Berlyne describes, more cognitively complicated animals have elaborately developed abilities to remember and, on the basis of those memories, to anticipate what will occur if somewhat familiar environmental conditions are present and previously used strategies are followed. Creatures with the ability to remember where predators have been, where water is to be found, where prey typically congregates, and so forth surely have survival advantages over their forgetful cousins.

As discussed above, Groos saw play as a refining of the instincts. The juvenile period of life exists so that animals have time to fashion the abilities they need as adults. At one level, this theory makes little sense, for animals that develop adult skills in the shortest possible time should have advantages over those that dawdle. Indeed, a study of killings of seal pups by animal predators (Harcourt 1991), showed that most of the killings (twenty-two of twenty-six) occurred while the pups were playing. Why extend the maturation period and have it filled with a self-indulgent, unvigilant, risk-taking activity such as play? Groos's theory makes sense only when it is understood in terms of its second theme. Play is not simply an exercising of the instincts; it is a behavioral pattern that supplements inherited dispositions with experience-based learning. The reason creatures play may be to develop a repertoire of memories and skills that can be called into action in ever-changing settings. Seal pups live in a complicated world of land and sea filled with prey and predators that come and go without warning. The death of some pups—like that of young primates falling from trees—is the cost of maintaining a developmental system that prizes exploration and risk-taking.

Robert Fagen (2005) offers a sophisticated presentation of these themes. In his view, play is one of five "gates of evolution," behavior patterns that support adaptation and change. Many followers of Darwin emphasize the economic gate of evolution, that is, the emergence of characteristics that make some members of a species able to survive in complicated environments. For Fagen, the second gate is sexual selection. Individuals choose mates on the basis of criteria other than sheer size and strength, qualities directly related to dominance and survival. Of special interest to Fagen is the third gate, aesthetic selection, the establishment of preferences for certain kinds of settings and stimuli. Much like sexual selection, these biases (for what feels right) differ from criteria that directly support survival. In other words, as part of their evolution, animals develop a wider array of subjectively maintained orientations. But how can these preferences change?

For Fagen, the answer to this question is provided by another gate of evolution, the playful, or "ludic." Play's function is to destabilize orientation patterns. It does this, first, by courting variation, improbability, or "driving noise" that loosens (or "springs the trap" of) aesthetic preferences. Second, play emerges as a specific behavior strategy that emphasizes discontinuity, disequilibrium, and novelty. Third and finally, play produces a "T.S. Eliot effect," the extent to which play's realizations cause creatures to rethink what has come before, indeed, to recast many aspects of their orientation regimes (pp. 24–30). To summarize, play is a force for disequilibrium and change that allows creatures to overcome the limitations of genetic direction and cultivates responses to widely varying situations.

Fagen's fifth gate of evolution is the "agapic." As part of their subjective trajectory, some species develop a deeper power of reflection which reveals that "beauty is skin deep, adds compassion to play's brittle brightness, and shows us the power of artificial selection at work in nature" (Fagen 2005, p. 33). As the reader can see, this approach emphasizes that creaturely success involves much more than economic adaptation. And it extends Groos's view that play disarms instinct and opens the way for

new patterns of behavioral commitment including, ultimately, appreciation for the transcendent.

Play as Expression of Surplus Resources

Gordon Burghardt (1984, 2005, 2010) has offered a theory that integrates
many of the above themes. He shares the commitment of Darwin and
the classic play theorists to trace the evolution of behavior patterns in
animals and humans. Much like Fagen, he decries the lack of appropriate
theory to guide ethological scholarship. Like Fagen as well, he emphasizes
the importance of distinguishing play from such similar expressions as
exploration (a behaviorally restricted, deliberate inspection that typically
precedes play's more energetic, behaviorally variable treatment of that
same object) and stereotyped behavior (extremely repetitive, limited actions such as a bear's pacing back and forth in its cage or a parrot's hop-
ping from one perch to another).

Burghardt (2005, p. 121) argues that previous research has been side-
tracked by disagreement over whether play should be seen as consequence or cause of species development: *"We now recognize that play
can be viewed as both a product and cause of evolutionary change:
that is, playful activities may be a source of enhanced behavioral and
mental functioning as well as a by-product or remnant of prior evolutionary events"* (italics in original). In that sense, he brings together the
ancestral legacy approach of Hall, the feelings of playful urgency in the
surplus energy theories, and Groos's commitment to seeing play as both
practice and progress.

Burghardt conceptualizes three levels of play. The first he terms
"primary process play," behavior that is pertinent to "animals that play
rarely or simply" (2005, p. 119). Many behaviors of animals (and humans)
are quasi-accidental in character. They are simply variations that occur
in response to sudden environmental challenges or as expressions of
"excess metabolic energy." Primary process play does not usually lead
to changes in behavior, but it can be a kind of "pre-adaptation," a new
possibility that might be extended.

"Secondary process play" is behavior that may have "evolved some
role, although not necessarily an exclusive or even major one, in the
maintenance or refinement and normal development of physiological
and behavioral capacities." Play of this sort may somehow prove useful
to predation, defense, food procurement, and so forth. Finally, there is
"tertiary process play," which has gained a major if not critical role in
modifying and enhancing behavioral abilities and fitness, including the

development of innovation and creativity" (p. 119). To summarize, some play seems to be a casual variation of the animal's behavioral repertoire; some should be understood as a more firmly established capability that maintains fitness, behavioral flexibility, and motor coordination; and some is a consciously regulated process that reorganizes behavior systems and cognitive schemas.

As the reader may note, this approach draws on Darwin's theory regarding the natural selection of distinctive qualities in species. Somehow, variation—in this case, the creature's development of new abilities to behave in certain ways—occurs. Creatures possessing the physical characteristics generative of such expressions may have advantages (in certain environments) over less flexible creatures. That drift toward increasing flexibility (and ultimately conscious regulation of behavior) continues through the centuries. Creatures occupy different niches in the ecosystem. Some species need extremely complicated behavioral repertories (and thus exhibit the higher-order play processes described above); others lead more settled lives and exhibit play of the lower types or do not play at all. Said differently, play can be an uncoordinated display of surplus energy; it can be more clearly mandated and regulated by biological structures; it can be consciously directed and strategic.

Burghardt's theory also expresses Darwin's view that species' traits do not evolve in isolation. Rather, they emerge as genetically supported patterns that aid survival in specific environments. This leads Burghardt to a multi-causal or even contextual view of play's origins and sustenance that he calls "surplus resource" theory. He understands play to be made possible by wide ranges of factors that he terms "affordances," that is, conditions that allow or facilitate play. Some of these are biological (metabolic, developmental, and neurological). Others are environmental (such as the character of the terrain, weather, and availability of food). Still others are social, such as supportive group structures and parenting styles. In that context, he argues that play occurs (1) when there is sufficient "metabolic energy" for this activity, (2) when "animals are buffered from serious stress and food shortages," (3) when there is "stimulation to elicit species-typical behavioral systems or to reach an optimal level of arousal," and (4) when there is "a lifestyle that involves complex sequences of behavior in varying conditions" (2005, p. 172). Warm-blooded, mobile species such as mammals and birds (which require periods of parental care and form social bonds) are exemplars of this evolutionary process. However, there must be a sufficiency or even surplus of these resources in order for play to occur; otherwise, responses to more basic survival needs will dominate.

The Playing Brain

Whatever the (scientifically based) reasons why creatures select play from the range of available behaviors, they seem to find enjoyment in their choice. Play has, to repeat Burghardt's phrase, an "endogenous component"; participants find the behavior satisfying enough that they choose to perform it in the first place and then continue it, sometimes against the objections of irritated adults and peers. What are those enjoyments? According to Groos's (1898, pp. 287–328) classic account, there is, first, the pleasure of "satisfying an instinct," of conforming to the body's frameworks for recognizing and responding to deeply established needs. Thus play expresses the remembrance or "recapitulation" of ancient practices that Hall discusses. The second pleasure is that of movement or "energetic action." Creatures, like hamsters on their wheels, seemingly select activity rather than continued rest. Another pleasure comes from being a "causal agent," that is, from demonstrating one's influence over the world. That pattern of awareness Groos (p. 290) describes as "delight in the control we have over our bodies and over external objects." The resulting sense of achievement, if it comes, he calls the "joy in success, in victory." To that degree, he accepts Nietzsche's dictum that satisfaction comes as much from the "struggle for power" (including power over members of one's own species) as it does from the "struggle for existence."

The pleasure of control expresses itself in other ways. There is the ability to develop and sustain pretense, to stipulate which framework will apply to the situation at hand. Gross calls this "consciousness of make-believe." In more cognitively complicated species, this process of treating objects in "sham" ways (as when a kitten pretends a ball of yarn is prey) leads to the "pleasure of experimenting" and ultimately, to creativity. When we create things, we re-present them to the world as something they have not been before. In such ways, Groos repeats his claim that playfulness (as an inherited propensity for behavioral improvisation) gradually diminishes the role of instincts.

Groos's account is basically a surmising about the character and causes of play's satisfactions. Much more difficult is the task of describing how the brain manufactures the internal conditions that players experience as satisfying or pleasant. Is there a neurochemistry of movement and pleasure that intrinsically rewards activity and (in its anticipation) motivates creatures to perform it?

As we have seen, structures of the body and brain afford the possibilities of play. Creatures with higher proportions of brain to body size are more likely to exhibit play, which is most frequent during periods of life when the brain is growing rapidly. This is especially true of the cerebellum, the region at the lower back of brain that is densely packed with neurons and is responsible for motor skills (Byers and Walker, 1995). Byers and Walker also note that, in mammals at least, play is most frequent during the developmental stage when specific muscle groups are altering their character. In such species, most muscles begin as slow-twitch (or slowly contracting) fibers. As creatures mature, individual muscle sets develop a distinctive ratio of fast- and slow-twitch fibers. Play is associated with these processes. Putting the case more strongly, Byers (1998) argues that physical play at the early stages of life helps creatures achieve this differentiation.

Mammals also exhibit brain development in another region that is associated with play. This is the frontal cortex, the region in the upper front of the brain that is responsible for planning, organizing thoughts and feelings, distinguishing relevant from irrelevant information, and directing concerted actions. More sophisticated forms of play involve this region or, to state this more precisely, feature an interaction between this and the older regions of the brain.

Would animals still play if the frontal cortex were relatively undeveloped or absent? As we have seen, some researchers claim that creatures with a small frontal cortex such as fish and reptiles sometimes exhibit playlike behaviors. To use two more of Burghardt's examples, certain species of captive turtles "play" with balls thrown into the water or interact in a teasing way with zookeepers; sharks nose balls around in much the same way. The implication is that play arises from brain regions other than the frontal cortex.

This point is supported dramatically by experiments on mammals such as rats and cats. Pellis, Pellis, and Whishaw (1992) have shown that if the entire cortex of a neonatal rat is removed surgically, the animal can still engage in the most common form of rat play, play-fighting, in which contestants wrestle and try to subdue one another by grasping the nape of the opponent's neck. But there are differences in the play of normal and surgically impaired rats. Those whose cortex has been removed are more likely to seek domination of their opponent, while normal juveniles adopt practices that make it easier for the subordinate to regain control. In other words, normal rats willingly weaken or destabilize their own advantages. The Pellises (see Pellis, Pellis, and Bell 2010, p. 292) argue that this is evidence for a theory that play is not simply "motor-training" but also "training-for-the-unexpected." Creatures need to understand not only what they can do but also what the world can do to—and with— them. That world includes the social community of other rats.

Affect in Play

Play may be contemporaneous with the development of certain brain regions. But does play itself do anything to promote that development? This extremely challenging question has been addressed by researchers working in a field of study that Jaak Panksepp (1998) terms "affective neuroscience."

To offer the briefest of summaries, the brain is the control center of highly developed organisms. By means of a system of nerves extending throughout the body, the brain receives sensory information, analyzes the significance of that information, and provides directives to bodily organs and muscle groups. Although some bodily reactions, such as pulling one's hand away from a hot stove, involve communication only between the spinal cord and the affected body parts, most bodily functions feature brain activity. The brain is composed of billions of nerve cells (neurons) as well as other kinds of cells that support and protect them. These cells are organized into three general brain regions, each with specialized functions.

From an evolutionary standpoint, the oldest region of the brain is the brain stem, the upper end of the spinal cord. The brain stem culminates in what is called the limbic system, composed of ancient structures such as the thalamus, hypothalamus, and pituitary gland. These formations regulate very basic (and autonomic) functions of the body such as heartbeat and breathing and help coordinate bodily responses to such conditions as hunger, thirst, the need to eliminate waste, and sexual excitation. The limbic system also is central to the patterns of bodily arousal termed "emotions." Furthermore, this region is particularly important as a coordinator of the endocrine system, which secretes chemicals into the bloodstream to trigger specific forms of development and behavior.

The cerebellum, as we have seen, is the second fundamental region (adjacent to the brain stem); it coordinates balance, posture, and movement. The Pellises' surgically impaired rats were able to play-fight by relying on this region. In higher animals, most of the brain is devoted to a third area, the cerebrum. Its extremely convoluted outer surface (the cortex) contains specific areas that process messages from sensory organs. Other areas of the cerebrum send messages to muscle groups to implement action, and still other areas store, analyze, and "associate" information. Beneath the cortical surface are vast networks of neurons that link the brain's various regions.

Although the brain is divided into specialized regions and possesses "hard-wired" channels of communication between these regions, other connections between neurons are not firmly established. Panksepp (1998) describes this distinction with computer terminology: ROM (read-only memory) is different from RAM (random-access memory). The RAM-like connections (between billions of neurons) are solidified through activity. What we call learning is the development of pathways that allow creatures to quickly notice, evaluate, and respond to occurrences or stimuli. This process can be compared to the pruning of a tree. Some connections (synapses) between the tree-like branching of nerves (dendrites) become strengthened through repetition and attributions of significance; other potential (but unused) connections fail to thrive (Allman 1999).

Are there biochemical processes that encourage the brain to perform these connections? Neuroscientists claim that the brain has its own internal reward system that facilitates connection and motivates activity in the world (see LeDoux 1996; Vanderschuren 2010). Of special importance is a group of signaling substances, or neurotransmitters, that promote experiences of pleasure. These include dopamine, endogenous opioids such as the endorphins (the best-known example being what people experience as a "runner's high"), and endogenous cannibinoids. Some of these secretions congratulate the brain and body for having performed appropriate actions, including the completion of neural associations. Alternatively, they allow the body to keep going in situations of extreme stress or pain by masking some of the danger of those situations.

The feelings of pleasure associated with these internally produced substances are sometimes discussed as reward states for ongoing or completed actions (a subject called *hedonics*). A different approach is to see some of these neurotransmitters as motivators for future actions. The latter function has been a theme of Panksepp's research. According to Panksepp (1998, 2010), there is hard-wired neural circuitry within the brain that he calls the "seeking/expectancy system." This system assists creatures oriented toward achieving some of their life needs (procuring food and sex, for example) by making their appetitive quest pleasurable. In that sense, creatures experiencing gnawing or even desperate hunger are motivated to keep going against the most difficult odds. Furthermore, creatures facing dire circumstances (such as being confronted by a predator or plunged into icy water) are given a kind of energy and courage. This will to accomplish one's goals (by approach or avoidance) is associated with dopamine production. Creatures fighting for their lives exhibit high dopamine levels; creatures that have reached their goals have dramatically reduced dopamine levels. So understood, dopamine is more a motivator and sustainer than a reward system.

Panksepp locates the specific neurocircuitry for the seeking/expectancy system in the mid-brain. He has produced appetitive urges in laboratory animals by electrically stimulating nerves along this circuit. His current research seeks to identify other basic circuits in the brain. The other six putative circuits are rage or anger, fear or anxiety, lust or sexuality, care or nurturance, panic or separation, and play or joy. His quest is to show that such patterns are deeply established neural pathways that are shared by many species. Rage and fear he considers pre-social formations; the other four are connected closely with sociality. Triggering any of these circuits is said to result in predictable behaviors and emotions (that is, patterns of alertness, physical gesturing, and action tendency). Finally, Panksepp applies the idea of deficit or deprivation to some of these expressive capabilities. That is, animals that have been deprived of play for long periods will energetically engage in that behavior as soon as more pressing needs are met.

Consciousness Reconsidered

This chapter ends where it began, with comments on the role of consciousness in directing human behavior. In that light, few academics are as forthcoming as William James, who said of consciousness: "Its meaning we know so long as no one asks us to define it" (James 1952, p. 147). Although it is exceedingly difficult to say what consciousness is, for most of us it is central to our ideas of subjectivity. Human beings seem special in their ability to interrupt or even uncouple entirely the stimulus-response relationship. Between our perceptions of something and our responses to it, we are able to ponder (often quite abstractly) the implications of what is occurring. We review behavioral strategies for the situation at hand. We choose one of these strategies—or we choose to do nothing. Most of us treasure the notion that we are the commanders of our sensibilities.

As important as these ideas of subjective agency may be, it is apparent that there are different levels of cognitive awareness. Sometimes people operate with the abstract symbol manipulation that Piaget extols. At other times, we indulge ourselves in sensorimotor activities of the most basic sort and take comfort in the concreteness and particularity of what is happening around us. Since the late twentieth century, neuroscientists have made substantial progress in understanding how the brain operates at these different levels of awareness and, by those operations, manufactures consciousness.

Some of the best known of these accounts are provided by Antonio Damasio (1994, 1999). He positions his work as a rebuttal of Descartes's famous argument about the centrality of consciousness (as the "reality" people can best know and trust) and about the relative disconnection of that citadel of awareness from external occurrences. Ideas of a subject-object distinction, which are fundamental to the development of Western philosophy, owe much to Descartes. Against that view, Damasio argues that consciousness emerges through the activity (and interactivity) of various brain regions, themselves the results of long evolutionary development. That is, the physical structure of the brain has emerged from interaction with its surrounding body and with a natural environment that is both the support system and the testing ground for species survival.

Most people are familiar with the idea that there are different levels of wakefulness. That is, we understand that a coma is different from a persistent vegetative state (in which there may be flickerings of wakefulness) and from deep sleep or deep anesthesia. Under such conditions the brain continues to function, but in limited ways. There are also higher levels of wakefulness. On the basis of studies of patients with brain injuries, Damasio points out that being awake but functionally immobile (as in an "absence seizure") is different from being stirred up by internal processes (what he calls "background emotions"). The latter state is different again from the dim awareness of external matters that he calls "low-level attention." Such patterns of low-level recognition he distinguishes from "focused attention," in which people bring to consciousness their perceptions of occurrences, both in the external environment and within the body. More highly focused yet are processes that identify particular thoughts and feelings and result in action strategies. Those directed states he calls "specific emotions," "specific actions," and "verbal reports" (1999, p. 89).

His general point is that the brain supports many bodily functions even in the lowest levels of wakefulness. To take an extreme example, patients in comas can exhibit arousal by sweating, having their skin hair stand on end, and regulating the diameter of their pupils (Damasio 1999, pp. 93–94). His special concern, however, is the rise of consciousness, that pattern of alertness that is built on "focused attention." He distinguishes two levels: "core consciousness" and "extended consciousness."

Core consciousness, which humans share with many species, is a creature's awareness of its own standing and operations in transitory, concrete situations. A rabbit knows that it is being chased and may experience "emotions" pertinent to that predicament. A fox interprets the same event from its perspective. As Damasio (1999, p. 125) defines it, core consciousness *"is the very evidence, the unvarnished sense of our individual organism in the act of knowing"* (italics in original). Creatures that possess this capability have the awareness that their organism is being changed by an object; as part of that process, they hold a "salient internal exhibit" of that object in their mind (p. 169). Another way of saying this is that this level of consciousness is expressed when an organism creates an "imaged nonverbal account" of what has happened to it and when this process "enhances the image of the causative object." To have core consciousness is to understand that one is in the thick of things and that some identifiable object is causing that difficulty.

The second level, extended consciousness, involves longer-term and more abstract frames of reference. It depends on a "gradual build up of memories" based on the "life experiences" of the organism with objects in its environment (p. 197). That gathering and arrangement of memories is the foundation of typifying or categorical intelligence—what behaviorists call "stimulus generalization." Moreover, creatures with extended consciousness need not be in concrete situations to trigger memories. They can call them up at will. That double ability to transcend immediate circumstances and to command an arsenal of remembrances and action strategies is critical to the development of the self.

In that context, Damasio claims that selfhood emerges in three stages, each prior to the next in evolutionary terms. Creatures limited to a "proto-self" operate beneath the level of core consciousness. As he (1999, p. 154) defines it, the proto-self is *"a coherent collection of neural patterns which map, moment by moment, the state of the physical organism in its many dimensions"* (italics in original). The proto-self has no powers of perception and holds no knowledge, nor can it express itself in language. It does, however, regulate sensory recognition from moment to moment and is the (continuing) foundation for the higher forms of self.

The second pattern of recognition, the "core self," is associated with the emergence of core consciousness. At this level, creatures live in the moment. But they are aware of *themselves* as being in predicaments and of the actions they are taking to address those challenges. Damasio's third and final level is the "autobiographical self," which is rooted in extended consciousness. Creatures at this level comprehend themselves as having lived through many times and places; they also possess some sense of what they might do in the future. Such a self depends on the tools of memory and flourishes amid a cultural environment of language and other symbols.

All this can be summarized as follows: the brain has evolved over millennia and exhibits different levels and kinds of informational and sensory processing. Many of these capabilities do not depend on (what we think of as) conscious awareness. Humans probably have the most highly developed abilities for abstraction and symbolic expression (exemplified by extended consciousness and the autobiographical self), but we share other levels of cognition with animals, and those abilities remain critical parts of who we are. Whatever powers for self-appraisal and self-direction we possess, we are dependent entirely on these older brain regions and their neural mapping systems.

When creatures play, then, they run through the possibilities for self-functioning. Some animals, as this chapter emphasizes, have highly developed abilities to select, regulate, and reflect on action strategies. Other animals rely on core consciousness and its concomitant, the core self. Regardless of its complexity and abstraction, play explores and exercises patterns of recognition and response. In animals with extended consciousness, play integrates symbolic and physically based meaning systems. At such moments, favored ideas and images are experienced as a series of biomechanical repercussions, deep-seated emotions are exhumed, pleasure and pain are revisited. To that degree, and to recall Sutton-Smith's argument, play is a form of consultation between matters manifest and latent, known and unknown. In consequence, players extend and secure their understandings of themselves.

6 Play and the Physical Environment

Humans are apprehensive creatures. We grasp reality with our bodies and minds. Those attempts at physical and mental control are intimately related. We handle objects in order to comprehend their character and implications; we reach conclusions about those objects so that we can manipulate them and others of their type more easily in future dealings. As the pejorative meaning of *apprehensive* suggests, we are always a bit uncertain how those handlings will proceed. What people need are activities that turn apprehensions into positive experiences. Play is that attempt to extend the circumstances within which confidence prevails.

This chapter explores the intersection between human capability and the physical environment. First, I view with an anthropological lens some distinguishing characteristics of our species, including its persistent immaturity. I next discuss different patterns of active play that emerge during the life course. Third, I consider the relation between environments—both natural and artificial—and playful expression, and follow with a discussion of some classic educational theories of object play. I conclude with comments on the character and consequences of physical play.

The Evolution of Human Capability

Seen from an evolutionary perspective, the human species has no beginning or end. We have many requirements and abilities in common with some other species (nearly 99 percent of our DNA is shared with chimpanzees). Other creatures seem less like us in form, behavior, and environmental circumstance (see Leakey and Lewin 1991; Campbell, Loy, and Cruz-Uribe 2005; Konner 2010). Like other animals, humans reached their current configuration by the splitting off and reconnecting of population groups that adapted in specialized ways to distinctive environments. Changes in those environments, predation, and competition from similarly situated groups led to extinctions of untold populations. Other groups found themselves possessed of endowments that helped them survive, prosper, and expand their range.

Our ancestors were part of a vast set of changes associated with the rise of the mammals about seventy million years ago. Among those mammals were small prosimians. Such creatures, whose closest modern relatives include the lemurs and tarsiers, became adapted to tree living. Their descendents included the New World monkeys (which split off from the lines that led to humans about thirty-five million years ago) and the Old World monkeys (which separated from the line leading to humans about twenty-five to thirty million years ago). Those early primates had several characteristics that anticipated our own. Among them were flexible hands (and feet) featuring an opposable thumb (and great toe), useful for grasping branches and objects. In addition, their forelimbs acquired the ability to rotate (that is, to alter the relationship of the ulna and radius). This capacity to reach and grab was also facilitated by the development of nails rather than claws, thus maximizing sensitivity at the ends of digits while still affording some protection. Although this new system meant a loss in defensive capabilities, it was useful for arboreal living, where falling is a constant danger for young and old alike.

Useful also for forest life was the development of visual acuity and (because the eyes moved toward the center of the face) stereoscopic sight. The latter quality promoted depth perception, which aided reaching and leaping from branch to branch. Also helpful was color vision, which allowed primates to make fine distinctions among distant objects, including estimations of ripeness in fruit. Those two qualities compensated for the weakening of a trait that is essential to ground dwelling: the sense of smell.

Because of difficulties in caring for the young in trees, monkeys give birth to few offspring at a time. Associated with that birth pattern is prolonged gestation and infancy. Instead of relying on the survival strategy of many species (large number of offspring, rapid infant development, and little parental care), the primates feature a pattern of close supervision, parental feeding, and the modeling of needed behaviors. Although group size among the primate species varies, creatures of this type tend to exhibit complex social behavior. In addition to having strong mother-child bonds, they frequently live in small groups, or "troops," with status hierarchies and recognition rituals such as greeting and grooming. As part of this more intensive sociality, elaborate communication systems consisting of calls and gestures are used to inform other group members about food, danger, sexual receptivity, and social standing. Making possible that sophisticated communication is an enlarged brain.

These traits are extended—and altered—by the apes. During the past twenty million years different lines of apes broke away from the path that led to humans. Our closest living relatives, the chimpanzees and bonobos, had ancestors that separated from ours about six to eight million years ago. Whereas monkeys tend to be tree dwellers that use all four limbs to get about, apes express a style of ground locomotion that relies more on the legs (and uses long arms for balance and support). Some ape species also exhibit a pattern of arm-swinging (brachiation) to move through the trees as well as a "suspensatory" pattern of feeding, whereby they hang from a branch by arms and legs and reach for food with the other available limbs.

These changes in posture and movement, featuring differentiation of arms and legs, were carried forward by our hominid ancestors. One of these changes, bipedalism, is associated with the adaptation to a savannah environment. On a relatively treeless plain, it is helpful to see predators—and prey—from far way. The ability to raise the body into an upright posture is useful in this regard. (Note that other species, including other primates, are able to stand erect for short periods.) Furthermore, having four legs instead of two surely is preferable in terms of speed, agility, and balance. However, the shift to two legs as a customary means of movement—a change which also meant alterations in the pelvis to redistribute weight, reconfiguration of the spinal column to its familiar S-shape, and repositioning of the skull—had one great advantage. It freed the upper limbs to perform other functions.

In hominids, the thumb became longer (extending to nearly the middle joint of the index finger in modern humans) and increasingly opposable to the other fingers. Hominids alone became able to form a pinching grip between the thumb and all their other fingers. New styles of grasping became possible; objects were picked up and manipulated easily. With no need to support body weight, arms became shorter and even more flexible in their range of movement. Hands developed in ways that favor sensitivity rather than strength. Unlike other animals, hominids could throw sticks, rocks, and eventually more sophisticated weapons with some accuracy for substantial distances.

The legs and feet changed as well. In hominids, the great toe became less opposable and the foot less flexible, for legs now had to support the body's weight. Similarly, legs became longer to allow faster movement. The ankle moved slightly toward the back of the heel and the arch rose. With this new setup, walkers (and runners) had a spring in their step.

Finally, consider changes in the skull. Like many animals, adult apes have faces that are snoutlike, or "prognathic." They have long, U-shaped jaws and pronounced canines that are used to tear fibrous plants and to defend themselves. The upper portion of the skull features a sloping forehead and prominent brow ridges, traits that protect the eye sockets and also support musculature helpful to crushing and tearing by the jaws. In contrast, hominids have flatter foreheads, a domed cranium, small faces, reduced brow ridges, small V-shaped jaws, small incisors and canines, and high molars. This configuration is suitable for creatures eating a diet of grains or seeds that require grinding. Hominids also feature a pronounced separation of lips and nose; the nearly total lack of a rhinarium (the strip of skin connecting nose and mouth) allows for great flexibility in facial expression.

The above description of a relatively slight, weak, slow animal without sharp canines, claws, or thick skin surely is a recipe for extinction in the African grasslands that are thought to be humanity's cradle. Yet hominid survival was supported by social and cultural inventions that intertwined with physical evolution (Dressler 2005). Stone, bone, and presumably wooden implements served as weapons and as aids to cutting food. The control of fire allowed hominids to frighten predators and drive prey. Fire also permitted cooking, needed to soften meat for creatures with diminished biting teeth, small jaws, and long digestive tracts. Inventions such as clothing and shelter allowed populations to migrate to harsher climates. Many other creations—fish hooks, bows and arrows, bone needles, pottery, boats, and so forth—came in the past fifty thousand years. In other words, it is now human nature to be part of a "culture." Both bodies and brains depend on material and informational resources for fulfillment and direction. Survival without these elements is unthinkable.

Much the same can be said of people's communication systems and social alignments. The patterns of the higher primates—including strong mother-child bonds, single births, long periods of immaturity, elaborate vocalization, and social learning—are extended in hominids. So is the prospect of long-term bonding between adult males and females. Changes in the estrus system led to year-round mating, new patterns of male-female social support, and the dispersion of births (over the course of a year) within the group as a whole. The repositioning of the birth canal allowed face-to-face engagement during sex. All these patterns are consistent with a species whose members depend on one another for the learning of needed skills, sharing of food, and other forms of long-term support. Furthermore, these social (and political) arrangements must be seen as the conditions of ongoing physical evolution (Goodman and Leatherman 1998). Societies, however modestly fashioned, establish the terms by which certain types of individuals prosper while others are cast aside. They regulate access to food and shelter and, more generally, create differences in lifestyle. They also create the contexts for sexual selection, in effect, the determination of what physical traits will be idealized and reproduced (Chick 2001).

These changes can be portrayed as an evolving set of characteristics—physical, psychological, social, and cultural. In a somewhat different vein, contemporary anthropologists, biologists, and neuroscientists now focus on the interconnections of these traits and on the question of which changes preceded others. One of the most fascinating accounts of these interrelationships is the neurologist Frank Wilson's book *The Hand* (1998). Presented as a contemporary reexamination of themes from the surgeon Charles Bell's classic 1833 work of the same title, Wilson's volume describes intricate changes in the skeleton (and its neuromuscular supports) and the connection of these to changes in the brain.

In addition to describing changes to the hand in much detail (for example, considering alterations in the joint surfaces of the fingers), Wilson shows how an extremely flexible, grasping hand was linked to a pronating and supinating wrist and to an arm that could not only contract to carry loads but also rapidly extend itself (through the actions of paired muscle groups). At roughly the same time, changes in the collarbone, shoulder blades, and shoulder sockets allowed for new ranges of arm motion. Anyone who has seen a baseball pitcher grasp a ball (with many different grips) and then hurtle it with this system of levers is impressed not only with the speed and distance of the throw but also with its accuracy. More fantastic yet is the manner in which this system of levers can be extended by the subtle gripping of an external lever (such as a stick, hammer, or golf club) to dramatically increase the speed (and thus the force) of the motion. And of course, what if the objects to be thrown could be sharpened and lengthened, as in the case of a spear (or by widening the arc even further with the aid of a "spear thrower" that cradles the spear and extends the point of release)? With weapons of this sort in hand, humans became, "at once, both the most delicate and the most dangerous of the primates" (Wilson 1998, p. 32).

Most of these profound changes in the muscular-skeletal system were well established by the time of *Homo erectus*, that is, about a million years ago. However, the brain of *Homo erectus* (with a cranial capacity of 900 to 1,100 cc) was still well shy of that possessed by modern humans (about 1,350 cc). In other words, changes in the size and configuration of the brain were not only slower to develop but also perhaps adaptations to the tool-based (that is, "cultural") environment of the early hominids (see Washburn 1960). Whatever the specific chain of causation, Wilson (1998, p. 36) argues that manipulative ability was a crucial element of a "hand-thought-language nexus." Some aspects of that nexus are described briefly below.

Having some ability to "map" or remember terrain arguably is useful to any creature that must search for food that is relatively scarce, and especially for carnivores hunting mobile prey. Still, carnivores—or at least those that hunt in a solitary fashion—do not tend to have especially large cortexes (the planning, analyzing, and communicating portions of the brain). By contrast, the hominids pursued large prey by means of group activity. The coordination of those groups would have been facilitated by a system of gestural communication, a predecessor of forms of verbal language that were made possible by changes in the throat and larynx. Facial expressions, as additional indicators of intent, may also have been useful. Some have argued that levels of social cooperation pertinent to killing and consuming were elements of tool-making (see Reynolds 1993). At any rate, processes of (collectively) modeling, remembering, planning, and executing behaviors may be the basis for what Merlin Donald (1991) calls a "mimetic culture." This, he states, "rests on the ability to produce conscious, self-initiated, representational acts that are intentional, but not linguistic" (p. 169). Modeling of this sort is not simply repetition of what has just been observed. It is the creation of general models that can be remembered and applied to wide varieties of situations.

These arguments parallel Damasio's claims about the different levels of consciousness in creatures. Some animals seem to have only core consciousness (awareness of themselves as active participants in specific situations). Creatures such as hominids also possess extended consciousness (reflections that transcend the particular situations they are in and that they can call up as they wish). Those abilities to represent situations from outside the present (that is, past happenings or future possibilities) as mental images and to share those representations with others become much more developed in members of our species that arose in the last hundred thousand years. Those recent ancestors have left behind examples of cave paintings, formal burial sites, decorated tools, and food containers, all of which make plain their fascination with a world of ideas and images that transcends the moments of life.

Such processes of mentally conjuring possible behavior patterns and then trading those representations with others are central to the present book. We hominids harbor action scenarios in our minds. Some of these are based on remembrances of things we have done in the past (and wish to do again). Others are based on actions that have just occurred, perhaps some happy combination of circumstances that we seek to re-create. Still others recall strategies used by others. The most complicated models are products of mental combination, pieces of strategies taken from various sources and re-presented in a new (to us) way. Whatever its origins, imagination is not enough. Humans are driven to explore the relation between possibility and actuality. And play's protected settings are perhaps the best places to test those projected chains of cause and consequence.

The Functions of Immaturity

Many species devote themselves to play while they are young and then abandon those activities for the responsibilities of adulthood. The great apes are different in that their play period is extended more deeply into the life course; adults (and especially mothers) may initiate play with the young. In humans, playfulness is manifested in all age groups. Arguably, that interest is the result of a continuing need for flexible behavior strategies based on learning. This continuing fascination with novelty Wilson (1998, p. 13) attributes to a "permanent immaturity" in the human brain.

Permanent or not, immaturity seems to be an important feature of humans and an essential ingredient in their commitment to play. That thesis was developed in a classic essay by Jerome Bruner (1976) in which he focused on what he (p. 30) calls the "evolution of educability." That is, he wished to know what factors led distant human ancestors—and ultimately *Homo sapiens*—to develop the innovative, flexible approaches to behavior that have been described above. For Bruner, two key themes were changes in social organization and new "structures of skill" that led to tool-using and language.

With regard to social organization, Bruner argued that monkey troops (as examples of mid-level primates) feature a distinctive "attentional structure." This means that group members must continually orient their attention to one another to ensure that issues related to security, food, and dominance are being addressed. Failure to maintain this attentiveness is punished by the dominant members. The great apes, on the other hand, are less threatened by predators and have greater access to food. For such reasons, they develop a looser group structure that is less hierarchical and less fear-based. That pattern is reflected also in the greater sexual access that subdominant males have to females and in expanded patterns of recognition and support within the group as a whole. Bruner claimed that these patterns of looser social connection led to "self-domestication," a softening of aggressive traits to enable individuals to fit in with the group. These themes became accelerated in the hominids.

This new pattern of group orientation—in which creatures look to one another as sources of support rather than punishment—influenced the socialization of the young. Wider spacing of births by mothers (often at intervals of three years) led to much longer periods of child dependency (sometimes five years or more). Furthermore, the presence of other non-threatening adults meant the young had many models to observe. Bruner emphasized that this learning was of a new type. Monkeys (again, as mid-level primates) tend to follow an imitative learning style in which behaviors are copied immediately. Chimps, on the other hand, display intelligent learning. This means two things. First, they are able to separate themselves from the task at hand (that is, to conceive of the task as a set of duties in its own right). Second, they can develop action plans based on combinations of components from different skill sets. This pattern of intelligence is displayed when chimps perform before a mirror. Unlike most creatures, chimps recognize that what they are seeing is a reflection of *themselves*, and they take pleasure in the behavioral improvisations that manipulate that image. All this suggests a somewhat distanced take on the action at hand and on the creature's involvement in it.

That dawning awareness of the self as one participant among other participants in the world is a milestone in the development of young humans. Recalling James's and Mead's arguments, we are capable of turning consciousness back on ourselves reflexively (that is, of seeing ourselves both as objects and as acting subjects). We can adopt the perspectives of other people's roles and imagine what a person so situated is thinking of us. Understood in that context, play activities are occasions when creatures develop abilities to think about the consequences of acting and being acted on, of seeing and being seen.

In Bruner's view, play has two primary functions. The first is that it provides opportunities for creatures to pursue lines of behavior without fear of serious injury, punishment, or censure. This is especially the case with regard to social play. By using "play faces," distinctive postures, and other signals, creatures let one another know that they are going to test the limits of their relationships but that this experimentation will be done in a context of mutual respect. The other function is that play frees creatures from the demands of necessity, or what he calls "reinforcement" (Bruner 1976, p. 42). Many behaviors fall into fixed patterns that are the most efficient ways of responding to a need or feeling of urgency (for food, sex, protection, and so forth). Play, by contrast, gives creatures permission to try out combinations of behavior that are not directly related to these obligations and thus might not otherwise occur. Play is an exercise in goal attainment.

Taken together, these two themes—a relatively pressure-free environment and the absence of reinforcement—form the groundwork for behavioral ingenuity. In a savannah environment—where there is no easy escape to the trees—hominids needed to be ingenious. Tool-using was necessary for survival. So was language. And play was a principal way in which these capabilities could be developed, tested, and modeled before others.

These themes have been developed by Brian Boyd, who argues that this set of changes (physical, psychological, and social) led to new "strategies for attention" in groups (Boyd 2009, pp. 218–19). Focusing on one another now as sources of positive support, hominids enhanced their status as brokers of communication and cooperation. Part of that entailed the development of story-telling as a device to coordinate behavior and to grant ascendancy to those who performed well in this capacity. Humans developed capacities to learn from observing and from listening to others. Boyd argues that those capabilities may be related to the development of "mirror neurons" (p. 103), which activate not only when a creature is performing an activity but also when it is watching one. Although the status and role of mirror neurons in humans remains controversial, such a possibility suggests that our species' proclivity for intersubjective feelings (including empathy and sympathy) may have physiological and emotional as well as cognitive foundations.

Bruner's approach has also been extended by David Bjorklund (2007), who claims that childhood must not be rushed because human maturation focuses on adaptation to several different stages of life, each with its own issues.

Bjorklund posits that the long juvenility of our species is necessary to learn the complexities—and especially the social complexities—of the human condition. Human infants are completely dependent on their caretakers. Toothless and without significant motor skills, they acquire these in stages. Even when they reach puberty, humans in traditional societies tend to have limited fertility for two to three years. All this time prior to the responsibilities of adult caretaking (often two decades or more in our era) is given to personal development. Moreover, our brains are especially slow to develop. At six months the brain weighs about 50 percent of its adult weight, at two years 75 percent, at five years 90 percent, and at ten years 95 percent (Bjorklund 2007, p. 51).

Bjorklund (p. 66) claims that "neuronal plasticity" is central to development. Although most of our ten billion neurons are produced during fetal development, cell growth continues in the hippocampus (which is central to memory). Distinctive of the human brain is the *extent* to which connections between neurons are being established as registrations of activity. Some patterns of recognition and response become well established as chains of neuronal connection; other potential patterns are not developed, and their disuse leads to cell death. The behavioral requirements of social experience—at least of the human sort—are, in his view, far too complicated to be hard-wired. People need time to allow the brain to establish and refine these memory-based linkages.

Why aren't babies born with larger brains? As Bjorklund explains, upright posture entailed changes in the pelvis. Extremely wide pelvises in females—of the sort facilitating easier births—would be hindrances to mobility, especially problematic when fleeing predators. So humans are born small in brain and body. Children reach about 20 percent of their adult weight at two years and 50 percent of that weight at age ten. Just as their brains are relatively uncoordinated, so their bodies need to become much stronger and to acquire the sophisticated skill sets that match physical movement and mental direction. The pausing-and-planning style of action our species exhibits requires time to develop. Although some body-brain pathways (such as those associated with basic emotions or with other autonomic physical responses) are maintained without learning-based direction, other infant responses (such as rooting, sucking, grasping, and startle reflexes) are largely overwritten by later patterns.

Bjorklund also claims that the retention of juvenile qualities, or "neotony," may have been pertinent to social bonding as well. In addition to being smaller, children—and women—exhibit a softer, more receptive physical style that seems less threatening to adult males and perhaps invites support. Finally, he asserts that humans physically are prepared by evolution to be attentive to certain classes of stimuli. Some of those patterns of receptivity and orientation (described as stages of development by psychologists) function as "deferred adaptations." That is, they are interests and behaviors that ready the young for adult responsibilities. Other characteristics and behaviors of youth are not preparations for adult life but rather "serve an adaptive function at specific times in early development" (Bjorklund 2007, p. 7). This idea—that activities are pertinent to the distinctive life stage in which they occur—he calls "ontogenetic adaptation." As more comprehensive patterns of relating to the world develop, these patterns are abandoned.

Patterns of Physical Play

The process by which physical play becomes established through the life course has been a special interest of play researchers, including Anthony Pellegrini and Peter K. Smith (see Pellegrini and Smith 1998, 2003; Smith 2010). These authors argue that different developmental stages feature different types of physically active, or "locomotor," play. In empirical terms, the expression of each of these types follows an inverted U shape. That is, the child, who heretofore showed little interest in a particular type of activity (or perhaps was unable to do it), suddenly becomes preoccupied with it. Then that interest fades, and new forms of activity take place.

The first of these types is what Pellegrini and Smith (1998, p. 578) call "rhythmic stereotypies." To recall a theme from Chapter 5, some activities (of both humans and animals) seem to be practiced simply for the satisfaction of making the body work. For example, infants commonly engage in bodily rocking or foot kicking. Some will do this for as much as 40 percent of a one-hour period (see Thelen 1980). Such activity tends to peak around six months and then declines. It can be argued that this seemingly compulsive movement is not play, or at least not a sophisticated, consciously controlled version of play, yet the actions of setting the body in motion, watching what it does, and experiencing a range of pertinent sensations are surely the foundations for more expansive and consciously directed excursions.

Another type of play is what Pellegrini and Smith call "exercise" play. This is the activity that most of us associate with toddlerhood, specifically, the use of large muscle groups to move about. Representative activities are running, jumping, chasing, and climbing. When movement of this sort is done for the sake of pleasure (rather than from necessity) it is usually described as play. Exercise play begins near the end of the first year and peaks at about age six. Just as adults commonly encourage rhythmic stereotypies in children (for example, by bouncing them on their knees or tossing them gently in the air), so they initiate games of chasing, hiding, and so forth with preschool children.

A further type of physical expression is "rough-and-tumble" play, activity that includes wrestling, restrained kicking and hitting, shoving, and others forms of tussling. Rough-housing of this sort peaks from age seven to age eleven. It is especially prominent in boys, owing to a combination of physiological and sociocultural factors. Like the other forms just described, rough-and-tumble is sometimes initiated by fathers, who take pleasure in play-fighting with their sons (Pellegrini, 2009).

The principal expressions of rough-and-tumble are found among peer groups. To recall Erikson's (1963) model of the ages and stages of life, preadolescents are preoccupied with skill development of many types (what Erikson calls the commitment to "industry") and with demonstrating these in forms of status rivalry. Success (judged as social standing in relation to peers) arises not only from accomplishment in school or in social activities but also in games of physical dominance. Such games also promote what Erikson calls "inferiority," the sense of diminished standing before others. Most of us know well what it means to be picked last when teams are selected or, having been picked, to perform poorly.

Supervisors of pre-teen children routinely wish that these tussling matches (which may be accompanied by teasing and lead to someone's getting hurt) were less frequent and less violent than they are. Yet rough-and-tumble play is a useful counterpoint to the idealized vision of play as routinely congenial and socially supportive. The agon, to repeat Huizinga's term, is one way in which people discover their qualities in relation to others. Violent or not, what is remarkable about playful social contests is the extent to which participants—human and animal—are able to restrict their deadlier impulses and to subordinate competition to the broader requirements of group cohesion.

Much like other forms of play, physical play in older children becomes more complicated. In that light, some physical play features collective opposition. Many games, such as king of the hill, feature chances for people to gang up on someone. Even the strongest person can be brought down. Chase-and-capture games commonly feature sides (based on existing social divisions such as gender or neighborhood). So do war games and, of course, team sports. Under such circumstances, participants explore the relationship between cooperation and competition. Ideas of "us" and "them" develop. Winning and losing are collective matters.

All these examples express an essentially competitive worldview. Players may cooperate, but their reason for doing so is to gain rewards—in the case of most play, symbolic dominance or victory—that cannot be attained by individual effort. Cooperation, represented both by rule-recognition and by commitment to team members, is mostly the means by which we get what we want. This approach disregards the fact that play can be *contestive* without being socially *competitive*. Many forms of play such as dancing, group exercises, jumping rope, singing in choruses, and playing in marching bands emphasize the coordination or matching of interpersonal movements.

In these examples of communal play participants are trying to do something quite difficult. They are challenging themselves to perform strenuous maneuvers and to stay together while doing them. Anyone who has been in a marching band or dance troupe knows that any person's being out of line or out of step destroys the group's effort. These play forms are contestive. That is, players challenge the limits of their bodies (in terms of strength, stamina, flexibility, and so forth) and do this in carefully controlled ways. Successful effort—measured as collective accomplishment—produces expanded feelings of power and resolve.

Sometimes, activities of this sort are organized as "indirect" competitions, in which groups perform their behaviors without interfering with other groups. This occurs in relay races (whose results are usually obvious to observers) and in sports such as cheerleading, synchronized swimming, and dance contests (where judges rate the teams). Social competition of this formalized sort is not, however, a necessary ingredient of play. Many activities such as rock climbing or group survival exercises feature people challenging themselves by collectively confronting environments. Such cooperative play has been an important theme of the so-called New Games movement, which explores ways for people to have fun without social rivalry (De Koven 1978). This includes activities that most of us are familiar with, such as throwing a football or Frisbee around, but it also invites groups to respond to interesting challenges involving time and space (discovering hidden objects, occupying small spaces, maneuvering through an environment blindfolded, scaling a wall, and so forth). Once again, the theme of this contestive activity is that *we* are trying to do something interesting or difficult, we are doing this *together*, and we are doing it in a way that respects the *satisfactions of everyone* involved.

Going Out to Play

How do people learn about their connections to otherness? How do they expand those connections? As we have seen, our human ancestors developed their characteristics and capabilities as responses to life in trees and, much later, to a savannah environment. Activities that we would consider physically challenging (squatting for hours, walking long distances, carrying heavy loads, and so forth) were elements of daily living. With the advent of the Agricultural Revolution five thousand years ago and the Industrial Revolution three hundred years ago, people became more sedentary. Recent developments that encourage people to sit for hours each day staring at electronic gadgets have accelerated this pacification process. Making all allowances for the wonderful flexibility of human beings and for the important role of culture in self-realization, contemporary living poses challenges to physical well-being. It is difficult to defend our proclivities to sit and ride, eat foods high in salt, sugar, and fat, dose ourselves with legal (and illegal) drugs, and prefer electronic to face-to-face discourse. Equally dubious is our belief that we can manage privately the risks of a complicated, changing world.

As discussed in the introduction, cultural changes of this sort are pertinent to child development. Fifty years ago, children played outdoors, often with physical objects. They gathered in neighborhoods for informal play. Physical activity on school grounds—before, during, and after school hours—was an important part of growing up. These practices have not been eliminated but they have been challenged by such factors as the enclosure of once-public spaces, school policies oriented to success on standardized tests, changes in the character of neighborhoods, and general concerns about child safety and the legal implications of behavior.

In some countries, such the United States, this has meant a reduction or elimination of school recess (Clements 2004; Jarrett 2003). That reduction occurs despite growing knowledge about how children learn (Pellegrini 2005). Within classrooms, children are more attentive and responsive when they are permitted physically active breaks. Outside classrooms, the playground is a setting where participants plan activities, design play structures, create and administer rules, negotiate disputes, and assume all manner of pretense. Players comprehend group alignment and dissolution, advances and declines in social status, creation and destruction as public affairs, and the vicissitudes of chasing and being chased. In profound ways, people learn the meaning of being "it." Those exercises in self-management (at the individual as well as the social level) are challenged by the bureaucratic impulses of modern schools.

The nature of playgrounds in contemporary societies has been a scholarly focus of Joe Frost (1992; Frost and Klein 1979). Although Frost does not romanticize the past, he is certain that the play spaces of his youth were different from what most children (at least in highly industrialized societies) know today. Rural settings and small towns allowed children immediate experiences with nature. Rocky hillsides, groves of trees, weedy fields, gardens, creeks, tadpoles, insects, and the like were elements of public life; children were freer then to wander and explore. Their wanderings led them to meet other children, encounters that could be unfriendly as well as friendly. Physical challenges—and their collective resolution—were part of growing up.

Frost is concerned less with reestablishing the past than he is with designing play environments that address the needs of growing bodies and minds today (Frost, Brown, Sutterby, and Thornton 2004). Both indoor and outdoor environments are important for child development, but outdoor settings provide wider opportunities. Children have greater freedom outdoors to be noisy and rambunctious. Messy materials—sand, dirt, branches, leaves, and water—can be transported without consequence. Wider variation in sensual experience—sights, sounds, smells, and textures—is possible (Olds 2000). Outdoors, children run, jump, climb, push, pull, and otherwise use major muscle groups.

Outdoor settings also permit the employment of large, humanly constructed items—carts, wheelbarrows, tricycles, construction materials, and the like. Frequently two or more children must cooperate to manipulate these objects. Furthermore, being outdoors permits an expansion of social scale. That is, players have more opportunities to interact with wider groups of children. Playground language tends to be more complex that indoor language (Tizard, Philps, and Plewis 1976). Girls, in particular, play more assertively outdoors than they do indoors (Yerkes 1982).

Indoor environments, especially in schools, typically feature age-segregated play. Against this pattern, Frost argues that a general "playground culture"—which integrates age groups—should be honored. In essence, children should learn from one another. A wide range of materials, both natural and human-made, should be available. Players should be encouraged to organize these in ways that suit their inclinations.

Furthermore, available spaces and materials should be appropriate to the age and developmental stage of the player (see Frost, Wortham, and Reifel 2008). For example, one-year-olds enjoy object play (afforded by blocks, grasping toys, and push-pull devices). Children a few months older profit from opportunities for gross-motor play, a range of challenges that becomes increasingly complicated as they move through childhood. These include swings, slides, climbing apparatus, and objects to test balance. Children aged two and older use objects for make-believe activities (encouraged by playhouses, wheeled vehicles, and loose materials). Those same age groups enjoy construction play (featuring elements light enough to be carried and arranged) as well as activities that combine work and play (such as gardening). Finally, children aged five and above enjoy physical games and require the large spaces, goal-posts, and equipment pertinent to them.

Designing public play spaces to accommodate all these age groups is difficult. Space must be balanced against potential use. Too little space promotes competition for equipment and even fighting; too much space inhibits interaction. Storage, utilities, safety, accommodations for disabled children, appropriateness of materials, and maintenance must be taken into account. Also critical are the anticipated functions of the activities that will occur there. Some spaces (such as settings for small toddlers) may be isolated; other spaces should encourage interaction across age groups. As careful as all this planning may be, it is important to not overdesign the spaces, for the broader goal is to offer children chances to transform the elements found there in self-directed, creative ways and to let them build social relationships with one another.

Themes of creativity and self-direction are emphasized even more in a process of play facilitation called "playwork" (see F. Brown 2002; F. Brown and Taylor 2008). Based principally in the United Kingdom, playwork arose as a response to the human challenges presented by urbanization, poverty, and related social problems. Playworkers and communities establish play spaces for children, furnish those sites with (intentionally rough) materials, and help children confront what is there. As Penny Wilson (2009, p. 269) explains, playworkers look at "what is around for the children [they] seek to serve and for what they are missing. Then [they] establish an environment that helps compensate for what is missing. Then [they] watch how children are using the space and share [their] reflections as a team. Together [they] make adjustments informed by those observations and reflections. Then [they] watch some more." Some themes of this system are distinctive. Playworkers facilitate play but do not consider themselves experts. Children are said to occupy that status. What playworkers do is encourage children in their collective creativity. Furthermore, playworkers usually don't endorse prefabricated bent-metal playgrounds but instead favor environments filled with many "loose parts," utilitarian materials of the most ordinary sort such as boards, tires, and garden hoses. Children are encouraged to build and maintain structures with these materials. In addition, playworkers take special interest in children who might be considered economically, socially, emotionally, and physically disadvantaged. This method draws some of its inspiration from the efforts of children to play amid the rubble of World War II bombings. Modern playworkers reaffirm the ability of contemporary children to construct, inhabit, and regulate their own interesting play worlds, however difficult the rest of their lives may be.

Finally, I should emphasize that frequently matters do not go as the playworker or any other caring adult wishes. Children can be uncooperative and mean; sites can be demolished; people can get hurt playing on nonstandardized structures. However difficult these circumstances may be, playworkers try to support the adventurous quality in every child and take their cue from one of their founders, Lady Allen, who said: "Better a broken arm than a broken spirit" (P. Wilson 2009, p. 277).

Although this section stresses the benefits of physical activity, note that playwork is committed to many other forms of social and cultural play. As Fraser Brown (2003, p. 52) defines it, "Playwork may be seen as a generalized description of work that includes adventure play, therapeutic play, out-of-school clubs, hospital play, environmental design, and much more—all those approaches that use the medium of play as a mechanism for redressing aspects of developmental imbalance caused by a deficit of play opportunities." In that light, practitioners conduct activity in many settings: helping mothers play with their children, encouraging community storytelling and theater, working with prison populations, supporting local art making, and assisting in hospitals and other public institutions with socially and emotionally deprived residents. Always, the theme is that people will create something interesting and meaningful if they are encouraged to combine the world's elements. That creative impulse is fundamental to the human spirit.

Object Play in Educational Theory

As discussed, professionals who design play environments are concerned not only with spaces but also with the objects that are found there. Many parents are familiar with the situation in which they have given their child a highly designed (perhaps battery-operated) toy. After a short time playing with the toy (sometimes ended by the object's failing to work), the child is found playing with the box it came in. Some objects seem to invite the child to make something out of them. Others are so complete that there is little for the child to do except perform small acts of manipulation and observance of the object's behavior.

Play ecologists Jane Perry and Lisa Branum (2009) emphasize this theme. Materials in a play setting, be it exterior or interior, should instigate activity. A block or sand table encourages planning and building. Art and writing areas—with appropriate materials—facilitate ventures in design and small-motor skills. Bamboo plantings suggest the mysteries of nature and encourage hiding. Climbing structures challenge people to learn about height, gravity, and the effort it takes to overcome these restrictions. In other words, play environments should have elements of many types that bring into focus distinctive ranges of ability. As they explain:

> When children playfully interact with their environment, they receive immediate information and feedback about how the world works, including how their bodies work in the physical world. During play, their own thinking, feelings, and experiences are tested again and again by the consequences of their actions. Playful interaction with objects and people in the child's world builds confidence, self-esteem, and an inner drive to seek out new information. (p. 196)

Such ideas are not new. The view that children—and the rest of us—learn via creative manipulation of objects was a theme of some great educational reformers during the nineteenth and early twentieth centuries. Those theorists argued that interaction with material objects is not only a way of developing physical skills but a foundation for organizing thought. Recalling Vygotsky's concept of the pivot, a stick horse carries much more than a child's body around a room; it transports a person's imaginings.

Prominent among these reformers is Friedrich Froebel, who at the end of the eighteenth century advocated the development of kindergartens (see Provenzo 2009). Froebel's vision was part of the Romantic movement in Germany, itself a protest against state centralization, bureaucratization, and industrialization as these were rising throughout Europe. For the Romantics, encounters with nature, especially in its wildest manifestations, were an important focus of self-experience. Strong feelings were not to be denied or subdued but instead encouraged through acts of physical exploration and challenge.

According to Froebel, the good society is a place where individuals are permitted to cultivate their imaginations and discover enriching experiences. For centuries, educational institutions had regarded unregulated play as dangerous. One of Saint Augustine's "confessions" had been of a childhood fondness for play that distracted him from his educational responsibilities; this suspicion of play (as disorderly and destructive) has persisted into modern times. Froebel opposed the view that self-directed play is dangerous. But as an educator he also wished to sponsor the conditions for active, inquisitive learning. Thus, he offered the world his ingenious system of "gifts" and "occupations," a series of twenty physical devices (with accompanying activities) that could be manipulated by the self-directed learner to reveal the relationships of the physical world. Froebel's true gift to educators was his insight that hands-on activity and curiosity-based expression might assist the child more effectively than teacher-dominated, standardized, abstract, and pain-enforced education.

Another theorist, the American pragmatist John Dewey, shared Froebel's commitment to individually directed activity. Dewey, however, was interested much less in spiritual edification (including the awareness of unity and proportion that comes from bringing together disparate physical objects) than he was in practical, goal-oriented behavior. Although Dewey strongly advocated individual freedom in democratic societies, he was equally committed to the good or "civil" society as a whole. In his view, personal and public good exist in a delicate, interactive balance; each depends on the other.

Such views influenced Dewey's vision of education and play's role in that process. Dewey opposed the older style of education, which honored only the academic subject, but he also rejected newer, child-centered philosophies that allowed personal interest to play too strong a role in development (Dewey 1902). Instead, students should be guided by teachers to engage with the curriculum in ways that capitalize on the students' interests and experiences. This means using material objects, with which the child interacts and which "impress the mind," as avenues to the more abstract forms of knowledge. The best forms of learning occur when teachers guide student ventures in practical problem-solving.

Dewey's theory of play is presented clearly in his 1910 work *How We Think*. In it he analyzes the work-play dichotomy, or rather the unfortunate consequences of schools' attempts to separate these two themes. Work is activity that focuses on products or results. Play focuses on processes. When people focus only on ends (as they do in work), activity becomes drudgery. When they indulge their enthusiasm for play, they fall into aimlessness and "fooling" (1910, p. 218). For Dewey, then, a combination of playfulness and seriousness of purpose is the "intellectual ideal." Stated differently, supporting the properly playful mind is "not to encourage toying with a subject, but to be interested in the unfolding of a subject on its own account" (p. 219).

One of Dewey's striking arguments is that "playfulness is a more important consideration than play" (p. 162). That is, he was interested in the spirit or attitude that players bring to their activity; play is only a "passing outward manifestation of this attitude." He continues, "In order then, that playfulness may not terminate in arbitrary fancifulness and in building up an imaginary world alongside the world of actual things, it is necessary that the play attitude turn into the work attitude." Purposive serious activity was Dewey's ideal. Play is merely its enabler.

The importance of combining work and play is also prominent in the approach of Maria Montessori. Her famous method, which continues to be used in alternative schools around the world, challenges the idea that children prefer play to work. As she recalls in her book *The Secret of Childhood* (1992, p. 123):

> Though the school contained some really wonderful toys, the children never chose them. This surprised me so much that I intervened to show them how to use such toys, teaching them how to handle the doll's crockery, lighting the fire in the tiny doll's kitchen, setting a pretty doll beside it. The children showed interest for a time, but then went away and they never made such toys the objects of their spontaneous choice. And so I understood that in a child's life play is perhaps something inferior, to which he has recourse for want of something better.

The broader lesson that Montessori learned was that young children have no aversion to work, at least if that work is organized in certain ways. What children do object to is being under the rule of adults who establish the terms of their activity and who make judgments about their performance in those settings. The reason children typically prefer play (and especially fantasy play or fairy stories) is that they wish to flee these adult requirements. In Montessori schools, children are encouraged to participate in activities often associated with adulthood (such as household duties) and handle objects that have pertinence in the real world. Some of these objects and settings are miniaturized to reflect this child orientation, and the students are encouraged to explore these and other environments at their own pace. The principal role of teachers is to provide interesting materials and offer support.

As Angeline Lillard (2007, pp. 188–89) explains, what Montessori calls "work" other theorists call "play." Montessori activities feature "embodied cognition," the practicing of behaviors using real if child-sized objects. Choice is emphasized; children get to do what *they* want much of the time. In that sense, schoolwork resembles the free play that children associate with recess. Furthermore, Montessori activities are rewarded intrinsically; there are no grades or gold stars. Finally, social communication is encouraged. Again, this contrasts with the solitary, quiet behaviors that are typical of school. Most generally, Montessori activities are based on the premise that children prefer serious occupations if these can be pursued on their own terms and timing and if they can engage with others of a similar age. Work of this sort is self-sustaining and even joyful.

Note that all these theorists deemphasize the play-work distinction. What children need is purpose-driven activity with real objects. The children's motivations can be extrinsic or instrumental (as in the case of work), or they can be intrinsic or consummatory (as in play). What matters is that children commit themselves to lines of action where they *transform* the materials before them in terms of their own visions for what those materials can become. Ideally, learners become fascinated by processes of inquiry and emboldened by the idea that they can discover the secrets of the world by performing practical manipulations.

Other educational researchers emphasize that object play takes many forms; those forms reflect the developmental stage of the child. As Piaget (1962) noted, children in the first year move from fairly undifferentiated, repetitious treatment of single objects toward more manipulative, sequential actions. This pattern is consistent with his view that the developing child is preoccupied with mastery. Initially, actions are repeated for *functional* reasons (to establish confidence in behavioral strategies); later play features *generalization* (the application of these schemes to wider categories of objects).

During the first months of life, children explore objects by mouthing, gnawing, grabbing, and hitting. After the first year, they treat objects in more specialized ways; that is, they use behaviors that are consistent with conventional understandings of specific categories of objects. For example, two-year-olds will push a toy car about and make the sounds that we associate with cars (see Belsky and Most 1981). This drive toward increasingly differentiated and behaviorally complex activity continues through childhood.

In that context, Sara Smilansky (1968) distinguishes between early patterns of essentially *functional* play (as Piaget defined it) and what she calls *constructive* play. That latter pattern, which becomes prominent at about age four, refers to goal-oriented behaviors whereby players arrange and create. In an extension of that process, older children use objects as props or pivots. That is, they are interested in objects that help them conceive and communicate ideas.

The specifically mental implications of one particular form of object play—block play—have been analyzed by Sarama and Clements (2009). With their different colors and shapes, blocks invite categorizing. Similarly, blocks make apparent the concept of size. They can be easily sorted, piled up, and (less easily) counted. Softer materials can be squished and shaped into this form; that is, a round ball of clay can become a block. Colored and decorated blocks can be combined to enhance the effects of patterns. Most interesting, perhaps, blocks can be arranged in ways that make people understand spatial relationships. Blocks can be placed on top, underneath, and beside. They can be inside or outside defined spaces. They can be moved about to illustrate processes of change.

For such reasons, Sarama and Clements argue that block play helps children "mathematicize" the world. Blocks facilitate understanding such concepts as big and small, straight and crooked, tall and short. They show us how things can be built and how they can be taken down. They reveal how complex wholes are made of individual parts. They provide concrete examples for sharing understandings with others. Some blocks we claim as "ours"; others are "yours." Negotiation skills (featuring ideas of parity and equity) can be developed—"If you give me that block I'll give you this one." In such ways, a mathematical vision of the world emphasizing how fluid, complex relationships can be simplified by establishing identical units and then counting these up is established. So we think, act, and communicate in terms of standardized measures of weight and volume, distance, degrees of temperature, money, units of time, and so forth. If at first only physical presences that resist our movements, objects become touchstones of our symbolizing abilities.

Conclusions

Does physical play produce developmental change? Are bodies and minds made different by it? According to Sattelmair and Ratey (2009, 366), physically active play has many effects on the player. Energetic play causes physiological stress on the brain that (after time for recovery) "promotes adaptation and growth, preserves brain function, and enables the brain to respond to future challenges." Physical activity inhibits mental decline in older people and more generally supports learning and memory. Aerobic activity causes the "release of neuronal growth factors," "promotes synaptic plasticity," and "stimulates the growth of new neurons in the hippocampus." Furthermore, play promotes physiological activity in the frontal lobe (where control of behavior occurs). This ability to inhibit as well as initiate behavior may be pertinent to "pro-social" behaviors (see also Panksepp 2008).

Such arguments are central to policy debates surrounding the place of physical education and fitness courses in schools. Sattelmair and Ratey argue that physical fitness has been shown to correlate positively with academic performance. Yet physical education courses, by themselves, do not have this effect. More important is the opportunity for students to experience periods of relatively intense aerobic activity each day. This activity need not be school-based. In addition, the researchers emphasize the value of self-directed, self-monitored exercise. In particular, they advocate such activities as climbing rock walls, riding interactive stationary bikes, and playing fitness-based video games that let participants regulate and receive feedback on their efforts (see also Ratey 2012).

I do not dispute that sustained physical exertion is important to body and mind at every age. Note, however, that vigorous activity is not a hallmark of play. Regimens that many people remember from physical education "activity courses," athletics conditioning drills, or the forced marches of scouting camps surely produce many of the same effects. The advantage that play has over compulsory forms of activity is that play (because it is self-directed, self-monitored, and self-rewarded) increases the likelihood that people will pursue patterns that respond to their distinctive ability level and that produce satisfying experiences. As we have seen, play is something people wish to repeat.

Instead of focusing on the benefits of aerobically vigorous play, then, this chapter has stressed the importance of physical play as a way of thinking concretely about the world. Through physical play, we discover who we are and what we can do. We crawl, walk, run, jump, climb, and swim so that we may learn how to propel ourselves through space. By such processes, we decide what is near and far, low and high, easy and difficult. For the same reasons, we handle wide varieties of objects. Such manipulations tell us what our hands are capable of. But they also inform us about the qualities of the objects that we handle. Like Goldilocks, we discover that some things are too big (for us) while others are too small, some too soft or hard, some too hot or cold. Equally profound are our understandings of what is inside and outside, above and below, firmly established or in continual change.

Those conclusions are pertinent to other species as well. Our primate ancestors also had to discover their own (quite individualized) abilities to run, jump, bite, climb, and grab. Some of those same abilities determined their safety from predators, access to food, sexual desirability, and the level of respect they could expect from peers. These abilities and evaluations—in them and in us—are not fixed. They must be developed by trial-and-error processes and then kept in a state of ready-reserve by periodic revisiting. If we humans are different from our animal relatives, it is in the extent to which our physical encounters become layered with symbolically orchestrated thoughts and feelings. We use physical actions to express our intentions to others—and to ourselves. By such processes, sensuous and abstract understandings of self are linked.

7 The Social Life of Play

Play is complicated by the presence of more than one player. When we play with others, we encounter those whose capabilities and intentions match our own. As opponents, those others give the event added dimensions of resistance and unpredictability; as teammates, they offer new possibilities for alliance and affirmation. Collective play immerses us in a world filled with other people's judgments. Those judgments, be they effusive approvals or angry rebuffs, are frequently the immediate outcomes of our actions and the basis for what we decide to do next. Amidst this flurry of recognitions and responses we reach conclusions about who we are and what we can do.

This chapter explores the fourth context for play: the social. As the patterning of human relationships, social context shapes play by offering behavioral formats or directives. Those directives—essentially claims by others that we should act in certain ways—both support and restrict our actions. Manifested in countless situations and at different levels of abstraction, they constitute the social reality of our lives. In the following pages, play is described first as a process of reality construction and maintenance. The remainder of the chapter extends this theme in treatments of three levels of social reality: self-identity, social relationships, and social structure.

Play as a Social Construction of Reality

In an influential book, Peter Berger and Thomas Luckmann (1967) argued that our knowledge of the world, including our most basic or commonsense understandings of people, situations, and behaviors, are developed through the interactions and agreements of persons. Berger and Luckmann identified three phases of this process. First is what they called *externalization, which is* when people express their will by creating material and social forms. The second phase is *objectivation.* Once something has been created—an object, idea, or practice—it confronts its makers as a thing in its own right. The world is now different because of the presence of this pattern or form. Third is *internalization.* This occurs when society's members take publicly proclaimed forms into their minds as guidelines for private decision making and action. Frequently, this acceptance process is so complete that they do not think about the fact that they are willfully applying these socially constructed and maintained norms and practices. In that sense, forms become taken for granted.

Although it may seem that the norms of groups and societies inevitably become internalized, this is not the case. Quite the opposite, society is a battleground in which individuals resist, negotiate, and otherwise assert themselves with the purpose of determining what meanings should apply. People disagree about projected lines of action; they dispute their own place in the relationships that ensue. Nothing is settled until participants give their approval, and even then disagreement and discontent are inevitable portions of all that follows.

In such terms, Berger and Luckmann instructed their readers that society is a sociopolitical as well as a cultural order. Beneath the surface of public conformity is the prospect of resistance and rebellion. Furthermore, social order is not simply a congenial agreement or social contract crafted by *equals.* Some individuals and some categories of individuals have more power and privilege than do others. Inevitably, individuals have specialized interests in what occurs; so do groups and organizations. At its broadest level then, society, as the vast configuration of all these personal and public commitments, is recognized as having an important role in the smallest of affairs. Widespread customs, laws, values, and practices are prominent forces in our lives and are very difficult to change. Although people must never forget that they are the makers of the social worlds they inhabit, they must also address the difficulties of refashioning those powerfully supported worlds.

Is there a setting where people are encouraged to explore the themes and tensions described above? I argue that play is that social laboratory. When we play with others, we create and administer a publicly acknowledged reality. Most of us know that this world we are building is only a momentary, fictive affair which nonparticipants are free to criticize or disregard. Still, we earnestly define our play occasion, establish its rules, assign roles to ourselves and others, and defend its boundaries against intruders. For the most part, this special occasion is for *us*. And it is *we* who decide what happens there.

Precisely because the play world is constructed so artificially and is so narrow in its scope and implications, it illustrates well Berger and Luckmann's three phases. In the first instance, play events capitalize on people's capacities for creativity, or externalization. Nothing exists—at least, nothing that is playful in character—until the participants decide to invest the moment with this quality. When they withdraw that energy and enthusiasm, the moment dies. Play makes people aware of their capacities for social agency.

Once created, the play world is recognized as something that possesses a clearly defined character and implications. This is objectivation. The general outline for the activity (which makes reasonable its constituent actions and interactions) is made public. People decide that they are at play, that their play is of a certain type, and that the event requires them to act in certain ways. They recognize that this play world is different from other social involvements and that they may need to defend this new reality against those would disrupt or destroy it.

Finally, play exemplifies internalization. The event's moving forward requires that people take seriously their respective parts. Like other activities, play does not require people to participate in their entirety, that is, to display all their personal qualities. Rather, it asks participants to take seriously specialized versions of themselves as jumpers, dancers, third basemen, goblins, and so forth. Accepting and then exploring the implications of these roles—in effect, internalizing their meanings—is the personal challenge of playing well.

Some of the best descriptions of these issues are provided by scholars who study the play of young children. One of these is Vivian Paley. In opposition to Montessori's views about the dangers of fantasy play, Paley (1992, 2005) emphasizes exactly that theme. Even more forcefully, she considers play of this type to be the child's "work." When children invent scenarios and play roles such as Batgirl and Spiderman or when they explore narratives such as Goldilocks, they are forced out of their habitual modes of thought. Necessarily, they think through the possibilities of their own cultures and those of others. Even spending a play period as a puppy or a kitten in the company of other children allows one to encounter the most fundamental social issues. In that guise, children learn to receive the attention of others, both affectionate and reproving. They enact the thoughts, feelings, and behaviors of their characters. Most important, perhaps, they learn that every social setting is a reality of its own sort that is maintained by consistent role performances. So understood, imagination is a public as well as a private affair.

None of this is meant to imply that play events or other social creations move ahead smoothly. Creativity is a disputatious process; so is the maintenance of what has been created. And getting anyone to participate wholeheartedly in such a fragile, perhaps trivial affair is a challenge of its own sort. Real play events display the negotiation of these difficulties.

Catherine Garvey explores this theme. For Garvey (1977; Garvey and Kramer 1989), playing together means reaching agreements about who will do what. This is especially true for activities featuring social pretense, in which participants invent behavioral scenarios, assign roles, and make one another perform actions that are consistent with those visions. If children are to play house, only one person can be the mommy; others must play supporting (and complementary) roles. The discussions that players have about how these lines of activity are to be developed are described as "meta-communication." Some of these conversations, which often feature bossy instructions from an older or more assured child, set general guidelines for what is to occur (for example, that the play scenario is to involve a sick baby). Others provide specific instructions within the terms of that scenario (that the baby is to start coughing). Players may not agree about the course of action. And getting people to play "right" or "fair" is one of the great challenges of the playground.

Still, the question remains: what is it that play "constructs"? In the following, play events are described as contributing to three critical aspects of social living. The first of these is *self identity*, how we as persons understand and enact our places in particular situations and in society more generally. The second issue is *social relationships.* When people play with one another they affirm that their activity is a proper form for human interaction and that their common support of this form binds them as a group. The third is *social structure.* Most abstractly, play endorses—and contests—the general organizing principles of societies, including the direction and reward of members.

Play and Self-Identity

In social studies of the self, the guiding theme is that individuals develop understandings of their placement in the social world by interacting with other people (see Branaman 2001; O'Brien 2006). Social recognition is the process by which young children reach conclusions about their own qualities and rightful spheres of action. It is also the means by which older people reaffirm and extend self-understandings. These identities can be positive or negative, welcome or unwelcome. Rarely are such matters settled. Instead, all of us continually seek the approval of others, who indicate to us by their words and actions that they accept or reject our assertions that we really are who we claim to be.

MEAD'S PLAY AND GAME STAGES OF DEVELOPMENT

For sociologists, the classic description of the intersubjective foundations of the self is that of George Herbert Mead (1964). In Mead's perspective, self-realization means managing our own visions of ourselves amid the visions that others have of us. But how do we know what others think? Much like his contemporary Cooley (1964), Mead argued that we can know something of the mental states of others because people participate in systems of publicly circulated ideas. We communicate these ideas to others using "symbols," agreed-upon meanings of concrete words and gestures. By exchanging these symbols, we acquire a fairly good (though never perfect) understanding of how others are reacting to our behaviors and to the wider situations in which we find ourselves. To that degree, social life is an intersubjective affair, a relatively assured trading of thoughts, feelings, and intentions.

As noted in Chapter 3, Mead's (1964, pp. 228–33) self has two aspects. The first of these is the objective sense of who we are, the "me." In that sense, we know—or rather, we have learned—that we exist as an object in the minds of other people. Part of self-development is learning to see ourselves in this more external perspective. Just as we consider what others are thinking of us, so we apply this view to ourselves reflexively, as when we ponder our qualities or get mad at ourselves for some misbehavior. However, we are not simply the passive recipients of others' or our own estimations. Instead, we actively inhabit our selves. We make decisions about courses of action. We adapt our behaviors to the reactions of others. Mead calls this more assertive, subjective stance the "I."

Mead (1964, pp. 209–28) presents a stage model of self-development in which play has a central role. The first of four stages is the newfound ability to see oneself as an object in a world filled with other objects, to learn the boundaries of body and mind. Thus, when an infant grabs her foot and pulls it into her mouth, she is effectively learning what is "her" and "not-her." The second stage, the play stage, builds on that period of infantile exploration. Preschool children learn to "take the role of the other." This means that they are able to adopt a viewpoint of someone not themselves. They do this by taking on the perspectives appropriate to statuses different from those they typically occupy. Examples include playing mommy or firefighter. In order to play these roles, children must anticipate how the occupant of such a position would think and act.

More impressive still is the ability to engage in acts of role-switching. Slightly older children can play both a firefighter and a baby who is being rescued in the same scenario and use the verbal and nonverbal behaviors pertinent to each. These one-person dialogues are in effect a practicing—and indeed, creating—of the social mind.

Third is the game stage. Understanding the way any occupant of a specific social role is likely to see the world (and from that vantage point to see the subject herself) is important. But how are these different roles tied together into bigger social complexes such as groups? Mead uses the example of a baseball game to illustrate this. To play baseball—let us say one is the shortstop—requires understanding all the different positions on the field and their expectations for any situation. When a ball is hit to the shortstop (with one out and runners on first and second, to make the example difficult), the player must anticipate every other player's intentions at that moment. Just as we enact our role in these particular moments, so we develop views of our position within the group. Such matters may include whether we recognize ourselves to be the starting shortstop, whether we are good at our position, and whether other people respect us.

The last of Mead's stages is the "generalized other." All of us play different roles in different groups. By complicated additive and integrative processes, we build these experiences into general understandings of who we are. Thus, we may think of ourselves as good students, committed to our families, religious, or shy. We also think of ourselves as being involved in, perhaps good at, such endeavors as surfing, poker, or tennis. In other words, self-identity operates at different levels. We harbor general estimations of our qualities, character, and life experiences. But we also maintain more limited identities that reflect our roles in groups and situations.

PLAY AS PERFORMANCE AND PRESENTATION

Although play events are often set apart intentionally from other life spheres, the question remains: how different are play identities from the identities that people routinely hold? One answer to this question emphasizes the creative, exploratory, and novel features of play. That approach, developed well by Vygotsky and some of his contemporary interpreters, I term the "performance theory" of self. Another answer is that play identities (and play worlds) are not so different from people's other commitments. That approach, which stresses the game-like features of all social interaction and the overlap in human commitments, is associated especially with Goffman's writing. I call it the "presentation theory" of self.

The view of play as a "making new" has been prominent in this book. For Huizinga, play is an act of social and cultural creation, and for Groos, it is the development of new strategies for the unseen challenges of adulthood. Play unleashes (heretofore restricted or not fully developed) ideas and images; it challenges participants to confront an increasingly wide range of forms and forces; it establishes new neural connections. Vygotsky's vision, which stresses the social and developmental aspects of play, exemplifies this theory. As noted in Chapter 4, Vygotsky focuses on children's desire to be a "head taller," to do what they have not done before. So motivated, they take on successively complicated challenges. People become themselves via their actions in the world.

His emphasis on the role of other people in these processes is pertinent in this context. Although some play is self-guided, more is the result of other people's challenging us and responding to what we do. This shifts the creative process from strategic displays of individual capability to patterns of co-creation (Edmiston 2008). Interaction is a dialogue that players improvise together. Those improvisations should honor the subjectivity of everyone involved. Understood in that light, playing selves are those who are situated in a collectively established, challenging, and changing world.

These ideas have been extended by contemporary psychotherapists and by practitioners who apply dramatic arts to community settings (Sawyer 2003; Lobman and O'Neill 2011). The contributions of Fred Newman and Lois Holzman (Newman and Holzman 1993, 2006; Holzman 2008) are noteworthy. Building on Vygotsky's general insights, these authors argue that play's creative processes are important to every stage of life. As therapists, their primary concern is to help patients move out of fixed identities and routines that block them from making connections to others. Play is the vehicle for doing so. Rather than asking clients to express themselves (or otherwise make themselves accountable to the therapist), they try to induce levels of involvement in social settings. Some clients, such as those with autism, may be able to participate initially in only the most restricted or passive ways. However, through processes of recognition and support, these clients take on incrementally more active roles in the creation of the event. This general approach of encouraging people to envision new selves by role play has been adopted in applied theater and arts programs in prisons, hospitals, schools, and neighborhoods. Better lives, and the fluid, responsive identities that go with them, are the concomitants of supportive communities.

The presentational vision of self emphasizes continuities between our playing selves and the more established selves that operate in other spheres of life. This theme is developed in one of the best-known books in sociology, Goffman's *Presentation of Self in Everyday Life* (1959), which describes social life as "impression-management" and "dramaturgy." So conceived, the book explores the many theatrical devices that people use— carefully crafted words and gestures, facial expressions, clothing, settings, and "props"—to make others believe the versions of self that are being displayed. Every human knows intimately the roles of actor and audience. Just as we display our character and intentions to others through controlled (and also through accidental) behavior, so we scrutinize the performances of others. In the former case, our hope is to have them see us as the characters we claim to be. In the latter, we wish to see through the stagecraft to discover their hidden thoughts and identities.

As his book title makes plain, Goffman speaks of presentation rather than performance. In play-acting and fantasy, we take on temporary identities and have some sense that what we are doing is false (and not to be taken seriously). In social life more generally, we usually play roles in earnest. We want other people to accept the often idealized characters we pretend to be. More than that, we ourselves want to believe we are these characters. And the best, and perhaps only, way to maintain that self-identity is to convince others of this. Seen in overview, social interaction is the playing out or expression of people's identity commitments.

Several of Goffman's other books (1961, 1967, 1969) develop the gamelike features of social life. Like play worlds, other social settings establish clearly marked physical boundaries, employ distinctive ideas of time, restrict entrance, have narrowly defined goals, and administer complicated rule systems. Individual success within these formats commonly follows the terms and techniques of an "information game" (Goffman 1969). Much of what we do, at least as he sees it, is strategic advancement. In order to achieve our ends, we reveal some information to others and withhold other things we know. Sometimes (and at great danger to ourselves), we lie. Most commonly, we craft or modulate what we say and do so that others will see us as we wish. We often find ourselves trapped in unwelcomed identities, what he calls "stigma" (Goffman 1963). Even then, we try to manage these "spoiled" statuses with all manner of deceit, bravado, seclusion, and social realignment.

I discuss Goffman's work because he makes clear the parallels between play and other social settings. Play is neither "exceptional" nor "exotic." More than that, his writing challenges the view that play features versions of the person that are completely disconnected from other life domains. To be sure, like factory floors, emergency rooms, beauty parlors, and army barracks, play worlds display specialized presentations of self. Still, other aspects of identity are not left behind entirely. What goes on in these settings—and what makes them both stressful and enjoyable—is the interaction between more transcendent and more temporary versions of self.

Such connections between play identities and other identities are the subject of Gary Alan Fine's book *Shared Fantasy: Role-Playing Games as Social Worlds.* Focusing on such games as Dungeons and Dragons, Fine (1983) emphasizes that people participate in the play world in three different ways. Most broadly, they participate as "persons." That is, players typically hold an ongoing status as members of a friendship group composed of those who know and care about one another. This is different from Fine's second level, that of a "player." After all, some of those friends may be good at the game in question; others are not. Being a (good) player refers to one's ability to develop and execute strategies to make his way within the game. Fine's third level of involvement is being a "character," a personage whose game role (including rights and responsibilities) is limited and who is expected to know some things, have certain powers, and so forth.

In addition to describing behaviors at these different levels, Fine emphasizes the way these three kinds of identity intersect. Inevitably, players invest their characters with their general qualities as people. They may also operate (inappropriately) in the game with knowledge that their character—perhaps a certain knight—is not entitled to possess. Furthermore, personal friendships may affect the playing of the game, and occurrences within the game may have repercussions for those friendships. Fine thus provides empirical details for Goffman's general point that people are not simply players of games. They are persons who have "gaming encounters" and who experience the human implications of what it means to do well or poorly in those settings.

To summarize, Goffman's person is the ever-strategizing (perhaps lonely) individualist who learns the rules of the game for every social situation so that he can advance on those terms. Such individuals want to occupy idealized positions in those settings; stagecraft is directed to these ends. Vygotsky envisions a more socially supportive world, where people bring each other upward and onward. Play is the testing ground for new identities that change not only persons but also communities.

Play as Social Relationship

To be sure, the individual causes and consequences of play (including the formation of self-identities) are important. Yet often what is at stake in social play is not the experiences of individual players but rather the coherence of the group. When people play, they agree to meet at certain times and places, establish shared lines of behavior, and honor one another as worthy participants. That sense of *collective* purpose and identity is significant enough that individuals and groups sponsor play with this end in mind.

SIMMEL'S PLAY FORM OF ASSOCIATION

To repeat Berger and Luckmann's thesis, people collectively establish idea systems regarding the character of society and their responsibilities within it. Once created, these forms confront them as objective forces in their own right. This general approach was developed earlier by Simmel, whose writing centers on the symbolically articulated forms that regulate the many different situations or "worlds" of human encounter. Simmel's insight is that play is one of these forms.

This theme is developed most clearly in Simmel's (1950) essay concerning sociability, the "play form" of association. He begins by noting that much of what people do is instrumental or necessitous; we operate according to long-range obligations and interests. There are times, however, when we suspend those concerns. In that light, he emphasizes the ways various play forms of the polite society of his time—balls, parties, fancy dinners, afternoon teas, and soirees—allowed (and indeed, expected) people to set aside their customary obligations and relationships. Abandoning those obligations permitted revelers to focus more clearly on the form in question (such as the manners and motifs pertinent to a dinner party). Indeed, people especially skilled in this specialized system of manners can elevate behavior into art.

On one hand, suspending ordinary relationships can be felt as freedom. When we play, we hold the world's concerns at arm's length. Conversations at such events, therefore, tend to be casual and free-floating. On the other, this new world possesses its own formal requirements. Conversations should, for the most part, be affable and light-hearted. When serious topics are introduced, they should be presented in a way that involves everyone and (more personally) displays the speaker's ability to engage them in a clever, amusing way. No topic should be explored at a depth that exhausts the circle's patience or capabilities. Nor should it be examined systematically or pedantically. Somewhat like dancers changing partners, conversations flow and then shift quickly before boredom (and worry) set in. Because of that, conversational circles form and re-form. The point of all this is to sustain a tone of collective exhilaration.

This commitment to public well-being is illustrated also by the banishment of certain topics that might disrupt the occasion. Distinctively, Simmel emphasizes that play forms must not be overly personal or subjective in tone. All of us have ongoing concerns such as difficulties with spouses and partners, fears regarding our children, health concerns, or anxieties about our jobs. These worries must not be allowed to dominate the event. If they are raised (for who of us can resist entirely?), they should be presented in a joking, ironic way that signifies our resilient spirit.

Just as conversations must not be overly personal, so they must not be dominated by objective public issues. Dwelling on the affairs of the world, especially in a dour way, effectively diminishes the status of attendees as people who can do something about their own circumstances. So participants in sociable events move carefully through a territory that lies between the personal and impersonal. Notably, the job of the host (at least in Simmel's world) is to see that this tone is maintained. When effervescence fades, new people and new topics are introduced. Music and food are ordered.

Rules for sociable gatherings today differ from those of early twentieth-century European upper-crust life. Simmel's general theme nonetheless still resounds. Play events, like other events, are regulated by their own symbolically interrelated standards. Party-goers know how they should dress, that they should arrive with a smile and perhaps a gift for the party-giver, that a successful event is one where everyone has a good time, that some topics are appropriate while others are not, and that excessive behavior on their part such as displays of anger or drunkenness may result in their being asked to leave. When we are invited to a party at the Simmels' (or the Smiths'), we know what we are getting into. And on that basis we decide whether to accept their invitation and present ourselves in the appropriate way.

GOFFMAN'S FRAME ANALYSIS

The ways in which people collectively organize their interactions is also the theme of Goffman's classic book *Frame Analysis*. Goffman (1974, p. 8) argues that people who come into one's another's presence must answer a question: "What is it that's going on here?" Once they have decided what *kind* of situation they are in, they can make judgments about how long the event is to last, what its goals should be, what roles they should play, what words and behaviors may be appropriate, and what motives and feelings they should have. Because individuals bring different concerns to situations (differences based on personality, mood, interests, values, and social circumstances), the prospect of coordinating any social encounter is daunting. Goffman's thesis is that people nonetheless are able to do this because they rely on preexisting models that help them organize their thoughts, feelings, and behaviors and communicate them to others.

Much like Bateson's monkeys (Chapter 1), we employ physical and verbal gestures to let our comrades know what kind of situation we *think* we are in (or wish to be in) and that we wish to receive signals from them that indicate their agreement to those terms. Once we've decided collectively that we are in a play situation, then the whole affair can move forward relatively smoothly. At the very least, we can eliminate competing ideas about what is to happen—that we are preparing ourselves to fight, seek food, groom each other, or have sex.

Anchoring. In opposition to Simmel (who identified but did not interrelate forms of social life), Goffman wished to show how these forms are supported and sustained by other patterns of social functioning. That process he called "anchoring" (Goffman 1974, p. 247). Certain conditions—physiological, environmental, psychological, and cultural—enhance the prospects for one form of activity rather than another occurring. These supporting conditions also help us "realize" the activity by allowing it to be acted out in physical ways before others. Goffman's emphasis was that our definitions of encounters typically conform to the various logics of the situations in which we find ourselves.

As a sociologist, Goffman's primary interest was in *social* factors as supporting conditions. These include such matters as the group of people who are brought together (including its traditions, size, and composition), the characteristics of pertinent organizations that have an interest in the proceedings, the specialized roles of the people involved (both external to and within the event), and the qualities of the event itself (as a pattern for human relating). People clearly do not participate in encounters in socially disembodied ways.

Transformations. Human playfulness stems from our ability to make subtle distinctions between possible social realities and to introduce new ways of looking at situations so that an event is suddenly not what it was a moment before. That is, we are able to take a basic pattern of activity that most people easily recognize and then *transform* it into a slightly different pattern that is built on (and refers to) the previous pattern. To make this plain, think of yourself approaching a crowd of people who have surrounded two young men who seem to be getting ready to fight. Many elements are in place to make you believe this is the situation at hand. The crowd is excited and attentive; the young men have squared off and have raised their fists. Most of us, I imagine, have some understanding of what will happen next if the event is indeed a fight. But perhaps it is not. The event may be form of pretense or display in which the men are only kidding and nothing serious will occur. It may be some sort of prank or stunt, something that is being put on to satisfy the needs of some group or organization (for example, some publicity-seeking affair). Or it could be some sort of test or hazing ritual, used to examine people's commitment to join a group. Perhaps it is a type of exercise or practice for a real, more serious fight to come. Yet again, it may be a dramatic enactment of a fight, something that is being filmed by nearby cameras.

All the above are what Goffman calls "keys" (1974, p. 40), transformations of an event that make it comprehensible to participants and observers alike. But darker interpretations are also possible. Perhaps the event is a distraction of some sort that will lead to some act of theft or violence within the crowd (such as a several persons' getting their pockets picked). It may be a hoax or ruse in which two conspirators try to display (disingenuously) to others that they do not like each other. Here is still another possibility: What if one of the participants believes that the fight is only in play while the other harbors murderous intent? This second type of transformation, in which some of the participants or observers are kept in the dark, Goffman (p. 83) calls a "fabrication."

Whatever the observer's conclusion, Goffman's point is that people are highly committed to produce accounts of what is going on and why it is occurring. We construct social reality by trying to fit occurrences to different models—tests, jokes, scams, practices, dramatizations, and so on—that we possess. Those models are based on or defer to other models of the behavior that we possess—such as a real fight. Play is one of those transformations.

Play as framing. In two different ways play is an attempt to frame or culturally organize an encounter. In the first instance, play is a basic transformation, in other words, a style of approach to, or a or take on, any encounter between people. As a key, then, playfulness is one of three forms of make-believe. The other two are fantasy or daydreaming and dramatic scripting. When we treat something in a playful way, we emphasize that participants are not to take it seriously (that is, they should disregard the usual implications of people's roles and behaviors). Thus, a famous actress may blow kisses to a crowd (as if she is interested romantically in any of them!); two boxers may swell and swagger at a weigh-in (as if they wish to fight at that very moment). Both are forms of public pretense, acting out that no one is expected to take seriously.

In addition to playfulness as a key, Goffman also was interested in "playful fabrications," in which some people are kept ignorant by a benignly intentioned prank, joke, or ruse. In the practical joke, participants know that the suspense (and ultimately the pleasure) of the occasion depends on the "butt" being kept in the dark for a short period of time. Those in on the joke work together to sustain a public fiction (perhaps the butt has been told that he has just won an award or that the boss wants to see him immediately). The perpetrators of the joke force the poor soul to confront the expectations that apply to anyone who receives such information. They make a spectacle of his (logically appropriate) reactions. Then they make him reveal his confusion when he learns that his expectations are ill-founded. By such (benignly cruel) processes, everyone at the scene learns the perils and pitfalls of human aspiration.

In both keys and fabrications, play is a "playing at" or modification of form (that is, a transformation). Yet play also can be a recognizable form or frame in itself. In that context, Goffman (1974, pp. 41–43) defines play as having seven characteristics. In play, the "ordinary functions" of the activity are "blocked" (that is, the behavior does not lead directly to the satisfaction of basic needs but follows a softer, more circuitous pattern). Second, there is "exaggeration" of some acts. That is, participants work through the implications of behaviors by producing them in extreme forms. Third is "interruption of sequences": behaviors are started and stopped, started and stopped again. The fourth characteristic is "repetitiveness." Like Freud's obsessive-compulsive acts, behaviors are produced repeatedly as if something is being engraved or refined. Still another characteristic is "voluntarism." Participants choose to make this activity happen and end it on the same terms. The sixth trait is "role-switching"; players commonly alternate roles, especially those involving dominance and submission. Seventh is the idea that play is disconnected from "external needs." It is not something that needs to happen; still it occurs. Play is funded by satisfactions found in the moment.

One can place Goffman's list beside the other lists of play's characteristics described in Chapters 1 and 2 of this book. A different way of looking at Goffman's characterization is to emphasize that these seven qualities also describe the "frame" of play. When we play, we understand that interaction will probably occur on the terms described above. We expect to encounter free choice, exaggerated action, repetition of small behaviors, and so forth. When play doesn't move forward in this way, we are surprised. Indeed, we may decide that what is going on isn't play at all.

Like Caillois, Goffman saw a gradient between play and games, a movement toward increasing formality and culturally induced complexity. As he (Goffman 1961, p. 9) asserted, games are "world-building activities." That is, they are human encounters wherein participants collectively affirm a set of rules for the ways their actions should be limited. "Fair play" is idealized; cheating is punished.

In that regard, his approach is distinguished by its identification of three kinds of *norms* that people rely on to build game worlds (Goffman, 1961, pp. 19–34). The first of these he called "rules of irrelevance." Players decide that some matters are outside the boundaries of the game and are not allowed to influence its character. What people were doing the previous night, what commitments they have later that day, what is happening on an adjacent playing field, and so forth are matters of no relevance. The second category is rules of "realized resources." Some patterns and processes from the outside world are brought into the setting and redefined as elements of play. A rock becomes a boundary marker; a stick is suddenly a sword or gun.

Most interesting is Goffman's third category, "transformation rules." Although players try to establish games as separate worlds, this separation is not always possible. Players get hurt and threaten to quit; mothers shout for children to come home; people want to talk about what they will do later that day. For such reasons, it is necessary to establish rules that forbid certain kinds of conversations (such as talking about family problems or work) and to introduce procedures that console or encourage players who have become distracted.

Goffman's typology of rules illustrates his general interest in play and games. He was not especially interested in the strategic actions featured in games (for example, playing one card and not another in a game of bridge). Instead, he wished to understand how games are connected to the wider social worlds of players. What is brought in from those external patterns, commitments, and identities and what is left out? How are the inevitable interruptions that threaten to destroy the delicate social world of the game handled? Such questions are for *groups* to answer. To be sure, individuals choose to play and draw private satisfaction from these activities, but they—or rather, quite specialized versions of themselves—are moved into and through those activities by established social procedures.

Play and Social Structure

When we expand the social context of any action, interaction, or activity, we multiply the possibilities for interpretation. Understanding how individuals operate in narrowly bounded events is challenging enough. Understanding how the ongoing external concerns of individuals, groups, organizations, and societies intersect with those settings is much more complicated. However pleasant our playful escapes, we conduct those activities with the knowledge that we are obligated, defined, and even constituted by wider social involvements. Those social commitments, like our physical and cultural commitments, have a momentum of their own. Two views of that intersection between play and social structure are described below.

PLAY'S SOCIAL FUNCTIONS

Introduced in Chapter 3, functionalism focuses on the perceived contributions of recurrent processes to the maintenance of some unit of analysis. Units of the social type include groups, organizations, communities, and societies. Such collectivities not only permit play but also actively sponsor it. To restate Parsons's terminology, recurrent human events are responses to a social system's requirements for adaptation, integration, goal attainment, and pattern maintenance. Traditionally, functionalist accounts emphasize repetitive and rule-bound events. Their general theme is that such activities, including sponsored play events, do more than bond people in privileged moments. They help them establish deeper and longer-lasting patterns of connection.

The case of sports, and specifically school sports, is instructive in this regard. It is often claimed that school-sponsored sports serve many functions for the host organizations (see Figler and Whitaker 1994; Coakley 1996). One of these functions is the development of school spirit, the focusing of student attention (in a positive, supportive way) on collective membership. The second function is social control. School sports channel young people's energies, provide tension release, and focus aggressive impulses. The third function is facilitation of interaction. School-sponsored sports provide occasions for otherwise dissimilar people to meet and form friendships.

Sports also provide a way to identify and reward students who are athletically gifted. They offer avenues for such people to achieve (and manage the implications of) status, both among peers and adults. A further function is the development of social skills, including qualities related to leadership, collective loyalty, and cooperation. Yet another is the integration of adults into school life. School sports offer ways for alumni and community members to honor their own past and to show their commitment to the younger generation. Finally, school sports function as sources of revenue and jobs for coaches, referees, media, vendors, leagues, and officials.

Many of these same functions can be claimed for company-sponsored teams, community recreation leagues, nation-based squads, or even professional teams carrying the names of municipalities. Arguably, contemporary sports function as a kind of "civil religion" that prizes individual achievement, equality of opportunity, competition, self-discipline, technocratic strategy, and team loyalty (see Forney 2010). According to that creed, people's fundamental commitment is to teammates; outsiders are comprehended as worthy competitors who acknowledge a similar scheme of values. In that context, civility is the courtesy extended to partisans.

Play events, including organized sports, support and sustain the social units that sponsor them. There are, however, criticisms of this approach. First, public events always have several different aspects; it is difficult to know which of these aspects performs which functions. Some parts of the event should be interpreted as work (expressed as skill development, job creation, and transfer of resources), others are ritual (affirming public values, structures, and positions). Still others are communitas (emphasizing group bonding and mutual respect). Play (as the contestive exploration of the possibilities of living) is only one aspect of what occurs.

Second, play events may have dysfunctions as well as functions. School sports, to continue the current example, may distract students from academic learning. Expenditure of money on coaches, stadia, travel, camps, equipment, and so forth is a diversion of resources from other important activities. The celebration of gifted athletes may have the effect of turning most students into spectators. And the guiding values of the sports setting, however worthy these may be, are a very limited way of thinking about human relationships. The "sports creed"—featuring competition, individual achievement, authority relationships, goal orientation, and ascetic attitudes toward the body—is one strategy for self-awareness and public involvement. But partisanship and personal advancement should not be overpraised.

Finally, the functionality of any activity (presumed or demonstrated) does not mean that other activities are not as beneficial. Other forms of play besides sports—art, music, theater, debating, and mathematics contests—accomplish many of the same purposes. Indeed, they may cultivate skill sets that are much more closely aligned with the academic values of the school. And nonplayful activities such as public assemblies, awards ceremonies, public service projects, and classroom exercises provide benefits of their own sorts.

PLAY, POWER, AND PRIVILEGE

Functionalism presents groups as relatively integrated wholes. Yet this quality of shared values and common commitment is only sometimes present. Some segments of groups and organizations—and some individuals—are positioned more prominently than others. The favored subgroups may benefit greatly from the activity in question while others, less favorably placed, benefit hardly at all. This is the position advanced by functionalism's most direct rival in sociology, *conflict theory* (see Figler and Whitaker 1994; Coakley 1996).

Represented well by Marxian theory and extended by more recent approaches, conflict theory emphasizes the extent to which social units are divided along lines of economic, political, and cultural interest. Some groups and organizations have privileged access to socially useful resources such as wealth, power, prestige, and knowledge. Far from wishing to share these resources, they attempt to consolidate their dominance by regulating the activities of those positioned beneath them. In order to speak of beneficial functions, then, it is necessary to ask: beneficial for whom?

As discussed in Chapter 2, the Marxian tradition emphasizes the importance of labor, especially as a historically situated system for producing and distributing resources. Although play studies, for the most part, has not focused on questions of economic disadvantage, that theme has been prominent in sociological studies of sport and leisure. Clearly, sporting at its highest levels is organized around economic interests (see Sperber 2001; Clotfelter 2011). This model is to be expected in the case of professional sports, in which athletes are public entertainers. But university sports, at least in the United States, are marked by many of the same issues. Any reader of the sports pages is familiar with recruiting scandals, multi-million-dollar coaching salaries, illegal payments by "boosters," construction of fabulous arenas, television contracts, conference realignments based on economic incentives, and academic violations by student athletes. The tremendous pressure on teams (especially within the so-called revenue sports) to win is generally accepted. Although most sports at the intercollegiate level—think of cross-country track, volleyball, and equestrian sports—hew more closely to an older amateur ideal, it is plain that a quasi-professional model now pervades athletic training and performance at lower levels of school and youth sports.

Accounts inspired by a Marxian perspective focus on the social and economic inequalities of the current arrangements. Coaches are paid vast sums while the student performers receive a stipulated maximum wage (under the best conditions, the opportunity for a paid education). Some athletes are tracked into athletic-department-approved courses and do not graduate. Athletes may be sequestered with other athletes and confront long hours of training, both in and out of season. They practice and perform in authoritarian organizational structures. They endure serious and sometimes life-altering injuries and may be expected to push themselves through pain. They are encouraged to sacrifice themselves for the good the program. Athletes receive public adulation only when they meet these expectations and otherwise achieve team goals.

To be sure, many participants are happy to be part of this athletics subculture and to play on these terms. Some scholars claim, however, that such involvement (and this is especially the case for minorities) is equivalent to Marx's alienated labor (see Edwards 1970). Others emphasize that highly organized play may be a social opiate, the publicly endorsed "circus" of the Roman metaphor (see Hoch 1972; Sperber 2001). In that sense, spectator sports distract people from their "true" (that is, class-based) interests. By such standards, the identities displayed by most formally organized sporting events (specifically, nation, city, community, region, and school) are false social divisions.

Theoretical extensions of Marxism emphasize patterns of political, social, and cultural hegemony (see Gramsci 1971) as well as economic dominance. Ideally, perhaps, our visions of the good life come from families, friends, and communities. But they also come from models placed before us in advertising, in television and films, and at sponsored public events. When people have few social influences to buffer these media images, they find themselves manipulated by economic organizations whose goals have little to do with the general well-being of viewers. This softer or "cultural" version of conflict theory, sometimes described as critical theory, is particularly germane to play studies. Media presentations focus increasingly on what people do in their free time, featuring issues related to leisure, lifestyle, and the acquisition of consumer goods (Jay 1973). In such presentations, viewers are encouraged to *realize* themselves, a process that involves choice-making (sometimes between nearly identical alternatives), pursuing culturally esteemed private satisfactions (because "we're worth it"), and estimating personal status relative to similarly situated others. Play—consummatory behavior, as I've defined it—fits easily into a cultural ethic that prizes pleasurable personal development. At any rate, play activities, and especially the versions of these that involve spending money, are presented by commercialized media as private entitlements (Rojek 1985).

Marxian accounts emphasize patterns of manipulation and exploitation. Related themes are exclusion and marginalization. Different categories of people hold specialized positions in play worlds. Some are encouraged to play; others are invited only to watch or are excluded entirely from the setting. Furthermore, leisure activities may be developed as the rightful preserves of specific status groups.

This theme is developed by Thorstein Veblen in his classic work *The Theory of the Leisure Class* (1934). Veblen argues that various forms of leisure function as status displays. Upper-class sports, in particular, demonstrate to others that the practitioner is able to spend great amounts of time and money on activities that are intentionally complex and unproductive. Those complexities include arcane rules, excesses of costume, elaborate equipment and playing grounds, and difficult skills. Just as graceful leisure marks off those who do not work for their living, so it presents a darker theme: barbarism. In Veblen's view, the world of horses, guns, and dogs revivifies patterns of military strength and economic predation that are the foundation of the upper class.

Such themes are not distinctive of early industrialism. As I argue in a study of preindustrial sport (Henricks 1991), forms of play and sport have long been signifiers of social standing, and access to playgrounds is routinely based on social, economic, political, and cultural criteria. An abiding question for play studies, therefore, is: What kinds of people get to perform what kinds of activities with whom before what kinds of others—and what meanings are attached to those events? Play may well be a vehicle of self-realization, as the present book claims. But only some people are steered in publicly valued directions. Others are blocked or scuttled off along entirely different paths.

Processes of class exclusion are paralleled by divisions of ethnicity, religion, nationality, and age. Especially pertinent are the experiences of girls and women, who have long been marginalized from many publicly celebrated forms of play, games, and sport (see Hargreaves 1994, 2000). Although much has changed since the extreme separatism of the Victorian era, the play of males continues to be celebrated through mass attendance at spectator events, television viewing, sports reporting, sales of sports paraphernalia, salaries and commercial endorsements of star athletes, playing facilities, and the like. Indeed, *sport* itself is sometimes construed to emphasize certain qualities—foot speed, upper-body strength, and punching or throwing force—that are usually considered to be male advantages. Boys are encouraged to extend participation in sports deep into adulthood; proficiency at a chosen sport (whatever the time commitment in achieving and maintaining it) is culturally esteemed (Messner 1990, 1992; Messner and Connell 2007).

Once again, the past forty years have featured important changes, especially dramatically increased participation levels by females in both informal and formally organized sports. Still, girls may be directed to specialized locations in the sports world (see Festle 1996). That sequestration process may include encouragement of activities that feature such purportedly feminine qualities as grace, flexibility, and balance (emphasized in gymnastics, figure skating, and diving). Prized also may be activities that feature indirect competition, in which players do not interfere with the progress of their opponents or performance is timed or judged. Less well supported are sports that maximize direct aggression, displays of strength, and physical contact such as wrestling, weightlifting, and boxing. In team sports, cooperation may be emphasized more than stardom. And females find that opportunities for vigorous team sports diminish as they move through the life cycle. In all these ways, girls and women have been seen as "athletic intruders" in a male-dominated domain (Bolin and Granskog 2003). Yet that same book emphasizes that these intruders are now erasing many of the barriers of a sex-segregated world and changing the ways women and men see each other.

Conflict theory's central theme—that people have differential access to society's valued resources—is important for play studies. What individuals choose to do is related to what they are encouraged or permitted to do. Real play is only sometimes a gathering of equals. Selected individuals and groups take the lead in choosing the activity, establishing the setting, determining rules, deciding who will play, and allocating rewards. Others may be encouraged to watch, applaud, and support or are allowed to play only with those of their type. In a more extreme case, people may be banished from activities considered unsuitable for them. Peer-based play, a guiding commitment of play studies, must be understood against this backdrop of social exclusion.

Like functionalism, conflict theories tend to emphasize certain kinds of play, specifically those that are highly organized, commercially sponsored, and culturally celebrated. Also like functionalism, focus is placed on serious play, that which has clearly instrumental purposes (making money for sponsors, securing a living for participants, and developing community pride). Conflict theories depart from functionalism, however, in their stress on the quite different stakes and outcomes for those involved.

I should emphasize that most play is not of this sort. Indeed, highly organized activities such as big-time sports are marked heavily by work and ritual. Moreover, leadership in play (as in other fields) is not necessarily exploitative or oppressive. Studies of play rightly celebrate the intersubjectivity of equals, but leaders such as teachers, coaches, parents, and older siblings may move the activity ahead without destroying its character (McDonald 1993). That pattern of challenge-setting and response is one of Vygotsky's themes.

Perhaps most important is the criticism that conflict theories sometimes overemphasize the coercive power of social institutions. Individuals and groups arguably are able to resist, or at least to hold at bay, the claims of vast organizations and their media outlets. This point has been stressed by those in the field of British Cultural Studies (Brantlinger 1990; During 1993). Essentially, this tradition claims that working-class and minority people are not dupes of the ruling groups. Nor are they unthinking consumers of commercial and media offerings. Instead, people use their local community institutions as settings to reaffirm their visions of life. Media offerings are chosen selectively and interpreted with group-based criteria. Community centers, pubs, churches, and playing grounds are places where these criteria are both sharpened and solidified.

This theme also is central to one of the most prominent books in sociology, *Distinction* by Pierre Bourdieu (1984). In it Bourdieu analyzes the leisure habits—television viewing, sports, hobbies, eating and drinking, nightlife, sex, and so forth—of different segments (what he calls "class fractions") of the French population. At one level, he recognizes the degree to which society is integrated by common cultural commitments. People's involvement in (or at least knowledge of) opportunities, pleasures, and entertainments is one of those integrating patterns. Yet Bourdieu also emphasizes that more direct participation in these activities is class-based. People are categorized along lines of wealth, prestige, power, and knowledge. People in those categories do not take the same vacations, eat at the same restaurants, attend the same events, or drive the same cars. All members of society are cognizant of these patterns of differential access and of their own places in the wider social system.

One might conclude that the lower classes inevitably are resentful of the more advantaged groups for the above reasons. Bourdieu offers a different interpretation. In the spirit of British Cultural Studies, he stresses that similarly situated groups of people develop their own tastes and style of life that afford them personal satisfaction and easeful interaction. According to his famous concept, members of these communities create and operate within a *habitus*, a clearly defined set of circumstances as well as physical and psychological orientations that allow them to acquire a distinctive feel for life. Within the terms of this sharply defined system of permissions (and constraints), most people seek similarly situated companions, take what pleasures they can, and ignore (for the most part) those situated differently. In that sense, playful leisure is an important aspect of one's adjustment to one's station in life.

Bourdieu's analysis provides a fitting end to this chapter. Humans construct social worlds that provide a rhythm to life, afford visions of advancement, and offer a manageable range of satisfactions and dissatisfactions. Play worlds buffer some of the influences of the broader society and offer formats for self-exploration. As pleasing as those expressions may be, they are not disconnected completely from the wider commitments of individual life. Nor are they set apart from concerns of communities. Most of us recognize that other persons, groups, and organizations are crucial formations by which we discover our human limits and possibilities. And play is the opportunity system that allows us to sharpen those understandings.

8 *Cultural Play*

The final context for play is *culture*, defined as the patterning of humanly created resources. Although it is common to conflate ideas of culture and society, they are not the same. The social (or "society") refers to the patterning of human relationships, essentially the ways people position themselves with regard to one another and coordinate their interactions. Culture, by contrast, is the much wider field of symbolically based (and thereby communicable) resources. To be sure, one very important part of culture is the informational resources used to direct individual and social life. But culture exists beyond this as a vast and ever-expanding range of abstract meanings and relationships. Most of us know only some of the words (and only some of the stated meanings of those words) in our dictionaries. Our comprehension of grammatical rules, theorems in geometry, research on heart disease, and the historical records of our home towns is similarly narrow. A novel, poem, or painting lives in a thicket of abstract implications. So does a video game, movie, or television show. A chess match features seemingly endless permutations. Computers run out possibilities no person can match.

Because the field of informational relationships is so great, individuals and groups adopt preferred, or privileged, ideas. That winnowing process restricts most of us to a certain language, code of manners, skill set, and set of beliefs, values, and activities. The sharing of these publicly accessible resources means that people are able to think, act, and feel in social settings with some confidence, at least with others that acknowledge their terms and techniques. That restricted sphere or *habitus*, to use Bourdieu's term, affords a certain comfort. But those formulations are also the outcome of sociopolitical processes, with rival groups pushing forward their views of the right and proper and differentiating themselves from those who do not meet their standards. Socially valorized culture, even in its most taken-for-granted manifestations, is at some level contested.

Thus a wide gulf exists between the ideas and practices that people are encouraged (or allowed) to possess and culture's great realm of known and knowable. Simmel (1971, pp. 227–34) describes this as the difference between *objective culture* (the range of publicly accessible abstract forms and understandings) and *subjective culture* (the individualized repository of these matters). In his view, the "tragedy" of modern culture is that we carry an ever-decreasing subset of objective culture within us. Culture expands exponentially and renders any of us insignificant.

Is there a way to alter the relation between or bridge the gap between socially preferred forms of culture and the wider possibilities for thinking, feeling, and acting? Following Huizinga, this chapter describes how cultural play represents that bridging activity. When we play culturally, we create, interpret, resist, and destroy patterns that are realities of their own sorts. Frequently, those engagements provide us with feelings of separation or difference from our customary routines. By its combination of imagination and activity, play permits us to become unusual personages doing unusual things and, from the vantage points of those roles, to reconsider our lives. So we tell stories, sing songs, offer jokes, try tongue-twisters, dance, paint, and play-act before our fellows. Some of our interpretations and improvisations align themselves with socially approved behaviors; others are nonsensical, rude, and obscene. In either case, we find pleasure in self-induced wanderings through culture's interiors. In play, the "tragedy" of receding possibility is converted into something familiar, manageable, and often comedic.

The first section of the chapter discusses briefly the ways in which other fields-of-relationships both express and resist culture's patterning. This leads to a discussion of three different ways in which play addresses culture. First, people and groups play *within* culture. Second, people play *with* or *at* culture. Finally, culture itself is *playing* and people adopt an appropriate, playful style of relating to these processes. As in other chapters, ideas of selected play scholars are given prominence.

Culture: Expression and Resistance

This book has developed the view that there are different kinds of goings-on in the world and that those occurrences are not reducible entirely to one another. Environments, bodies, psyches, societies, and cultures feature their own kinds of patterning. When we play, as when we do other things, we manage behavior that confronts these external happenings. For the most part, we accept the world's formations and adjust our orientations to them (descending meaning); sometimes, we confront, resist, and transform selected patterns (ascending meaning).

Although this chapter stresses the ways people play with cultural elements (through imaginative activity), it must be emphasized that culture has its own intersections with the other fields of relationships. On one hand, this means that environmental, bodily, social, and psychological patterns are influenced heavily by culture. On the other, it makes plain that these patterns resist and transform culture.

Consider first the relation between culture and environment. If Twain's Connecticut Yankee were to reappear now after being in Arthur's mythical era, he would find himself equally astonished by the sights, sounds, and smells. Motorized contraptions replace the horse. Roads, fences, and utility lines are the new geometry. Houses and factories overwhelm the landscape; cities are monuments to human enterprise. A significant proportion of humans scurry from one flashing electronic screen to another; the artificial is adored. Such changes are only of type and scale, for people have always marked their environments. Still, the natural world is not entirely domesticated. Storms, droughts, and other fits of weather destroy in an instant culture's plans. Small shifts in temperature, water levels, and atmospheric quality are determinative. And invasion by the tiniest of organisms can change profoundly the pattern and pace of life or indeed, end the reign of humans.

Much the same can be said of culture's relation to the body. It is clear that culture configures, even manufactures, the human form. Culturally defined patterns of eating, exercising, grooming, dressing, and doctoring condition our movements through the world and our experiences of self. In every society, bodies are what Mary Douglas (1996) terms "natural symbols." In her view, those physical forms are central sites for the display of social organization and for the cosmological principles on which that organization is founded (p. xxxvi). For Lévi-Strauss (1967, pp. 251–52) as well, bodies are opportunities to exhibit public comprehensions. To use one of his examples, Maori tattoos "stamp onto the mind all the traditions and philosophy of the group." This process of marking and positioning is just as conspicuous in modern societies. As expressed prominently in the writings of Foucault (1975, 1991), bodies are comprehended now with a medical, or clinical, spirit. "Healthy" bodies, minds, and behaviors conform to objective (scientifically justified) standards;

deviants are set apart and rehabilitated by similarly based protocols. To be modern is to be measured and managed quantitatively.

In contrast, bodies resist cultural demands. By the lights of the Pre-Socratic philosophers and modern apologists such as Nietzsche (see Spariosu 1989), the body is not compliant. It is a surging, transgressive force that evades discipline. Humans need and want; such desiring is the energy of history. The relentless urge for stimulation and satisfaction is also central for Caillois and Bakhtin, whose views of play are described in what follows. Bodies assault culture as much as they express it.

The psyche's relation to culture illustrates similar tensions. Mind is dependent on a cultural surround. We think and feel in ways we are taught; our actions are regulated by publicly approved standards. Behaviors that signal our commitments—and the ideologies by which they are justified—are sociohistorical matters. Freud's theories, as we've seen, offer a contrary view, however. As important as our internalized moral censors may be, we also attend to dimly understood psychobiological wishes. Desires come from many places, including the deep recesses of the past. We find satisfaction in the completion of our wants; we enjoy also the process of wanting (Deleuze and Guattari 1984). The psyche can never discover peaceful integration, for unsettled issues abound, and unsettling processes are life-long. Far from blandly accepting culture's directives and placements, most of us find ways to evade, finagle, and rebel.

This chapter's special focus is the relation between society and culture, and play's role in addressing it. As shown in Chapter 7, the social construction of reality features creation, negotiation, and resistance as well as rule-bound conformity. Some status groups are pleased with their lot, others less so. Individuals and groups have interests arising from their various circumstances. A related point should be stressed. Society itself is organized at many different locations and levels. Each of these sites has its own subcultural themes, and these differences inevitably produce tension and change. It is a sociological commonplace that different institutions—economy, polity, religion, family, education, and healthcare—endorse somewhat different goals and operating procedures. Social classes, ethnic groups, genders, age cohorts, generations, and religions may embrace distinctive commitments. Communities emerge and operate within specific sociohistorical and geographic contexts.

To extend this theme to its smallest levels, each group or organization functions as its own "idioculture" (Fine 1979). That is, each has its own history, beliefs, and regimens; each is populated by specific rather than generic persons. Within those groups, different roles articulate distinctive rights and responsibilities (which, together, align with distinctive perspectives). And, to reprise Simmel's theme, it is arguably the case that individuals are subcultures of their own sort. The implication of this is that groups and organizations—like psyches, bodies, and environments—have differentiated commitments that inevitably destabilize unified societal patterning. Publicly sanctioned or ideal culture must confront the (often cherished) ideals of people situated in smaller social categories, groups, and relationships. And real culture (the actual practices that people expect and follow) is different again from idealized proprieties.

Thus there are many kinds of social commitments that effectively disrupt the establishment of unified public understandings. Similar tensions and instabilities are found in environments, bodies, and psyches. And in a theme to be developed, culture itself features its own kinds of inconsistency and incompletion. In a world so ordered (and disordered), how do people establish meaning systems appropriate to their lives? Consistent with what has been presented above, play is said to be one pattern—along with ritual, communitas, and work—of imposing meaning. Players destabilize ideals by testing them against the realities of behavior and experience. And they introduce new ideals that contradict those that are publicly proclaimed.

Playing in Culture

Despite my focus on play's spirit of rebellion and resistance, I must stress that many of the most notable studies of play have emphasized how that activity expresses—and thereby reproduces—wider societal concerns and practices. To translate this into the terminology of previous chapters, play of this type features some measure of ascending meaning within the event as participants build their own understandings via self-directed assertions and resistances. But beyond the event, people conform to the guiding precepts of their societies and develop skills that are requisite to living there. In that restricted sense, descending meaning, as accommodation to publicly proclaimed terms and techniques, prevails. Explorations, games, and frolics may exhibit fervent creativity, but this creativity is bounded by socially condoned frameworks.

PLAY AS CHILDHOOD SOCIALIZATION

Studies of child play have sought to demonstrate that such behavior is neither irrelevant to society's wider purposes nor aimless. At times, children embrace idiosyncratic goals and procedures, but they also enjoy institutionalized games, songs, and stories. Those shared forms allow wider groups to participate, move interaction through coherent phases, and inspire imaginative responses to the perplexities generated by their narratives. The legitimacy of studying children's playground culture in its own right has been championed by folklorists including such modern representatives as Peter and Iona Opie (1959), Brian Sutton-Smith (1959), and June Factor (see Dow and Factor 1991). Relying for the most part on children's description of their own activities, such studies emphasize the way each generation perpetuates these traditions, introduces subtle variations, and instructs newcomers.

Other scholars focus on the degree to which ritualized games, songs, and stories are linked to broader cultural themes. And because societal cultures differ, games and play also vary historically and cross-culturally. Such themes are emphasized in some important cross-cultural studies of child socialization led by Beatrice Whiting (see Whiting and Whiting 1975; Whiting and Edwards 1988). Focusing on children's experiences in Kenya, India, Mexico, the Philippines, the United States, and Okinawa, Whiting and her colleagues found that the extent and type of play—and the role of adults in this activity—varied dramatically. Variable also was the treatment of boys and girls, including such issues as access to available play spaces, pattern of parental encouragement, and segregation of play activities. According to these studies, play socializes boys and girls in different ways.

This theme also is central for Helen Schwartzman (1978). When children play, they learn to inhabit and negotiate their society's view of important status distinctions (adults versus children, boys versus girls, people versus animals, and so forth). They discover how power and leadership work. They practice activities (domestic chores, economic provision, social courtesies, and so forth) that will be useful to them later in life. They develop language skills, both verbal and nonverbal. Just as Groos argued that play is a practicing or refining of instincts, so Schwartzman showed that play is a refining of social and cultural capabilities. When people play, they *project* themselves into situations. The character of those self-projections is influenced powerfully by culture.

Cross-cultural studies of children's play continue to be important (see Roopnarine, Johnson, and Hooper 1994; Lancy 2008). In particular, researchers have emphasized that understandings of childhood are themselves culture-bound. That is, Western comprehensions of childhood as a period of innocence and protected exploration are not widely shared. In some societies, adults do not play regularly with children, encourage play, or otherwise see its pertinence to development. In much of the world, the dominant condition of childhood is work rather than play.

A different version of the socialization thesis is that play replicates some of the tensions, issues, and challenges that are created by value frameworks. In other words, what play activities *reproduce* is the characteristic problems of the host society. In culturally supported games, people are given the chance to confront those challenges, albeit in socially protected ways. This approach, developed by John Roberts and his colleagues, is termed "conflict-enculturation" theory (see Roberts, Arth, and Bush 1959; Roberts and Sutton-Smith 1962; Roberts, Sutton-Smith, and Kendon 1963).

In the view of these authors, games can be categorized according to the ways in which people try to control their standing in the world. Three of these techniques are *strategy* (essentially cognitive calculation), *physical skill* (exemplified by vigorous activities such as running, fighting, and building), and assessments of *chance* (that is, the tempting or appeasing of fate). Relying on ethnographic data collected for the Human Relations Area Files, Roberts and his colleagues tried to discover the cultural correlates for different societies' preferences with regard to game type. A guiding premise of the theory is that the dominant child-rearing procedures in societies create distinctive challenges and tensions.

In that light, children's games are understood both as responses to these tensions and as socialization devices in which players use culturally approved skills sets—cunning, physical prowess, and spiritual power—to confront those challenges and, more generally, to become successful in that society's terms. A major finding is that games of physical skill are the predominant type in economically simpler traditional societies. Games of cognitive strategy are prevalent in economically more complex societies. And games of chance or spirituality represent an intermediate type.

ADULTS AT PLAY

As we have seen, Huizinga's primary concern was play as a culture-building enterprise. By sponsoring ritually organized competitions (the agon), societies encourage people to craft new possibilities of living. Ultimately, disorder (albeit bounded and regulated) produces symbolic order. However, Huizinga also was intent on showing that the character of play has been altered by the advances of modernity. In traditional and archaic societies, the public play of adults is set within the "play-festival-rite" complex (Huizinga 1955, p. 31). A spirit of exuberance, privileged abandon, and faux combat prevails. Because play of this sort is cut off intentionally from the typical repercussions of human claims and counterclaims (and especially from material consequences), it allows the symbolic implications of the activity to flower. Under the guise of public ritual, play is converted from its ordinary status as psychologically pre-occupied behavior into a pattern of stylized display or posturing. As he stresses, play in its "higher forms" appears as "a contest *for* something or a representation *of* something" (p. 13; emphasis in original). Such competition is with, against, and before others. Play draws people out to become something different from their normal selves. It expresses—and encourages—the magnanimous or "public" person that was esteemed in earlier ages (Sennett 1992). For such reasons, Huizinga expressed little interest in private play or in the play of children.

The last two chapters of *Homo Ludens* describe play's course in Western civilization. With some overstatement (see Henricks 2002), Huizinga celebrated the reign of the playful spirit in Europe's preindustrial period. As he saw it, "medieval life was brimful of play, the joyous and unbuttoned play of the people" (1955, p. 179). Shortly thereafter, the "whole mental attitude of the Renaissance was one of play" (p. 180). Whatever its social and religious rumblings, the seventeenth century is depicted as a period of glorious affectation, and this only prepared the way for the great and culminating century of play: "If ever a style and a Zeitgeist were born in play it was in the middle of the 18th century" (p. 189). All this ends with Europe's political revolutions. Gaiety, extravagance, and the wig are abandoned for somber attire and middle-class sensibilities. The new orthodoxy embraces large organizations, instrumentalism touted as progress, moralistic religion, materialistic (including money) relations, city living, individualism, and narrowly defined class relations.

Play, like other life activities, becomes bureaucratically organized and functionally specific. In societies fascinated by occupational achievement, play focuses on private satisfactions, accomplishment, and displays of expertise. This pattern is especially clear in the case of "sports," which now replace "games" (p. 197). As he continues, contemporary sports—at least those that dominate the public imagination—are pried loose from the ancient play-festival-rite complex. They are surrounded with technical rules, clubs, and gambling. Standings, statistics, and "records" become public concerns (Guttman 1978). Huizinga's commitment was to show how contemporary play has become managed or even "false." But the more general, and perhaps more important, theme is that play is shaped by social and cultural circumstances.

Caillois's extension of Huizinga. As described in Chapter 2, Caillois thickened Huizinga's vision of play. *Mimicry, ilinx* (vertigo), and *alea* (chance) are added to *agon* as irreducible impulses in play. Ludus and paidia are established as formal and informal poles of playful expression. Play and the sacred are set up as antinomies (Caillois 2001a, pp. 152–62).

However, and like Huizinga, he wishes also to show that play's actual expressions are culturally conditioned. In Caillois's account (2001b, pp. 81–98), traditional, community-based societies emphasize ilinx and mimicry as forms of expressive behavior. That is, such societies sponsor occasions when people surrender portions of their individuality to forces that stand beyond themselves. Through those activities they experience self- (and collective) transformation. Examples of this include group dancing, masking, and mythic reenactment. Although Caillois makes it clear that this festive participation is not identical to earnest communication with the sacred (his point in *Man and the Sacred*), play of this type does conform to the more general emphasis of early societies, namely, that humans understand themselves as living amid great (and often unpredictable) social, cultural, physical, and spiritual forces.

More recent societies highlight such qualities as individualism, contract relations, orientation toward progress, secularization, and organizational gigantism and complexity. In Caillois's (2001b, pp. 99–128) view, modernizing societies are fascinated with agon and alea, and especially with the combinations of contest and chance that are built into many modern games. Such forms of game playing showcase the strategic attempt of individuals and groups to establish new connections to others and, within those relationships, to advance their own standing. Yet self-advancement in modern societies is not the result of personal effort alone. It depends also on ascribed factors (accidents of birth, for example) and on sheer chance. Contemporary games explore these themes. Indeed, rare is the contest which allows no role for chance (chess being one exception), and chance is the dominant theme in the various forms of gambling. Although every society is interested in these issues, competition is much more "systematized" in the modern context (p. 126). Similarly, he continues, chance in earlier societies is "not an abstract expression of a statistical coefficient, but a sacred sign of the favor of the gods."

Caillois's second distinction, paidia versus ludus, is related to his four types of play. In his (2001b, pp. 27–35) view, ludus—the elaboration of rules, techniques, record-keeping, and the like—tends to accompany the forms just emphasized (agon and alea). He believes that ludus also can be connected to mimicry or role playing, but ludus and ilinx, or turbulence, are entirely incompatible. As he sees it, people do not rush into whirling, destabilizing events to experience artifice and convention but to escape those controls. My aim is not to analyze Caillois's typology in depth or to evaluate criticisms of his work (see Henricks 2011). Instead, I emphasize here his point that societies selectively make certain forms of play their own. The occurrence of those forms is not idiosyncratic but reflects the overarching cultural commitments of the society in question.

Civilizing play. The connection between historically emerging value frameworks and expressive life also is central for Max Weber. Famously, Weber (1958a) declared that the development of Western civilization can be seen as an extensive process of "rationalization." That calculating, systematic approach expresses itself in economics as capitalism, in politics as parliamentary government, and in knowledge-making as science. In administration, it produces bureaucracy; in religion, it encourages a certain style of Protestantism. Weber wished to know if this relatively dispassionate instrumentalism would also transform the softer, more emotional spheres of life such as family relations, art and music, sexuality, and play. For example, Western art is marked by an observer-centered, linear perspective; its architecture exploits the scientific possibilities of the arch; its writing is forwarded (and altered) by mechanized printing. Although Weber died before completing this massive project, he did produce a book about the rationalization of Western music (Weber 1958b). Its general theme is that a series of rational inventions such as the repositioning of notes in the scale, the mathematical reconfiguration of harmony, tunable instruments, written scores, and the separation of writers and conductors from players led to more abstract understandings of music and to playing by large, highly coordinated units. Although Weber remained uncertain whether the expressive dimensions of life would continue as necessary counterbalances to the bureaucratic impulses of his time (think of the Jazz Age), his book about music shows clearly how rational inventions can shift people's ideas of beauty and enjoyment.

Weber's interest in the "civilizing process" was pushed forward and modified by Norbert Elias (2000), in a two-volume work of that title. In it Elias focuses on the transformation of physical experience and bodily control during the Renaissance. He shows that many practices related to table manners, urination and defecation, coughing, spitting, sexuality, and other bodily displays became much more "private" and tightly regulated during this time. The cause of these changes, in his view, was the "courtization" of formerly dispersed nobles. Both competing and allying with one another, courtiers supplemented their military connections with new forms of scheming, statecraft, and personal embellishment. These changes made their way into the ambitious middle classes, in part because of mechanically printed "courtesy" literature and the new requirements of urban life.

Elias (with Eric Dunning) extends this thesis in a study of the development of sports. *The Quest for Excitement* (Elais and Dunning 1986) argues that modern sports result from several structural changes in European society, especially in England. In contrast to the older, community-centered model of sports and games, sports became reestablished as specialized activities supported by clubs of gentleman gamesters. Rules, leagues, standardized play, private sporting grounds, and the like facilitated interaction among a rising segment of the population, promoted a model of the "good society" as cooperative competition, and enabled gambling. This associational style of relating (as opposed to the older communal style) celebrated social order as a contract established by loosely affiliated peers. Put briefly, the "parliamentarization" of society leads to the "sportization" of pastimes.

Still, and like Weber, the authors ponder whether increasing pressures for civilized interpersonal relationships generate their own tensions and reactions. Many contemporary forms of sports emphasize violence, and this fighting sometimes spills over into fan behavior. Because of the character of modern civilization, people have a quest for excitement. What sports represent, then, is "an enjoyable and controlled de-controlling of the emotions" (Elias and Dunning 1986, p. 44). People act out their aggressions, but they do so in carefully formatted ways.

My own attempt to describe these changes during the pre-industrial period (Henricks 1991) focuses on the ways sporting activities became disconnected from their earlier practical contexts. Hunting sports shifted from arduous quasi-martial pursuits to social activities featuring smaller (sometimes emparked) prey and more refined, distanced modes of killing. Fighting sports changed from rough military training and collective battles to individualized, rule-bound, and display-oriented activities. Ball play was elevated from its humble beginnings to become a proper focus of higher-class adults espousing thoroughly civilian virtues. Pertinent to all this was the attempt of social groups to articulate their character and identity via leisure style and to distance themselves from others considered different or inferior. In such ways, play both joined and distinguished people.

Furthermore, play was removed from its holiday context to become a formally organized, commercialized activity. I have summarized that "modern" style of play (Henricks 2006, pp. 90–100) as follows. (1) Modern play tends to express the active, manipulative capabilities of individuals. That constructivist bent threatens older themes of collective immersion, spontaneity, and exuberance. (2) Modern play prizes order-making. Competition is commonly used to create hierarchies of winners and losers, an arrangement justified by an ideology of fair play. (3) Modern play features instrumental commitments, both as end states within the event and as extrinsic motivations and rewards. In such ways, it challenges the concept of play presented in this book. (4) Modern play tends to occur in institutionalized "game" formats. (5) Modern play is amoral and technical in spirit. It celebrates partisan achievement instead of moral and spiritual exploration. (6) Modern play is organized bureaucratically; that is, it is commonly surrounded by associations, rules, regimens, and records. Once again, none of this is to say that play in this (or any other) period is of one type or that there are not reactions to the dominant type. Rather, well-supported cultural elements shape the way people pursue creativity and enjoyment.

Playing at Culture

It is time to develop the opposite viewpoint: play activities represent instances of resistance to prevailing cultural patterns more than expressions of them. Put differently, people play to explore alternative life stations and strategies and to contemplate the feelings that these provide. Of course, "resistance"—in play or elsewhere—can mean different things. For one, play is a relatively direct confrontation with established cultural patterns. Play of this sort is an act of defiance or reversal, an attempt to undo what is normal. Second, resistance can be seen as a pattern of withdrawal or escape. Players evade their customary obligations rather than challenge them openly.

Third and finally, playful resistance may be a celebration of independence. According to this perspective, play worlds are fairly isolated settings that (like other settings) operate by their own standards. This more situational or pluralistic view of play presumes that participants are not concerned with dominant patterns of authority relations or value complexes. Instead, players' chief interest is simply to explore the possibilities before them. Such activity may have the effect of social resistance (as alternative life strategies are inevitably fashioned and tested), but this resistance occurs without the participants' having any rebellious intentions.

The view of play as cultural disturbance or resistance has been prominent in play theory, especially among thinkers who are drawn to themes from Romanticism, Nietzsche, and Freud (Spariosu 1989). To recall a discussion from Chapter 5, it is especially important to Sutton-Smith. Against the idealization or civilization of play, he consistently emphasizes that play is an unsettling or pushing outward. This theme is developed explicitly in his descriptions of "the imaginary" (Sutton-Smith 1997, pp. 127–29) and "child phantasmagoria" (pp. 151–52). Players love to test limits, not only cherished cultural beliefs and social norms but also the limits of their own psyches. We all are fascinated by the dangerous, the gross, and the obscene. Perhaps even more interesting to us are our own reactions to these circumstances. In play, we intentionally exhume the negative primary emotions of fear, anger, disgust, and sadness as well as the more usual modalities of surprise and happiness. Our pursuit of variability means learning how we can manage ourselves in such occasions and how others will respond to us when we act out in these ways.

CAILLOIS'S COMMITMENT TO DISORDER

I have described one element of Caillois's thesis, namely, that different kinds of societies encourage different kinds of play. But this theme must not occlude his more general point that play is a fundamental human urge that imposes itself on worldly affairs. In this, he followed Huizinga. However, Caillois revised Huizinga's (and Schiller's) ideas of a relatively unitary and form-giving play drive by his presentation of four types of play. Much more than Huizinga, he wished to comprehend the psychobiological foundations of imagination, including desires for destabilization.

Following Freud and the surrealists, Caillois was intrigued by the idea of a death instinct, which he understood to be a quest for non-utilitarian expenditure and even self-extinction (Caillois, 2003, pp. 69–81). Like a praying mantis that is to be devoured by its mate at the end of copulation, humans seem compelled to do things that counter narrowly defined self-interest. These universal urges are portions of our physical inheritance. Indeed, in his essay he proposes the existence of "objective ideograms," crystallized psychological associations that are transmitted via evolution.

Similar ideas dominate another of his best-known essays, that on the connection of "mimicry" and "psychasthenia" (Caillois 2003, pp. 89–106). In it, he argues that animals that have developed the ability to camouflage themselves (by mimicking environments or other more dangerous creatures) do so in order to move into experiences of otherness. Such animals are said to possess an "instinct for abandonment," a desire to discover a "dark space" that stands beyond the requirements of routine functioning (p. 100). Applied to humans, *psychasthenia* denotes this quest to escape the boundaries of the self, to immerse oneself in otherness.

As the reader may note, Caillois's typology of play emphasizes our desires to be out of control (ilinx and alea) and to inhabit the guises of otherness (mimicry). Furthermore, it is pertinent to note his more general commitment to develop an interdisciplinary approach to human experience, what he (2003, pp. 343–47) called "diagonal science." Such an enterprise should unite the natural sciences and the humanities. It should include both collective and individual explanations of behavior. And it should address the evolutionary heritage of our species.

BAKHTIN'S CARNIVAL AND CARNIVALESQUE

Another historically based view of the disruptive possibilities of desire is provided by Mikhail Bakhtin. In a study of the Renaissance writer Rabelais, Bakhtin (1984) explores themes of indulgence, excess, and monstrosity that were cultural fascinations of the medieval and early modern periods. Pertinent for my purposes is his analysis of carnivals as events celebrating fleshly disorder.

Bakhtin (1984, p. 9) distinguishes carnivals from "official" festivals, events that idealize the status of social authorities and their proclamations of public values. Those latter activities vouchsafe routine social hierarchies, feature carefully established protocols, and are usually serious in tone. By contrast, carnivals explore the possibilities of free and familiar relations. A source of religious legitimacy for carnivals was the Feast of Fools in some of the continental monasteries, when those in lowly positions might be allowed to mock or assume the privileges of their superiors (Cox 1969). In the wider application of the event, revelers surged over public (and sometimes private) spaces and committed physical excesses of every type. This behavior was all the more important because medieval society was marked by clear divisions of estate, guild, sex, family, and age. Suddenly stripped of these traditional commitments, "people were reborn for new, purely human relations" (p. 30).

Medieval carnivals were not social chaos, however. They emphasized special activities such as foolery and encouraged the mocking of both secular and sacred authorities. Another theme was masking, which magnified the unfamiliarity of the event and reduced the prospects for social consequences. Laughter and drunkenness trumped sobriety. Integrating these themes, carnivals overturned customary hierarchies of thought and feeling, sacred and profane realms, humans and other creatures. More than that, they insisted on the mixing of these distinctions. Honorees were degraded, the disreputable elevated. To use Bakhtin's language, "Degradation digs a bodily grave for a new birth; it has not only a destructive, negative aspect but also a regenerating one" (1984, p. 21).

Carnival is clearly an expression of the pre-modern context. Furthermore, Bakhtin emphatic that these events should not be seen as social safety values or releases of tension. Instead, carnival is a "second world and a second life outside officialdom" (p. 6). It stands on its own as an alternative set of principles for comprehending human affairs. But it is less a set of ideas than an invitation to free-flowing interaction or dialogue. Imagination—indeed, mind itself—arises from this sensual, immediate interchange, a thesis he treated more fully in his book *The Dialogic Imagination* (Bakhtin 1981).

Modern carnivals are altered, usually commercialized versions of their medieval ancestors that are diminished further by the presence of spectators. Indeed, Renaissance authors such as Rabelais were starting to lose the older view that "normal" and grotesque are complementary aspects of human life and that grotesquery is not a condition to be abhorred or eliminated. Their "carnivalesque" works exploit instead the sociopolitical possibilities of mockery, physically provocative imagery, and crude humor. Textual involvement substitutes for human interchange.

GEERTZ'S DEEP INTERPRETATIONS OF TEXTS

Bakhtin's account emphasizes the idea that revelers maintain a double commitment. They celebrate a new world founded on customarily denied ideas and behaviors, but they also keep in mind the world that is being rejected. A similar if much more cognitive approach is presented by Clifford Geertz. In a noted essay, "Deep Play: Notes on the Balinese Cockfight," Geertz (1973, p. 412) claims that such ritualized events as Balinese cockfighting can be seen as complicated expressions of the cultural traditions and tensions of societies. As he puts it, "The culture of a people is an ensemble of texts, themselves ensembles, which the anthropologist strains to read over the shoulders of those to whom they properly belong" (p. 452). As this statement implies, ideally those readings reflect the cultural perspectives of the people being studied. And although it is tempting to simplify the meanings of what is occurring (in the manner of positivist social science), the more challenging and anthropologically appropriate approach is what he calls "thick description," that is, a vigorous attempt to think through the possible connections of the event to numerous personal, social, and cultural themes.

In his essay Geertz explains that the cockfight, a series of formally organized weekly matches, is central to Balinese society. The fighting cocks are recognized openly to be symbols of masculinity and of the status of local groups. When two cocks—each sporting sharp spurs—are set at one another in a fifty-square-foot ring, the result is a frenzy that usually results in the death of one of the combatants. Geertz's interest,

however, is not the fighting of the animals as much as it is the social relationships of the human participants. In Bali, cockfighting is attended
by two kinds of betting: the solemn pooling of money (ringlets) from
kin and community that forms the central bet between the two principal competitors, and the noisy profusion of individual side bets by those
who are less closely affiliated. Many of these bets, in Geertz's view, are
examples of what the utilitarian philosopher Jeremy Bentham called
"deep play," wildly dangerous risk-taking. In the worst cases, land and
reputation are lost in a few moments of passionate speculation.

The willingness of individuals and groups to risk their social status in
such an aggressive fashion and to express themselves so vehemently might
not be remarkable but for the fact that Bali historically has been among
the most poised, ritualistic, and courteous of societies. On one hand, this
means that the cockfight is a kind of counterbalance to some of the tensions generated by that society's overriding focus on order, polite standing, and social harmony. On the other, Geertz believes, Bali's definitions
of masculinity and status or honor are critical social themes that find (and
perhaps need to find) expression in this form of fighting. In other words,
the cockfight is less an escape from prevalent societal pressures than it is
a chance to work through the implications of such fundamental human
themes as death, masculinity, rage, pride, loss, beneficence, and social affiliation. Play events are ways to make prominent certain values that are
addressed less clearly in other forms of human dealings.

TURNER'S CONCEPTS OF THE
LIMINAL AND LIMINOID

The extent to which ritualized events offer people chances to explore
alternative (and trans-structural) relationships has also been central to
the writing of Victor Turner (1967 1969, 1979, 1982). Like many other
anthropologists, Turner was interested in how rituals—as symbolically
orchestrated formats—help community members display their commitment to one another through the public enactment of their thoughts
and feelings. The articulation of that common vision stabilizes society.
Turner's work was distinguished, however, by its emphasis on ritual as
a dramatic performance (bonding actors and audiences) and by his concern with ritual as a *process* that moves people through time and space
and ultimately changes their status in society at large. In that sense,
rites associated with birth, puberty, marriage, and death are more than
affirmations of collective values. They are processes that help communities understand that the principal participants in such events (or at

least, those who complete them successfully) should now be seen quite differently than they were before.

Turner's views of ritual (and play) were influenced strongly by the writings of Van Gennep (1960), who argued that ceremonial events tend to feature three stages that guide the transitions in status of those involved. The first of these is separation, the stage when participants are asked to shed their old identities (think of military recruits surrendering their possessions, freedom of movement, and bodily adornments). The second is a period of initiation, test, or trial. Frequently, in this stage participants are sequestered together in socially deprived circumstances and subjected to physical and mental ordeals (think of recruits having a lowly place in their new organization and facing training rigors that are intended not only to disorient them but also to challenge them to reach new levels of accomplishment and experience). The third and final stage is return. This is the point when those who have proved themselves worthy are admitted to the group under new terms, perhaps with a clearly defined status and enhanced rights of membership.

Turner's special interest is the middle stage in the ritual transition. Such a time might be an occasion for intense peer bonding (his version of communitas) and for the enactment of an unusual range of statuses and behaviors. Borrowing from the Latin, he argues that some of these less clearly structured moments can be described as "liminality" (that is, as being in a doorway or threshold between normal social experiences).

In traditional and agrarian societies, public festivals commonly showcase participants playing out different possibilities for existence. These possibilities should be seen as "inversions" rather than "subversions" of the social order (Turner 1979, p. 494). That is, people take on alternative statuses (such as men dressing up as women, animals, or dangerous spirits) and imagine themselves in these circumstances. This imaginative recreation is an act of play, or rather a combination of rite, play, and festival, as Huizinga emphasized.

Ritualized statuslessness, or liminality, manifests its profoundest meanings in traditional societies. Yet modern, complex societies also feature their own version of this, what Turner calls the "liminoid." Traditional societies, as we have seen, feature ceremonies in which there is little division between participants and audiences and experience is intensely collective. In the modern age, specialized forms such drama, dance, art, and sport have broken away from the (religiously defined) ritual context to become their own formats for experience. Now audiences are separated from performers, emphasis is placed on individual accomplishment and experience, and social and cultural patterns are seen as problems to be addressed and resolved by acts of personal enterprise. Such occasions, like the carnivals of the contemporary era, are times to subvert ordinary routine. Novel behaviors and experiences are expected.

If true liminality is conditioned by collective, religiously inspired worldviews (operating as descending meaning), its modern version—and here Turner includes creative exploits in science and philosophy—is more secular and dependent on individual insights for its direction. He does not see this version as inferior to the prior form, only different from it. In either of its variations, the liminal moment "is full of potency and potentiality. It may also be full of experiment and play. There may be a play of symbols, a play of metaphors. In it, play's the thing" (Turner 1979, p. 466).

HANDELMAN'S TOP-DOWN AND BOTTOM-UP EVENTS

In the modernist tradition, culture and society are relatively well-ordered affairs; that is, the public meanings in which people operate are coherently integrated and anchored by the stable commitments of organizations and individuals. Culture in that sense is a reality of its own sort whose meanings are there for people to interpret, or "get." Cultural patterns such as religion, language, and ideology may even be seen as "systems" with their own boundaries and interdependencies (Geertz 1973). When we make meaning, we assess and interrelate symbolic themes from the vantage point of our respective social positions. Much as Huizinga stated, we court (somewhat) disorderly situations so we can construct symbolically based resolutions. On that basis, we gain assurances for how to live. But what if meaning systems are more pluralistic, fragmented, contestive, and open than this? That is the theme addressed by Don Handelman.

Handelman (1992, 1998) argued that many societies have been guided historically by religiously inspired worldviews that are *not* monotheistic, centralized, or orderly in spirit. Instead, the universe is seen as de-centered, ever-changing, and filled with countervailing demands. A prominent example of this, which he developed in his own writing, is Hinduism. In cosmologies of this sort, the universe itself is recognized to be at play. When members of such societies participate in ritualized or symbolic play (such as that found at religious festivals), they step knowingly across a boundary into turbulent circumstances. Although their activity can be described as play, it can also be said that they are "in play." And in those circumstances, many of the customary or neat divisions of secular life fall away.

Handelman considers this type of festive play to be "top-down." That is, it is understood to be an entry into swirling sacred forces that cannot be controlled entirely by the player. This style of play is to be contrasted with what he calls "bottom-up" play. This latter pattern is characteristic of Western societies (and their cosmologies). Whereas Indian festivity encourages participants to enter deeply into sacred turbulence, the monotheistic societies of the West tend to emphasize the distant, broken, or otherwise separated relationship of humans to the divine. In the modernist West, play tends to celebrate personal resistance, rebellion, and creativity. Players take on the established social, cultural, or spiritual order and show how *they* would manage things if given the chance. Western players are fascinated with order-building and with their own roles in establishing and maintaining those constructions (my themes of modern play noted above). By contrast, non-Western societies are more aware that orderliness,however firmly it is imposed by secular authorities, is not life's guiding aim.

SCHECHNER ON PLAYING AND PERFORMING

Many of the themes mentioned above are developed in the work of Richard Schechner, who gathers elements from ritual, play, and theater into a wider vision of human behavior. This project parallels Turner's attempt to analyze advanced industrial societies with concepts generated for the study of traditional and non-Western societies, and it draws also on Schechner's special insights as a theater director. Perhaps the clearest statement of his view of play is presented in his book *The Future of Ritual* (1995).

Although Schechner acknowledges that play is difficult to define, he emphasizes that "playing fast and free with play acts has precipitated much confusion in the name of theory" (1995, p. 26). Against such mystification of play, he believes definitions are necessary to identify the different genres of play and to distinguish these from acts of playing, from "how it feels to be playing," from what play does for individuals and groups, from "ideas encoded in play," and from "the signals players and spectators use to communicate" (p. 26). He states that "play and ritual are complementary, ethologically based behaviors which in humans continue undiminished throughout life." Play has "boundaries or realms," but these are permeable. Versus claims that play is normally innocent or safe, he asserts that play is dangerous. Its "multiple realities . . . are slippery, porous, and full of creative lying and deceit." The fun of playing comes from disruptions of accepted social hierarchies and routines. Finally, play is "performative"; it features not only players but also directors, spectators, and commentators who interact and exchange ideas. Persons of each type have their own interests in the affair. What is play for one may be non-play for another.

Schechner stresses three themes. The first is that play features "multiple realities." Although modernist accounts of play (such as those of Goffman and Bateson) attempt to frame—and thus frame out—the discrete forms of human encounter, Schechner advocates a much looser conception of framing that he calls "netting" (p. 41). This means that human events are semipermeable, with various meanings running in and out of the frame. Goffman, it may be recalled, also stresses this theme, but for Goffman the challenge is to keep outside occurrences from confusing the commitments of everyone involved. Schechner is much more reconciled to the interpenetration of inner and outer, near and far. More than that, he believes that play's loose, exploratory orientation, which prizes ambiguity and change, is the fundamental mode of human relating. More formalized activities such as work are largely sociohistorical constructions that channel this curious, open spirit.

In order to support this vision of play, Schechner employs two Sanskrit terms, *maya* and *lila. Maya* has various meanings, but in particular it indicates acts of making or bringing into being. In the first instance, this involves creating what was not there before. Later, it takes the form of altering or transforming that which was (or is) there into something else. *Lila* is "a more ordinary word, meaning play, sport, or drama" (p. 29). In etymological terms it is connected to *ludus, illusion,* and *elusiveness.* In combination, then, *maya-lila* connotes "a performative-creative act of continuous playing where ultimate positivist distinctions between 'true' and 'false,' 'real' and 'unreal' cannot be made" (p. 29). When we play, we engage in acts of creation. Alone or with others, we establish a living presence that was not there before. That moment of involvement must not be declared inferior or unreal (as play so often is in the West), for there is no fundamental, originating ground that can be used to critique or demean it. To embrace *maya-lila* is to acknowledge that "all relationships are provisional" (p. 34). Because the contours of ultimate reality (if such a thing exists) cannot be known, it is best of speak of "playing" rather than "play" (p. 43). For humans the quest is not to represent or dramatize some firmly established external (or eternal) reality but instead to make one's way through the world by confronting openly its multiple claims, contradictions, and ambiguities.

Another theme is "dark play." As we have seen, visions of civilized play feature people acting openly and fairly with one another. Clear rules that detail boundaries, procedures, motives, and consequences are set forth. Participants stay "in frame" for the duration of the event and then return to routine affairs. Dark play blurs these boundaries. Much as Goffman details in *Frame Analysis*, play can be a fabrication or deceit. That is, some participants in the situation may be kept in the dark about the intentions of others. The result is that those not in the know can be "put on" or played with, sometimes quite cruelly. However, these qualities of deceit and confusion may also mark solitary play, as Goffman also makes clear in his comments about self-deception, hallucination, and compulsion (see Chapter 8). Sometimes, people play in ways that defy both conventional ideas of the right and proper and their own rational standards for behavior. They take extreme risks, indulge carnal desires, and revisit childhood fascinations. At such times they may be unsure whether they are in or out of control, under the spell of hallucination and frenzy, or indeed amid events that have turned into something quite different. Such themes were anticipated by Pre-Socratic fascinations with lust and power, Nietzsche's Dionysian rituals, Freud's obsessive-compulsive acts, and Geertz's deep play.

Third and finally, playing is described as a process of doing or performing. Sometimes this doing is formalized in culturally defined activities such as art, music, theater, dance, and sports that can be described as "performances." These forms acknowledge clear boundaries and procedures. As a theater director, Schechner is interested both in the ways these forms are infused with playing and in their possibilities for moving people's life commitments in and out of the frame. He is perhaps more interested, however, in "generating performances" (p. 39). In that sense, he wishes to show that the act of playing is the more fundamental project by which people create the (always suppositional) worlds in which we live. As he discusses elsewhere (Schechner 2002, pp. 30–37), acting in the world is performance when it occurs within the culturally established patterns of expression noted above, but it can also be done *as* performance without these protections and assurances. There is "make-believe" (recognized forms of pretense) and "make-belief" (the attempt to construct and operate within social and personal "realities"). Once again, to play is to embrace the confusions or "blurriness" of existence and to live actively amid these conditions. As Schechner (1995, p. 40) summarizes it, "playing is a creative, destabilizing action that frequently does not declare its existence, even less its intentions."

Playing Culture

In the discussions above, play is presented as an active commitment of persons. Players act, and by their actions create meaning. Playing in culture emphasizes the way people fit their activity to society's broader terms. Even as we explore the personal implications of these formats in play, our performances are, in effect, exercises in socialization, civilization, and cultural reproduction. The section about playing at culture extends the idea of performance to a much wider consideration of the possibilities of living. Play is a seeking of alternatives to established cultural patterns; it may even be a rebellion against forms and forces of any sort. As they do with other elements of the world, players create symbolic patterns, fiddle with them, destroy them, and begin again.

It is possible, however, to think of play in a less person-centered way. That is, play can be seen as symbolic interaction of its own sort, a running *through* or *out* of the possibilities of meaning. In such a view, culture itself is said to be *at* play (Hans 1981; Kuchler 1994; Henricks 2001). And humans are *in* play as they find themselves in the midst of chance-laden, swirling processes without clearly marked beginnings or ends.

All this presumes that culture can be seen as a patterning of relationships that goes on without the supervision of its human originators. Recalling discussions of Caillois and Handelman, some traditional societies understand this viewpoint profoundly. The sacred intervenes in the affairs of the world and, indeed, establishes people's terms of living. Top-down play is participation in that which never can be controlled or comprehended. By contrast, modernism's conceit is that humans *can* create and regulate their life-ways, both as a manufacturing of ideal societies and communities and, more narrowly, as a refining of individualized selves.

On one hand, modern people's fascination with their own creativity weakens the power of the sacred. On the other, that commitment to artifice severs connections between cultural and social locales for experience. If humans relied once on face-to-face communication as a stimulant for thought and feeling, a series of technical inventions—writing, printing, the telegraph, the telephone, the phonograph, radio, movies, television, the computer, and satellite communications—changed the character of cultural production, distribution, and consumption. Now, interlinked machines permit new forms of culture-bearing and new patterns of cultural involvement for persons.

Especially pertinent are so-called virtual or hyper realities presented to us on our electronic screens. Many of these publicly accessible scenes feature (seemingly three-dimensional) moving images with sounds, characters, and plausible narratives. Today computers allow us to influence the development of these scenes and stories and, by extension, to alter our experiences of them (Wardrip-Fruin 2009). Whether we choose to intervene in such artificially configured worlds or not, there is a sense that all this is going on without our direct involvement or at least sits there waiting to be turned on. Under these circumstances, what does it mean to play culturally? I describe two responses to this question below.

DERRIDA AND THE PLAY OF TEXTS

Modernism celebrates the prospects for rationally configured, widely shared symbolic form. Humans create, modify, and monitor idea systems. More than that, they desire to see psyche, society, and culture in grand scale and beyond this, to see how the intimacies of personal life are connected to wider patterns. As Piaget, Erikson, and Mead showed, human development can be seen as the establishment of enduring, expansive, and integrative cognitive-moral frameworks. Play helps us assemble and test these frameworks.

Post-structural and postmodern theories challenge modernism's quest to discover the firm principles that give order to events. Instead, a key task of cultural interpretation is to expose the frequently dubious assumptions and logical fallacies inherent in grand, universal, or "totalizing" narratives (Lyotard 1986). Post-structural thinkers commonly stress intellectual and political resistance to the administrative schemes of dominant groups and emphasize the legitimacy of viewpoints from differently (and less advantageously) situated people. Frequently, the terms for this resistance can be found within the very idea patterns that are being challenged (Butler 1990). Proposed changes should respect the particularities of the persons and communities involved. To abet this resistance, special attention is given to the uses (and abuses) of language as a device that categorizes, pacifies, and otherwise controls people.

An important representative of this tradition is Jacques Derrida (1976, 1981). He rejected the idea that society and culture are composed of solid ordering principles. Nor are such structures—as habits or orientations—foundational to individual personality. Instead, people operate inside settings that are themselves comings-together of profuse meanings. Existence is a movement from one of these intersections to another. Memory and consciousness are fluid. For the cultural interpreter, then, the challenge is not to display the most important or "best" meanings of any cultural form (a modernist understanding of hermeneutics). It is to open up and publicize the range of possible meanings.

Derrida was interested especially in the meanings of language. His thesis is that cultural patterns can be read as texts, and these texts contain widely diverging trails of meaning. When we explore these trails, we find contradictory and ambiguous statements. Although it might be thought that language helps us nail down and evaluate meanings, in his view the words we use are rarely defined precisely, even in dictionaries. Looking up any word's meanings, we find ourselves in a pattern of continual deferral or circulation that he (1982, p. 3) calls *différance*. Ultimately, what texts do is make claims that one element of the world is different from another. When we try to learn what these differences are, we fail to reach any solid end point that defines or grounds the statements that have been made.

The reader can see that this viewpoint is a contrarian response to those who try to define the meanings of cultural events objectively or scientifically or to those who define them on the basis of their own subjective standards. Instead, texts are openings of possibility that invite readers to think, feel, and act. Much like the reader—or writer—of a poem, we follow symbolic concourses, where one thing leads to many others. We may persist along these endlessly branching trails of intracultural reference, or we may turn back. What we can know most certainly is that we are no longer where we were before. *Deconstruction* is this process of puzzling, dissembling, and unpacking—and to that extent playing with—the meanings of ideas, images, and artifacts (Derrida 1988, pp. 3–12).

GADAMER'S INTERPRETIVE APPROACH

In several visions of play presented above, people are challenged to recognize the extent to which all of us are embedded in circumstances that are, in many ways, chance-based intersections. To be a contemporary person is to confront life's moments without assurances that there are enduring conditions that support, direct, or ground our ventures. As Schechner claims, we live provisionally. For its part, play is the behavior that helps people address interpersonal and cultural circumstances with immediacy, creativity, and consideration.

Such ideas are developed in the writing of Hans-Georg Gadamer. Influenced strongly by Heidegger, Gadamer sought to understand the ways in which people are situated in the world. In an important work, *Truth and Method* (1989), he argued that philosophical efforts to address the two terms of his title commonly run at cross-purposes. At least, that is the result if one adopts (in his view) such overly simple approaches to knowledge-making as subjectivism (focusing on internal structures and processes of awareness) and relativism (focusing on external cultural frameworks as contexts for interpretation). Rather, the human predicament is to be situated inside concrete, historically conditioned settings. Our awareness of this predicament arises not from abstract thought or from some privileged perspective but from practical, context-based activity. Such activity is itself a kind of dialogue with occurrences. Truth, if such a term can be used, is experienced as a form of un-concealment or revelation, when we suddenly (and always partially) sense some of the ways in which we are connected to and bound by that which prefigures and contextualizes our efforts.

Gadamer's approach is pertinent to the study of play (see Kuchler 1994; Steinsholt and Traasdahl 2001), for, again following Heidegger, he believed that the experiences and sensibilities developed in art and play are the proper pathways to understanding. For Gadamer, neither play nor art is a process of enforcing one's private vision on externality. Rather, those activities should be seen as processes of involving oneself in pre-existing patterns of language, rules, and material elements. It is by operating in these ongoing patterns that we discover life possibilities.

Finally, experiences of art and play are not just sudden flashes of insight. When we participate in these realms we in effect create new versions of space and time, settings where we linger, gain an alternative perspective on other moments of our life, and establish new forms of community. In all these ways, play both uncovers our ongoing predicaments and prejudices and establishes the conditions under which new forms of awareness arise.

Like other theories explored in this chapter, Gadamer's approach centers on play as a special pattern of—and receptivity to—engagement in the world. Like other post-structuralists, he sought to move past modernist divisions of self and other, activity and passivity, resistance and compliance. As a strategy for becoming aware of one's ever-shifting placement in circumstances, there is much to recommend this approach. Note, however, that his conceptions address communitas as much as they do play. At best, they represent a blurred genre that gathers the virtues of both these pathways.

9 The Play of Possibility

This chapter gathers and applies some of the book's major themes. I summarize my view that play is a distinctive strategy of meaning-making that finds its end in self-realization and revisit the distinction between ideal play and real play. In that analysis, I give special attention to the historical transformation of play. Concluding remarks address questions of whether and how play should be evaluated. Central to that discussion are comments on the relation of play to freedom.

A General Theory of Play

I have advanced the thesis that play is fundamentally a sense-making activity and that the broader goal of this process is to construct the subjectively inhabited sphere of operations and understandings called the self. People play in order to learn who they are, how they are situated, and what they can do.

In brief, sense-making moves forward on two related fronts, the physical and the symbolic. As shown in Chapters 5 and 6, people make sense of their circumstances by processes of physical recognition and response. We feel our way through life, relying on deeply established biological formations we have little power to regulate. Many forms of play feature these bodily assertions and adjustments. We find satisfaction in consciously controlling our bodies, but we also enjoy moments when we are modestly out of control—when our bodies (and the environments in which they operate) prove so forceful or unpredictable we can only marvel at their capacities. So understood, play is self-managed physical education.

Chapters 7 and 8 describe a later evolutionary theme: our capacities for symbolic creation and manipulation. That pattern of sense-making, which builds on physical recognitions and responses, features the application of publicly communicable ideas and images to circumstances. To be human is to create and use informational resources and, more than that, to reflect on those creations. In that light, Chapter 8 stresses players' ability to confront beliefs, skills, values, and norms. Chapter 7 focuses on abilities to conceive and explore relationships with other people. Both express the theme that humans try to fit the goings-on of the world into symbolically articulated frames. Complementary to that order-seeking enterprise is the continual erecting, modifying, and dismantling of those frames.

The discussion of play's psychology (Chapter 4) emphasizes that our quest to ascertain physical and symbolic meanings is, on the one hand, a subjectively managed movement into diverging fields of relationships (body, environment, society, and culture). On the other, play is a confrontation with multifold mental capabilities and commitments. As a psychological process, it is an integrative behavior that melds conception and sensation in the crucible of action-based experience. It teaches us both the implications of those aspects of our nature and how they align and misalign.

Is there a broad commitment that makes reasonable our seemingly contradictory desires to organize and disorganize the world? Why should we give ourselves enthusiastically to the frequently silly, disruptive, repetitive behaviors we call play when we might better spend our time fashioning and repeating a narrow set of commitments? Arguably, such behaviors as ritual and communitas are better guides for discovering the world's more enduring patterns and for learning one's place within them. And work, which leads to clearly defined products and possessions, is perhaps a more effective way of judging personal character and capability. At any rate, all three of these behaviors are important pathways of self-realization.

Play is just as significant, specialized, and ordinary as the other forms. What distinguishes play is the way it develops, maintains, and assesses action strategies. Unlike ritual and communitas (both of which celebrate otherness as a guide for fulfillment), play honors personal enterprise. Although individually sustained in a fashion similar to play, work differs by its commitment to instrumentality. Ultimately, workers adore their creations—and the consequences of those creations—more than their acts of creating.

Like communitas, play allows people to realize themselves in the moments of their involvement. Unlike communitas, play emphasizes people's transformative and contestive proclivities. For such reasons, play brings into focus processes of goal attainment and cultivates the general skills pertinent to this planning, coordinating, executing, and revising of action strategies. Assessment of such activity is based not only on play's effects on the world but also on how it makes us feel during those processes. To that extent, play is a distinctive mode of personal functioning.

I have stressed that a general theory of play must embrace a very wide vision of self. Self is not simply psychological involvement (the way any person is thinking, feeling, and behaving). Nor is it only social involvement (a position in relation to other humans). Selfhood is equally a condition of bodily, environmental, and cultural participation, where we claim certain connections to the world as our own. In all these settings, play focuses on personal recognizance.

Exploration of other aspects of the play-self connection showed that play is not a quest for a privatized, highly bounded self. Comprehensions of "I" and "me" (as the subjective and objective modes of personal involvement) are important. But so are themes of "us" and "we," the self considered collectively as a shared predicament and set of action commitments. Similarly, selfhood entails ideas of "you," the sense of being called out as a subject capable of initiating meaningful responses to another. As we have seen, many theorists discussed in this book stress that play is a kind of intersubjective dialogue between self and other. But play can sometimes turn its play objects (and playmates) into an "it" such that they feel only the force of the player's assertions. Seen in this broader way, play is an invitation to several, at times alternating and conflicting, patterns of personal involvement.

Four types of "assertive" play were stressed. *Dialogical* play, in which subject and otherness are engaged in a relatively equal give-and-take, is one pattern. Play can also be *rebellious*, a pattern that occurs when otherness is so powerful that the player can only tease and taunt. Different again is *manipulative* play, in which the subject is able to control a relatively weak or passive form of otherness. Finally there is *exploratory* play, in which self and otherness hold each other at a distance and imagination flowers. Once again, the point is that neither play nor selfhood should be seen in a limited or static way. Play is altered by the quality (and power dynamics) of its relationships. Players' standings change from one moment to the next.

Just as these relationships (privilege, subordination, engagement, and marginality) produce differences in play, so they influence the character of work, ritual, and communitas. To take play's opposite as an example, some rituals are exercises in manipulation and privilege (such as brushing one's teeth in the morning), and some acknowledge subordination (adorations of the sacred). Still others are examples of dialogical engagement (greeting rituals between peers) or marginality (explorations of life's meanings). Although these forms differ in their color and dynamism, all express the general qualities of ritual described in Chapter 2.

Another theme was the variability of the settings in which the self finds itself situated. According to Csikszentmihalyi, players may feel themselves deeply inside an event, where they think only of the particularities of the moment. That quality of being embedded (or in "flow") is important, but play also draws on more general qualities of persons and worldly affairs that are brought in and out of the event. In other words, play features both a particularizing of broader commitments of the self and, in consequence, a generalizing from the particularities of the event that has just occurred. Much of the play's pleasure derives from this intersection of wider and narrower meanings of self-involvement. According to Goffman, we play in order to experience ourselves, both as players performing intricate maneuvers and as persons who have chosen to play. The playful self must not be restricted to either within-the-event or beyond-the-event modes of being, for its project is to combine the immediate with the transcendent.

Finally, self-realization should not be equated to ideas of steady personal development or "progress." As Vygotsky stresses, players commonly desire to advance themselves by expanding their capabilities. But play can also feature regression, the revisiting of what was once familiar. And it can be digression and introgression; that is, it can be a willful investigation of life stages that are neither ahead nor behind. Players run off in many directions; each run presents its own (usually unanticipated) challenges to recognize and respond to.

All this is based on the view that human existence, and the qualities of awareness that support that existence, are at some very basic level a process of continually repositioning oneself amid the occurrences of the world. That positioning process acknowledges many kinds of external elements and features involvements that vary in their stability. It is based on biological patterns of recognition and response that become elaborated as symbolic processing. It addresses and manages both extreme particularity and patterns that transcend most of life's moments. It features experiences of continuity and discontinuity, and comprehends these as complementarities. Like the other three pathways, play is an inquiry into the possibilities of self-standing.

Ideal Play, Real Play

Early in this book I defined play as a distinctive way of behaving and emphasized that such behavior can be seen (with an increasingly wide lens) as action, interaction, and activity. As action, play is *transformative* and *consummatory*. As interaction it is *contestive* and *unpredictable*. As activity it is *self-regulated* and *episodic*. Play's distinctive disposition is *curiosity*; its emotion sequence is *fun-exhilaration-gratification*. Both within the event and beyond the event, play features an ascending pattern of meaning construction. It opens up, rather than restricts, interpretive possibility.

The above listing represents an attempt to formalize—and situate— the definitions of contemporary play scholars. As part of that process, play was set apart from work, ritual, and communitas. Of special pertinence is the distinguishing of play from communitas, though the two patterns are commonly united in play studies. Also controversial is the view that play and ritual, rather than play and work, are opposites.

Chapters 4–8 gave greater attention to the theories of other authors and to "real" play. As discussed in those chapters, human events are usually blurred genres that combine not only goings-on from different fields of relationships (body, psyche, environment, society, and culture) but also organizational principles from the four pathways of behavior. As exhibited in figure 2, all behavior is shaped by many ordering processes, or inputs. When we play (or conduct other behaviors), we draw on these patterns to move action forward. Much of this borrowing is done without conscious reflection. In play, individuals bring to consciousness certain of these goings-on and reconstitute them as elements of contest. On one hand, this gathering and consolidating of resources is an order-making process. On the other, it is an opportunity for interpretation and revision and even for the ransacking of those resources.

Just as players create frames for their behavior and then pull elements in and out of those frames, so real events effectively combine, and alternate, the four categories. To recall Freud's obsessive-compulsive rituals and Schechner's dark play, it may be unclear, even to the player, if she is playing. Montessori and Dewey willfully combined work and play. Piaget's repetitive exercises seem to be work, ritual, and play at once. Several of the anthropologists mentioned in Chapter 8 combine ritual, play, and communitas. Such complexities are heightened if one acknowledges the many kinds of occurrences (bodily, environmental, social, psychological, and cultural) that have been described. Taking account of all these combinations and potential combinations leads to wonderful interpretive possibilities, including some that seem oppositional or paradoxical.

Clearly, the dispositions of real players and the categorizing inclinations of academics are different matters. We play in order to feel ourselves moving through the world, and it is often the combinations of things (for example, what our bodies do when challenged by changing environments) that surprise and excite us. Sometimes, this experience is consciously anticipated; sometimes, it is a happenstance of the course we've chosen. Regardless of its initiating conditions, play prizes—and intentionally convolutes—patterns of recognition and response.

For such reasons, no play scholar should disregard play's wonderful confusions and uncertainties. But play is neither confusion nor disparity, nor is it the pleasurable habitation of these conditions. Instead, players combine order and disorder strategically. Although we intentionally court disorder, our aim is to see what we can do with it. Leaping into precarious circumstances, we try to find our balance. Unsatisfied with our newfound security, we destabilize ourselves again. What marks play—and separates it from ritual, communitas, and work—is the way players manage discontinuity by developing their own behavior strategies and by reaching their own conclusions about what just occurred. That teasing, provoking style is orderliness of its own sort.

Real Play Is Historically Situated

Whatever the merits of the above claims, it should be clear that real play is constructed from many sources and that those constructions commonly reflect the organizing principles of societies. That shaping of the play impulse, sometimes in ways that contradict this author's ideal type, is Huizinga's other theme. This section offers a brief summary of play's sociohistorical transformation, a coherent set of changes that include not only the shifting character of public events but also new meanings for self.

Play in traditional societies. As we have seen, anthropologists are attentive to the symbolic meanings of public events, especially those in traditional societies. Combining Huizinga's themes of play, festival, and rite, these gatherings allow community members to act out—sometimes in highly energetic and improvisational ways—a variety of sacred and secular roles and even to combine these rival spheres of life. Play of this festive type is not mere frivolity. Dramatized events and personages may have much spiritual or mythic importance. Activities can be seen as attempts to awaken the sacred and have it intervene benevolently in ordinary affairs. So understood, symbolically charged events are occasions when people play out the cultural commitments of their societies and make public their allegiances to one another. And the most important of these occasions are avenues between the momentary and the eternal (see Eliade 1957; Henricks 2006).

As Handelman's work makes plain, traditional societies vary in the orderliness of their cosmologies and in the extent and stability of their secular hierarchies. Sometimes, as Geertz explained, play events redress tensions and cultural "omissions" generated by prevailing societal patterns. Sometimes, as Bakhtin noted, the festival is a fully established "second world" that holds its own against traditional authority structures. In most cases, however, traditional societies recognize the importance of bringing people together periodically to collectively create meaning. Such occasions are all the more important because such societies rely on face-to-face oral transmission for the sharing of beliefs. Recalling Turner's theme, communitas is an important stage of the ritual process, and play's spirited improvisations may be elements of this process as well. In a blending of these three forms, playful creativity is more than a quest for private capability; it is an attempt to locate oneself within a sacred realm and within the human community that survives by its graces.

For such reasons, I describe the playful self of traditional societies as *embedded* (Henricks 2010). Because people in these settings are fairly local in their commitments and affiliations and because they do not have access to external informational resources, they tend to look "within," "above," and "below" their communities for sustenance. Descending meaning, especially in the form of tradition, is critical. Play interprets, reassesses, and personalizes those guidelines.

Play in early modern societies. Traditional societies situate individuals within collectives that transcend their living representatives and establish the terms for their existence (Kahler 1956). Those same collectives monopolize information sources. Culture is carried in the minds of society's members; the sacred trumps secularity. Modernity, by contrast, features the growing independence of individuals from these centuries-old affiliations and beliefs. One effect of this change is the development of a more reflexive, enterprising, and narrowly centered person.

New social organizations parallel (and support) these changes. Modern inventions such as the nation-state, congregational church, school, legislature, business, labor union, and sporting league reflect a distinctive, constructionist style of human relating. That is, dispersed individuals, protected by recognized rights or freedoms, convene to erect new social arrangements that express and coordinate perceived commonalities. These institutions (for example, the joint-stock corporation) transcend older ties of language, community, and ethnicity. Primarily future-oriented, these organizational forms are understood to be human (rather than godly) creations. They are maintained as long as they meet the requirements of their members, who continually estimate their productivity. Collectivities of this type are created in order to be modified or improved reflexively.

This social style is expressed in play. As we saw, Elias and Dunning equated parliamentarization and sportization. Handelman spoke of "bottom-up" play. In either case, public affiliation is something to be manufactured intentionally by individuals. That "social contract," which prizes the agreements of socially equivalent (if otherwise disparate) persons, presumes that human discourse is appropriately a pattern of regulated competition. Such regulation includes specific agreements about terms of engagement, including protections of opportunity and acceptance of results. In that sense, social order is established, maintained, and, if necessary, rearranged by fully fledged persons.

Consistent with this portrait, I see play of this type as generative of the *associational* self. In an age of organizational expansion and individual mobility, people desired opportunities to forge new social connections. Instrumental to that process was the display of valued personal qualities to would-be associates. As Weber and Elias made clear, civility (as a bridling of self-interest) is key. Associational play celebrates people's capacities for order-making and self-regulation. But it also makes clear that such activity is but an artifice. Beneath society's veneer lie the desires of those whose interests are blocked by the new arrangements and, more profoundly, by the physical and emotional commitments of every person. That proclivity to disavow and reassociate is Bakhtin's theme.

Play in industrial (late modern) societies. For Huizinga, the major change in play occurred during the Industrial Revolution. In the political and economic realms in particular, activity became systematized and regimented. Social organizations grew in size, scope, and abstraction. Less formal, personal styles of administration gave way to bureaucracy. Organizations and individuals tried to expand their spheres of operation. As Weber stressed, the age became dominated by a calculating, instrumental ethic.

By increments, social institutions and the organizations they spawned became specialized. Society became organized as a contracting for services. Businesses, churches, governments, schools, and hospitals maintained formal relationships with one another in order to meet specific goals and needs. Individuals, as well, found themselves dependent on large organizations for the services they offered and, more than that, for the employment that sustained their living.

Like other institutions, play became specialized. That is, sports, games, music, art, and dance became separate endeavors marked by distinctive arenas, terminologies, rules, training, records, and roles. The sponsors of earlier forms of public play—communities, guilds, prominent families, and even associations of gentleman gamesters—were replaced by stable, abstractly configured organizations. Much as Marx described labor, play became organized systematically by nonplayers.

Huizinga was concerned with the politicization of play during his time, especially its being appropriated by totalitarian governments as elements of their festivals. Even more, perhaps, he objected to play's commercialization (see Plumb 1973; Walvin 1978). In the first instance, it means the ascendancy of a pay-to-play ethos, according to which money is the conduit of pleasure. Community-controlled spaces are replaced by privately controlled arenas, playhouses, and parks. Second, it means a professionalization of entertainment such that customers become watchers instead of active participants. For Huizinga, play loses many of its sociocultural functions when it becomes specialized, professionalized, and otherwise dominated by a commitment to expertise.

Because of this systematizing of play by formal organizations, I describe the playing self of this era as *managed.* This management occurred on two fronts. Directed by the formal representatives of organizations, creativity became goal-oriented or worklike. People manufactured or "produced" play. Split apart from such participation, although equally intentioned and organized, was the observation of play. The character of this consumption is a theme of Marxian analysts. None of this is meant to imply that industrial play destroyed entirely the earlier forms of relating, but it is claimed that the formal organization of play and the bifurcation of the play role presented challenges of its own sort. That concern, stated in much broader terms, animates Weber's rationalization thesis.

Play in advanced industrial (postmodern) societies. Because of the numerous social and cultural changes that have taken place since the 1970s, many social commentators now question whether we continue to live in an industrial or modern age (Jameson 1984; Rosenau 1992; Bertens 1995). To be sure, the role of machines has not lessened; neither has the importance of large organizations. But the development of information-processing machines has meant new patterns of work and leisure and, more generally, new possibilities for human relating.

The distinctive play setting of this putatively postmodern era is electronic media (see Aarseth 1997; Wolf 2001, 2008; Swalwell and Wilson 2008; Wright, Embrick, and Lukacs 2010; Wardrip-Fruin 2009). Television, computers, video games, and various social media alter cultural participation and, in a related way, permit social participation at a distance. In both individual and social settings, contemporary persons now take part in a (reconceived) public domain without confronting the issues historically associated with face-to-face communication.

These changes allow people to experience many of the emotions of social interaction via encounters with machines. This ability is heightened in the case of computers and video games, users of which match levels of challenge to their playing skills. Such technically induced flow (often prizing rapid physical and mental reactions to on-screen happenings) is augmented by player-controlled decisions and movements that advance complicated narratives. As in real life, virtual situations feature concrete (faux existential) challenges that require immediate responses. But these momentary events are also placed into trajectories that link back-stories to future-oriented quests. Much like the industrial-era consumers of novels and then films and television, players of electronic games achieve pseudo-social experiences, but they are deepened by embodied participation. To use Peter Stromberg's (2009) phrase, participants both play and are "caught in play," as they are carried forward by their own physical and emotional momentum. Players do not simply watch and interpret on-screen worlds; their movements bring these worlds into being. Increasingly, players control the character of the narratives they inhabit (Waldrip-Fruin 2009).

Similarly, social encounters change. Via computers, people participate in online multi-player games with others from around the world. To extend Fine's argument, separations between "characters," "players," and "persons" widen and the relationships between these three modes of personal functioning become complicated. In many instances, players do not have to—indeed, are not allowed to—exhibit themselves as persons (that is, as individuals with a recognizable physical appearance, established identity, biography, geographical location, and ongoing social commitments). To that extent, mediated participation encourages people to present specialized versions of themselves to others. These on-screen versions may contrast radically with the persons behind the controls. Furthermore, the presented self can be withdrawn at any time simply by exiting the playing field, an abandonment that is much more difficult in face-to-face settings or when one acknowledges ongoing obligations to others.

This identification process is especially prominent in games featuring the explicitly personalized versions of self known as "avatars." At such times, players manufacture characters and witness their exploits as they encounter a range of difficulties. Frequently, they observe the "death" (indeed, a succession of deaths and rebirths) of their persona and, more pleasingly, build its history of accomplishments and relationships. Once again, other media exalt spectatorship and permit vicarious identification (Debord 1977). Computers allow people to inhabit self-styled characters and manipulate their destinies.

In the case of social media, this representational self is entwined even more deeply with the routine self (or selves). As Turkle (2005) emphasizes, many on-screen personas are jaunty, socially idealized renditions of the individual. But they can also express his deepest fears and longings. In either case, on-screen selves are built and revised, often daily, with text and photos. They are visited both to experience one's public incarnation and to learn how others have interacted with the site. Thus blogs and web pages are ongoing cultural existences that display the lifestyle, social commitments, and psychological acumen of their creators. Bloggers and their like exist in a macro-sphere of interested observers or "followers" that no flesh-and-blood person can rival. The success of a site is measured by its visits or "hits." Sometimes the site lives on after the originator has died.

The creation and management of these publicly visible images may serve extrinsic purposes. But they are also expressions of the play impulse, which is to create versions of self and to put these forward in the world. Material added to sites may produce long trails of reaction from visitors. By means of such dialogue, electronic communities are built and stabilized, along with codes for civil conduct (Consalvo 2007). That cultivation of the "we" and "us," marked by patterns of inclusion and exclusion, is also an act of play.

Based on the foregoing, it seems reasonable to adopt Schechner's view that contemporary players are *performative* selves. Because of interactive media, many of us have opportunities to display ourselves to others and to interact with their displays. Those dramatizations can parallel our routine lives, but they can also veer wildly from ordinariness. Like other actors, we collude with those who share our interest in bringing quite specialized worlds into being. So thickly do our play activities mix with our off-screen commitments that it becomes difficult to determine which setting is true and which is false, which essential and which merely preparation for what sustains us.

Evaluating Play

Should play be judged? According to the above account, real play is set within sociohistorical circumstances. Societies play in their own ways, or rather, the members of those societies play to address beliefs, values, norms, and skills that are pertinent to their living. As Chapters 7 and 8 showed, different groups in those societies have distinctive concerns arising from shared predicaments. Play may be an affirming or idealizing of one's standing in life, but it may also be a rebelling against or ignoring of that standing. Different groups—and individuals—pursue their own visions of self-realization. We should not expect two persons to play in the same way.

Nevertheless, in this book I follow Huizinga in asking whether there are better or worse forms of play. Posing this question assumes the existence of some standard that can be applied to our life-ways. In the ideal-type approach of this book, human events are judged to be more or less playful according to their consonance with some list of defining characteristics. In contrast, play activities can be judged morally, that is, as promoting conditions that honor the principled integrity of individuals and groups. Play can also be considered aesthetically, by judging the quality of the experiences it generates. And standards of utility—whether play leads to effects that forward the interests of participants and organizers—can be imposed as well.

For his part, Huizinga (1955, pp. 206–13) believed that some forms of play are "false" and other forms true or, at least, truer. When leisure furthers the interests of abstract social forms rather than communities of persons, it ceases to be play, properly defined. As Marx's workers ideally set the terms for their own activity, so Huizinga's players do the same.

Huizinga (1955, pp. 204–6) objected to another aspect of the public entertainments of his age: what he called "puerilism." In his view, gatherings that revel in exuberant drinking, raucous singing, and pledges of unthinking loyalty are not equivalent to play. Boozy confraternity may have its place, but it is all too often regressive rather than progressive, childish rather than childlike. For him, play is not simply indulgence in collective affiliation; it is activity that encourages individuals to express themselves thoughtfully and creatively. Puerilism, for its part, evokes a simplified (and dangerously romanticized) past. To a large extent, Huizinga's critique is an aesthetic one. Enjoyments such as Nazi festivals can be judged.

Two other criteria for judging play, utility and morality, lie beneath the surface in Huizinga's account. As we have seen, he disliked utilitarian, instrumental, and functional explanations. Play is not purposive, nor do people understand the implications of their actions. Nevertheless, his book is a commentary on play's role in the transformation of societies. The proper society is the well-played society; interpersonal rivalry and creativity express and cultivate a style of living. Finally, he concludes by asserting that play "lies outside morals. In itself it is neither good nor bad" (p. 213). This does not mean, however, that people should refrain from judging play or from estimating its place among the array of human occupations. To quote his final sentence: "Springing as it does from a belief in justice and divine grace, conscience, which is moral awareness, will always whelm the question that eludes and deludes us to the end, in a lasting silence."

To be sure, Huizinga's criticisms reflect his idealist, agrarian inclinations. In a century maddened by economic depression, totalitarianism, and war, it was appropriate to remember the immediate joys of human engagement. Persons and person-based communities matter. In the twenty-first century, his concern stands. So also does his view that members of any society should have opportunities to creatively consider the character of that society, including its forms of play.

It is not to be expected that critics will apply Huizinga's standards to contemporary events. But some framework is necessary for perceiving and evaluating the world's turnings. In the following, I extend the theory of play as ascending meaning to focus on one important theme of playlike events. That theme is the degree to which persons control what occurs and administer the meanings of those occurrences.

Play and Human Agency

If play has a central quality, it is that this behavior (as action, interaction, and activity), first of all, celebrates people's abilities to craft their own responses to circumstances free from interference. That distinctive process of making and interpreting, what I have called ascending meaning, is connected intimately to the project of human freedom. In Western societies, freedom is often seen negatively, that is, as a condition of non-interference. We consider ourselves free when we do not have to take the dog for a walk, pay taxes, or watch a television program we dislike. According to a more positive, and more complicated, view, freedom is the ability to draw on resources that help us realize our ambitions. Achieving goals such as receiving a promotion at work or going on vacation customarily entails gathering socially valued skills and resources. Non-interference is not enough; indeed, connections to other people often are vital.

As ascending meaning, play is the process of bringing resources into settings and using them without external restriction or reproof. In that light, I introduce a third quality of play—and a third aspect of freedom. Players must know what to do with the resources they have garnered. That creative capability to select elements of the world, coordinate their application, and judge the implications of that application is critical to sustaining a successful trajectory through life. Play cultivates those strategies of goal attainment.

Unstated to this point are the different issues pertinent to conceiving and managing behavior. Four of these issues, each posing specific challenges for decision making, are presented below. By definition, "playful" events are those which emphasize the subject's role in fashioning what occurs.

To be sure, ritual, communitas, and work also feature choice-making. But play accentuates this process and changes its terms. Arguably, play is less restricted than are ritual (which is laden with obligation and other-direction), communitas (with its integrative and cooperative focus), and work (which is harnessed to end products and external purposes). More clearly than other activities, play prizes personal decisions. As one of June Factor's (2009) Australian schoolchildren put it, "It's only play if you get to choose."

Choosing to play. If play is a recognizable activity, then choosing to play is a statement of public intention. To declare one's readiness to play is to acknowledge that other commitments have been set aside. As discussed in Chapter 8, many categories of people are not able to make this declaration easily. Historically, authorities have prevented some people from playing publicly or have doled out opportunities within the context of ritualized events. Play's history is one of permissions and prohibitions. It is also a history of people permitting—or denying—themselves the right to play. Many of us feel too busy, serious, or dignified for play's improprieties. Or we allow ourselves to play only in ways that match our broader identities.

Establishing the frame for the event. As intensely particular activity, play must have its persons, objects, and formats. That means making decisions about who, what, when, where, how, and sometimes why. Ideally, players themselves make these choices and thus construct the frame that channels action. A description of five choices follows.

The first is that of *specific play activity*. Action cannot move forward, even in the most solitary behaviors, without some focus (a *what*) that gathers and expresses intention. In social play, this decision is more complicated. Most people have been involved in heated decisions about whether to play checkers or dominoes, tag or hide-and-seek. Institution-alized game forms (essentially, packaged choices) make collective selection easier. Whether choosing from pre-established forms or not, players should control this process.

The second choice involves the *setting for play,* in effect, *when and where* the event will occur. Preferably, players decide when to begin and how long the game will last. Alone or collectively, it is determined that play is to be outside rather than inside, in one yard rather than another. And within those latitudes, specific boundaries are established. One stump is fair territory, another foul. Some zones are "safe," others not. And nonplayers are stationed outside the field of play or given narrow, non-interfering places within it.

The third choice concerns *membership,* that is, *who* will play. Typically, social play involves processes of inclusion and exclusion. Sides are chosen; only some people are picked, or they are chosen belatedly. Procedures may be needed to ensure that sides are even. Within teams, specialized positions are assigned, and agreements are reached about who will be starters and who will be replacements.

The fourth choice entails *rule-setting.* Decisions must be made about proper goals, turns, movements, and equipment. Recalling Goffman's theme, some external resources are "realized" as play elements; others are declared irrelevant. And still other rules ("transformations") are established to keep within-the-event and beyond-the-event worlds at a proper distance. Once again, the use of established forms accelerates these decisions and allows players to fine-tune their activity to the people, places, and times at hand.

The fifth choice is another of Goffman's themes, *setting of stakes.* Ideally, events are played for fun. But the motivation can be sweetened by monetary rewards, honorific statuses, and additional opportunities to control the play space (such as continuing to play the next team up the ladder). In such ways, play is linked strategically to other valued aspects of life.

Administering within-frame events. Constructing the reality of the event is one thing; administering it is another. Play activities are not simply forms for behavior; they are emergent processes filled with strategic oppositions, disagreements about rules, improbable occurrences, and unsettled outcomes. Only some people find themselves happy about what is transpiring. Somehow decisions must be made that will keep a willfully unpredictable affair on course.

In this context, one choice involves *starting and stopping action sequences.* Solitary play is remarkable for the extent to which participants control the pattern and pace of their own behavior. This control is not unqualified, for game forms inspire us to complete them, and machine play sometimes draws us into its iron logic. In social play, these issues are more complex; allotting play opportunities usually means taking turns. Players should administer those transitions.

Another choice is *controlling action sequences.* Some forms of solitary play allow the player to mercilessly manipulate an object, as when one bounces a basketball. Even then the player may accentuate the difficulty by dribbling with her less skilled hand or by attempting fancy maneuvers with the ball. In social play, this issue is of great importance. So the stronger participant may handicap herself or voluntarily assume a subordinate position. In order to be effective, play requires strategic tensions or imbalances that result in uncertain outcomes. Ideally, players establish and reposition these tensions in ways that honor the subjectivity of all.

The third choice is *administering rules.* Once again, setting rules is different from applying them. Most people understand what it means to win or lose, to play fair or to cheat. Play's challenge—and charm—is learning what it means to have those labels applied to us personally. By being called "out" and accepting that decision, we learn how success and failure are intertwined with others' judgments.

Players must also *determine a conclusion.* Some games are fairly brief and have clear end points. Others exhaust the patience of all. Still other forms of play feature largely unstated goals or involve repetitions of small strips of behavior. When is the activity completed? Nonplayers may try to keep players in harness for the entirety of the event. But less formal and player-directed activity offers many stages at which satisfaction can be declared. Ideally, a party, music jam session, or spate of teasing continues until it loses the inspiration and commitment of its participants. Then, it's over.

Determining beyond-the-event connections. The comments above have focused on ascending meaning within-the event, choices that set up and administer activity of this type. The final process is deciding what to make of what is going on and how this connects to other life concerns.

In this regard, players need to *select resources to bring into the frame.* As Simmel, Goffman, and Schechner maintain, play's boundaries are semipermeable. External concerns, qualities, and commitments such as values, skills, beliefs, and norms are alternately pulled into and pushed out of the frame. Some play is a key that allows us to treat any issue in a light-hearted, socially protected, and publicly accessible way. Other forms of play are fabrications in which some participants are kept in the dark about the event's meanings. In either case, players test the boundaries of acceptable impropriety and, more precisely than that, discover what they personally can get away with. More generally, play involves people's bringing their own broadly useful capabilities into particular situations. Singing, running, fighting, and arguing are general skills. In play these are given specificity. The question is who decides what capabilities will be employed.

Another choice is *leaving the play setting*. Some play ends by collective assent. Much does not. Goffman's transformation rules represent attempts to keep people in-frame when they get calls to come home, are worried about a blister, or have their feelings hurt. Like all rules, these prescriptions work only some of the time. Ideally, play features the right of people to leave the playground just as they entered it, voluntarily. More profoundly, permission to quit is recognition that participants can determine the place of play in their own registries of daily commitment.

The final decision is *declaring what the experience "means."* Instrumental (that is, worklike) play often has predetermined meanings. Participants seek some valued end state, reward, or enhancement of personal functioning. Nonplayers may be even surer about their goals for the event. However, play differs from work in the way meanings are derived. In play, beyond-the-event implications are not specified. No one can predict in advance whether the event will produce estimations of pleasing self-regard or whether embarrassment, hurt feelings, and broken spirits will ensue. One person leaves the playground believing that something interesting and important occurred. Another draws no weighty conclusions. To say that play happens without firmly established links to the outside world is not to criticize that activity. For play's strength is its opening of possibilities, which people are free to gather on their own terms or to disregard entirely.

Conclusions

Play may be a socially protected strategy for engaging the world, but those protections do not make it immune to criticisms that pertain to any human endeavor. By whatever standards the reader employs, certain forms of play may be declared morally good. By plan or by happenstance, some events gather people together in ways that honor valued principles. Other examples of play—perhaps killing animals, vandalism, and other forms of injury—are morally suspicious. Much as pre-modern societies extolled virtues different from our own, so contemporary people are not expected to agree on any listing of honorable and dishonorable pursuits or on the role of communities in promoting some forms and opposing others. Still, play is neither innocent nor trivial. Actions done in the name of play, including many species of self-indulgence, are rightly questioned.

Much the same can be said for play's aesthetic implications. Distancing themselves from Schiller, Huizinga, and Groos, few scholars today see play as an avenue to the beautiful, harmonious, and sublime. Rather, and in the spirit of Sutton-Smith, it is emphasized that play courts disunity as well as unity and with this, emotions of anger, fear, and unhappiness. Although players seek difficulty and disarray (and the feelings that attend them), it is my view that such experiences are not play's end. Rather, and still following Sutton-Smith, the business of play is to exhume these discontents as a way of learning how to manage them. Players want the full arsenal of emotions and emotion-based behaviors. Still, it is not play's spirit to leave people in misery. Rather, play converts negative feelings into positive ones by providing opportunities for people to extricate themselves from simulated distress and damage. In that sense, play celebrates the qualities of subjective agency described above.

Are some forms of play more useful than others? Much of the scholarship described in the preceding pages concludes that play has enduring effects on its practitioners. Active play promotes bodily strength and agility, symbolic learning, emotion management, artistic creativity, complexity of imagination, and social awareness. The present book has adopted the extremely broad view that play is a project of self-realization. We play in order to distill our personal capabilities and to test them by means of specific challenges. What effect any one play experience—or multiple experiences—has on other life pursuits is difficult to establish. Still, play need not be justified by chains of causation. Self-exploration is legitimate simply because it expands the spectrum of human possibility.

Although self-realization as a general principle has been honored in this book, this activity must not evade the moral and aesthetic concerns described above. Human behaviors arise out of social contexts and, on that foundation, can be judged by others. More profoundly, perhaps, they can be evaluated by the self. Some play is aimless and ill-considered; at worst, it harms. By breaking play into its constituent elements, I have suggested the importance of examining what kinds of play carries what kinds of meanings. To that extent, this book encourages scholarly conversation about effective and ineffective, good and bad, satisfying and dissatisfying play.

Finally, it is important to understand that play as action is not equivalent to play as interaction or to play as activity. Private behaviors may feature manipulations of every sort and cultivate freedom in that re-stricted sense. Such play can be ill-tempered and cruel. But interactive (and thus intersubjective) play should respect the freedom of all partici-pants. And play as activity invites the most complicated inquiries into the expanded conditions within which participants assert and adjust, compete and cooperate, expend and regenerate, and in all other ways consider the implications of what it means to be involved with others. If play has a legacy, it is its continuing challenge to people of every age to express themselves openly and considerately in the widest human contexts.

REFERENCES

Aarseth, E. 1997. *Cybertext: Perspectives on ergodic literature.* Baltimore: Johns Hopkins University Press.

Ackerman, D. 1999. *Deep play.* New York: Random House.

Allman, J. 1999. *Evolving brains.* New York: Freeman.

Bakhtin, M. 1981. *The dialogic imagination.* Translated by M. Holquist and C. Emerson. Austin: University of Texas Press.

———. 1984. *Rabelais and his world.* Translated by H. Iswolsky. Bloomington: Indiana University Press.

Bateson, G. 1972. A theory of play and fantasy. In *Steps to an ecology of mind,* pp. 177–93. New York: Ballantine.

Baumeister, R. 1999. The nature and structure of the self: An overview. In *The self in social psychology,* edited by R. Baumeister, pp. 1–24. Philadelphia: Psychology Press.

Beck, U. 1992. *Risk society: Toward a new modernity.* London: Sage.

Bekoff, M. 1995. Play signals as punctuation: The structure of social play in canids. *Behaviour* 132:419–29.

Bekoff, M., and J. Byers, eds. 1998. *Animal play: Evolutionary, comparative, and ecological perspectives.* New York: Cambridge University Press.

Bell, C. 2009. *Ritual theory, ritual practice.* New York: Oxford University Press.

Bell, D. 1976. *The cultural contradictions of capitalism.* London: Heinemann.

Belsky, J., and R. Most. 1981. From exploration to play: A cross-sectional study of infant free play behavior. *Developmental Psychology* 17:630–39.

Berger, P., and T. Luckmann. 1967. *The social construction of reality: A treatise in the sociology of knowledge.* Garden City, NY: Doubleday.

Berlyne, D. 1960. Determinants of subjective novelty. *Perception and Psychophysics* 3(6): 415–23.

———. 1966. Curiosity and exploration. *Science* 153:25–33.

Bertens, H. 1995. *The idea of the postmodern: A history.* New York: Routledge.

Bjorklund, D. 2007. *Why youth is not wasted on the young: Immaturity in human development.* Malden, MA: Blackwell.

Bolin, A., and J. Granskog, eds. 2003. *Athletic intruders: Ethnographic research on women, culture, and exercise.* Albany: SUNY Press.

Bourdieu, P. 1984. *Distinction: A social critique of the judgment of taste.* Translated by R. Nice. Cambridge: Harvard University Press.

Boyd, B. 2009. *On the origin of stories: Evolution, cognition, and fiction.* Cambridge: Harvard University Press, Belknap Press.

Branaman, A., ed. 2001. *Self and society.* Malden, MA: Blackwell.

Brantlinger, P. 1990. *Crusoe's footsteps: Cultural studies in Britain and America.* New York: Routledge.

Brown, F., ed. 2002. *Playwork: Theory and practice.* Philadelphia: Open University Press.

Brown, F., and C. Taylor, eds. 2008. *Foundations of playwork.* New York: Open University Press.

Brown, N. 1966. *Love's body.* New York: Vintage.

Brown, S. 2009. *Play: How it shapes the brain, opens the imagination, and invigorates the soul.* New York: Avery.

Bruner, J. 1976. Nature and uses of immaturity. In *Play: Its roles in development and evolution,* edited by J. Bruner, A. Jolly, and K. Silva, pp. 28–64. New York: Basic.

———. 1978. Learning how to do things with words. In *Human growth and development,* edited by J. Bruner and A. Garon, pp. 62–84. Oxford: Oxford University Press, Clarendon Press.

———. 1986a. *Actual minds, possible worlds.* Cambridge: Harvard University Press.

———. 1986b. Play, thought, and language. *Prospects: Quarterly Review of Education* 16(1): 77–83.

Bruner, J., A. Jolly, and K. Sylva, eds. 1976. *Play: Its role in development and evolution.* New York: Basic.

Buber, M. 1996. *I and Thou.* Translated by W. Kaufmann. New York: Simon and Schuster.

Burghardt, G. 1984. On the origins of play. In *Play in animals and humans,* edited by P. K. Smith, pp. 5–41. Oxford: Blackwell.

———. 2005. *The genesis of animal play: Testing the limits.* Cambridge: MIT Press.

———. 2010. The comparative reach of play and brain: Perspective, evidence, and implications. *American Journal of Play* 2(3): 338–56.

Butler, J. 1990. *Gender trouble: Feminism and the subversion of identity.* New York: Routledge.

Byers, J. 1998. Biological effects of locomotor play: Getting into shape, or something more specific? In *Animal play: Evolutionary, comparative, and ecological perspectives,* edited by M. Bekoff and J. Byers, pp. 205–20. New York: Cambridge University Press.

Byers, J., and C. Walker. 1995. Refining the motor-training hypothesis for the evolution of play. *American Naturalist* 146:25–40.

Caillois, R. 2001a. *Man and the sacred.* Urbana: University of Illinois Press.

———. 2001b. *Man, play, and games.* Urbana: University of Illinois Press.

———. 2003. *The edge of surrealism: A Roger Caillois reader.* Edited by Claudine Frank. Durham: Duke University Press.

Campbell, B., J. Loy, and K. Cruz-Uribe. 2005. *Humankind emerging.* 9th ed. Boston: Allyn and Bacon.

Carlisle, R., ed. 2009. *Encyclopedia of play in today's society.* Thousand Oaks, CA: Sage.

Chick, G. 2001. What is play for? Sexual selection and the evolution of play. *Play and Culture Studies* 3:3–25.

Christie, J., ed. 1991. *Play and early literacy development.* Albany: SUNY Press.

Clements, R. 2004. An investigation of the status of outdoor play. *Contemporary Issues in Early Childhood* 31:68–80.

Clotfelter, C. 2011. *Big-time sports in American universities.* New York: Cambridge University Press.

Coakley, J. 1996. Sport in society: An inspiration or an opiate? In S*port in contemporary society: An anthology*, 5th ed., edited by D. Eitzen, pp. 32–49. New York: St. Martin's.

Cohen, L., and S. Waite-Stupiansky, eds. 2012. *Play: A polyphony of research, theories, and issues.* Play and Culture Studies 12. New York: University Press of America.

Colie, R. 1964. Johan Huizinga and the task of cultural history. *American Historical Review* 47:607–30.

Collins, R. 2004. *Interaction ritual chains.* Princeton: Princeton University Press.

Connery, M., V. John-Steiner, and A. Marjanovic-Shane, eds. 2010. *Vygotsky and creativity.* New York: Peter Lang.

Consalvo, M. 2007. *Cheating: Gaining advantage in videogames.* Cambridge: MIT Press.

Cooley, C. 1962. *Social organization: A study of the larger mind.* New York: Schocken.

———. 1964. *Human nature and social order.* New York: Schocken.

Cox, H. 1969. *The feast of fools: A theological essay on festivity and fantasy.* Cambridge: Harvard University Press.

Csikszentmihalyi, M. 1991. *Flow: The psychology of optimal experience.* New York: Harper and Row.

———. 2000. *Beyond boredom and anxiety: Experiencing flow in work and play.* 25th anniversary ed. with a new preface. San Francisco: Jossey-Bass.

Damasio, A. 1994. *Descartes' error.* New York: Grosset-Putnam.

———. 1999. *The feeling of what happens: Body and emotion in the making of consciousness.* New York: Harcourt.

Debord, G. 1977. *The society of the spectacle.* Detroit: Black and Red.

De Koven, B. 1978. *The well-played game.* Garden City, NY: Doubleday Anchor.

Deleuze, G., and F. Guattari. 1984. *Anti-Oedipus: Capitalism and schizophrenia.* Minneapolis: University of Minnesota Press.

Derrida, J. 1976. *Of grammatology.* Baltimore: Johns Hopkins University Press.

———. 1981. *Positions.* Chicago: University of Chicago Press.

———. 1982. *Margins of philosophy.* Chicago: University of Chicago Press.

———. 1988. *Limited, Inc.* Evanston, IL: Northwestern University Press.

Dewey, J. 1902. *The child and the curriculum.* Chicago: University of Chicago Press.

———. 1910. *How we think.* New York: Heath.

Donald, M. 1991. *Origins of the modern mind: Three stages in the evolution of culture and cognition.* Cambridge: Harvard University Press.

Douglas, M. 1996. *Natural symbols: Explorations in cosmology.* London: Routledge.

Dow, G., and J. Factor, eds. 1991. *Australian childhood: An anthology.* South Yarra, Australia: McPhee Gribble.

Dressler, W. 2005. What's *cultural* about bio*cultural* research? *Ethos* 33:20–45.

Dumazedier, J. 1967. *Toward a society of leisure.* London: Collier Macmillan.

Duncan, M. 1988. Play discourse and the rhetorical turn: A semiological analysis of *Homo Ludens*. *Play and Culture* 1:28–42.

During, S. 1993. Introduction to *The cultural studies reader*, edited by S. During, pp. 1–28. London: Routledge.

Durkheim, E. 1961. *Moral education: A study in the theory and application of the sociology of education.* New York: Free Press.

———. 1965. *The elementary forms of the religious life.* New York: Free Press.

———. 1972. *Emile Durkheim: Selected writings.* Edited by A. Giddens. New York: Cambridge University Press.

Eberle, S. 2011. Playing with multiple intelligences: How play helps them grow. *American Journal of Play* 4(1): 19–51.

———. 2014. The elements of play: Toward a philosophy and a definition of play. *American Journal of Play* 6(2): 214–33.

Edmiston, Brian. 2008. *Forming ethical identities in childhood play.* New York: Routledge.

Edwards, H. 1970. *The revolt of the black student athlete.* New York: Free Press.

Ekman, P. 1994. All emotions are basic. In *The nature of emotion: Fundamental questions,* edited by P. Ekman and R. Davidson, pp. 15–19. New York: Oxford University Press.

Eliade, M. 1957. *The sacred and the profane: The nature of religion.* New York: Harcourt.

Elias, N. 2000. *The civilizing process: Sociogenetic and psychogenetic investigations* Rev. ed. Edited by E. Dunning, J. Goudsblom, and S. Mennell. Translated by E. Jephcott. Maldon, MA: Blackwell.

Elias, N., and E. Dunning. 1986. *The quest for excitement: Sport and leisure in the civilizing process.* Oxford: Blackwell.

Elkind, D. 2006. *The hurried child: Growing up too fast too soon.* Cambridge, MA: Da Capo.

Ellis, M. 1973. *Why people play.* Englewood Cliffs, NJ: Prentice-Hall.

Erikson, E. 1963. *Childhood and society.* 2nd ed. New York: Norton.

Factor, J. 2009. "It's only play if you get to choose": Children's perceptions of play and adult interventions. In *Transactions at play,* edited by C. D. Clark, pp. 129–46. Play and Culture Studies 9. New York: University Press of America.

Fagen, R. 1981. *Animal play behavior.* New York: Oxford University Press.

———. 1995. Animal play, games of angels, biology, and Brian. In *The future of play theory,* edited by A. Pellegrini, pp. 23–44. Albany: SUNY Press.

———. 2005. Play, five evolutionary gates, and paths to art. In *Play: An interdisciplinary synthesis,* edited by F. McMahon, D. Lytle, and B. Sutton-Smith, pp. 9–42. Play and Culture Studies 6. Lanham, MD: University Press of America.

Fein, G. 1981. Pretend play: An integrative review. *Child Development* 52:1095–1118.

———. 1989. Mind, meaning, and affect: Proposals for a theory of pretense. *Developmental Review* 9:345–63.

Festle, M. J. 1996. *Playing nice: Politics and apologies in women's sports.* New York: Columbia University Press.

Figler, S., and G. Whitaker. 1994. *Sport and play in American life: A textbook in the sociology of sport.* Madison, WI: Brown and Benchmark.

Fine, G. A. 1979. Small groups and culture creation: The idioculture of Little League baseball teams. *American Sociological Review* 44(5): 733–45.

———. 1983. *Shared fantasy: Role-playing games as social worlds.* Chicago: University of Chicago Press.

Forney, C. 2010. *The holy trinity of American sports: Civil religion in football, baseball, and basketball.* Macon, GA: Mercer University Press.

Foucault, M. 1975. *The birth of the clinic: An archeology of medical perception.* Translated by A. Sheridan Smith. New York: Random House.

———. 1997. *Discipline and punish: The birth of the prison.* Translated by A. Sheridan. London: Penguin.

Freud, A. 1965. *Normality and pathology in childhood.* New York: International Universities Press.

Freud, S. 1958. *On creativity and the unconscious.* Edited by B. Nelson. New York: Harper and Row.

———. 1963. *Character and culture.* Edited by P. Rieff. New York: Collier.

———. 1967. *Beyond the pleasure principle.* Translated by J. Strachey. New York: Bantam.

Freysinger, V., and J. Kelly. 2004. *21st century leisure: Current issues.* State College, PA: Venture.

Fromberg, D. 1992. A review of research on play. In *The early childhood curriculum: A review of current research.* 2nd ed. Edited by C. Seefeldt, pp. 42–84. New York: Teachers College Press.

Fromberg, D., and D. Bergen. 2006. *Play from birth to twelve: Contexts, perspectives, and meanings.* 2nd ed. NewYork: Routledge

Frost, J. 1992. *Play and playscapes.* Albany: Delmar.

Frost, J., P. Brown, J. Sutterby, and C. Thornton. 2004. *The developmental benefits of playgrounds.* Olney, MD: Association for Childhood International.

Frost, J., and B. Klein. 1979. *Children's play and playgrounds.* Needham Heights, MA: Allyn and Bacon.

Frost, J., S. Wortham, and S. Reifel. 2008. *Play and child development.* 3rd ed. Upper Saddle River, NJ: Pearson.

Gadamer, H.-G. 1989. *Truth and method.* New York: Crossroad.

Garvey, C. 1977. *Play.* Cambridge: Harvard University Press.

Garvey, C., and T. Kramer. 1989. The language of social pretend play. *Developmental Review* 9:364–82.

Geertz, C. 1973. Deep play: Notes on the Balinese cockfight. In *The interpretation of cultures,* pp. 412–53. New York: Basic.

Geyl, P. 1963. Huizinga as accuser of his age. *History and Theory* 2:231–62.

Giddens, A. 1991. *Modernity and Self-Identity: Self and Society in the Late Modern Age.* Stanford: Stanford University Press.

Goffman, E. 1959. *The presentation of self in everyday life.* Garden City, NY: Doubleday.

———. 1961. *Encounters: Two studies in the sociology of interaction.* Indianapolis: Bobbs-Merrill.

———. 1963. *Stigma: Notes on the management of spoiled identity.* Englewood Cliffs, NJ: Prentice-Hall.

———. 1967. *Interaction ritual: Essays on face-to-face behavior.* Garden City, NY: Doubleday Anchor.

———. 1969. *Strategic interaction.* Philadelphia: University of Pennsylvania Press.

———. 1974. *Frame analysis: An essay on the organization of experience.* New York: Harper and Row.

Göncü, A., and S. Gaskins. 2007. *Play and development: Evolutionary, sociocultural, and functional perspectives.* Mahwah, NJ: Erlbaum.

Goodman, A., and T. Leatherman, eds. 1998. *Building a new biocultural synthesis: Political-economic perspectives on human biology.* Ann Arbor: University of Michigan Press.

Gordon, G. 2009. What is play? In search of a definition. In *From children to Red Hatters: Diverse images and issues of play,* edited by D. Kuschner, pp. 1–13. Play and Culture Studies 9. New York: University Press of America.

Gramsci, A. 1971. *Selections from the prison notebooks of Antonio Gramsci.* Edited by Q. Hoare and G. Nowell Smith. New York: International.

Groos, K. 1898. *The play of animals.* Translated by E. L. Baldwin. New York: D. Appleton.

———. 1901. *The play of man.* Translated by E. L. Baldwin. New York: D. Appleton. (Orig. Pub. 1898.)

Gruneau, R. 1980. Freedom and constraint: The paradoxes of play, games, and sports. *Journal of Sport History* 7:68–85.

Guttmann, A. 1978. *From ritual to record: The nature of modern sports.* New York: Columbia University Press.

Hall, G. S. 1931. *Adolescence.* 2 vols. New York: D. Appleton. (Orig. pub. 1904.)

Handelman, D. 1992. Passages to play: Paradox and process. *Play and Culture* 5:1–19.

———. 1998. *Models and mirrors: Toward an anthropology of public events.* New York: Berghahn.

Hans, J. 1981. *The play of the world.* Amherst: University of Massachusetts Press.

Hansen, P. 2013. *The summits of modern man: Mountaineering after the Enlightenment.* Cambridge: Harvard University Press.

Harcourt, R. 1991. Survivorship costs of play in the South American fur seal. *Animal Behaviour* 42:509–11.

Hargreaves, J. 1994. *Sporting females: Critical issues in the history and sociology of women's sports.* New York: Routledge.

———. 2000. *Heroines of sport: The politics of difference and identity.* New York: Routledge.

Henricks, T. 1991. *Disputed pleasures: Sport and society in preindustrial England.* New York: Greenwood.

———. 1999. Play as ascending meaning: Implications of a general model of play. *Play and Culture Studies* 2(1): 261–81.

———. 2001. Play and postmodernism. In *Theory in context and out,* edited by S. Reifel, pp. 51–72. Play and Culture Studies 3. Westport, CT: Ablex.

———. 2002. Huizinga's contributions to play studies: A reappraisal. In *Conceptual, social-cognitive, and contextual issues in the fields of play,* edited by J. Roopnarine, pp. 23–52. Play and Culture Studies 4. Westport, CT: Ablex.

———. 2006. *Play reconsidered: Sociological perspectives on human expression.* Champaign: University of Illinois Press.

———. 2009. Orderly and disorderly play: A comparison. *American Journal of Play* 2(1): 12–40.

———. 2010a. Play and cultural transformation; Or, what would Huizinga think of video games? In *Utopic dreams and apocalyptic fantasies: Critical approaches to researching video game play,* edited by T. Wright, D. Embrick, and A. Lukacs, pp. 15–42. New York: Rowman and Littlefield.

————. 2010b. Play as ascending meaning revisited: Four types of assertive play. In *Play as engagement and communication,* edited by E. Nwokah, pp. 189–216. Play and Culture Studies 10. New York: University Press of America.

————. 2011. Roger Caillois's *Man, play, and games:* An appreciation and evaluation. *American Journal of Play* 3(2): 157–85.

————. 2012. *Selves, societies, and emotions: Understanding the pathways of experience.* Boulder: Paradigm.

Hoch, P. 1972. *Rip off the big game: The exploitation of sports by the power elite.* Garden City, NY: Doubleday Anchor.

Hollier, D., ed. 1988. *The college of sociology, 1937–1939.* 2nd ed. Minneapolis: University of Minnesota Press.

Holmes, R. 1999. Kindergarten and college students' views of play and work at home and at school. In *Play contexts revisted,* edited by S. Reifel, pp. 59–62. Play and Culture Studies 2. Westport, CT: Ablex.

Holzman, L. 2008. *Vygotsky at work and play.* New York: Routledge.

Homeyer, L., and M. Morrison. 2008. Play therapy: Practice, issues, and trends. *American Journal of Play* 1(2): 210–28.

Huizinga, J. 1936. *In the shadow of tomorrow.* New York: Norton.

————. 1954. *The waning of the Middle Ages.* Garden City, NY: Doubleday Anchor.

————. 1955. *Homo ludens: A study of the play-element in culture.* Boston: Beacon.

Inkeles, A., and D. Smith. 1974. *Becoming modern.* Cambridge: Harvard University Press.

James, W. 1952. *Principles of psychology.* Chicago: Encyclopedia Britannica.

Jameson, F. 1984. Postmodernism, or the cultural logic of late capitalism. *New Left Review* 146:53–92.

Jarrett, O. 2003. Urban school recess: The haves and the have nots. *Play, Policy, and Practice Connections* 8(1): 1–3, 7–10.

Jay, M. 1973. *The dialectical imagination: A history of the Frankfurt School and the Institute for Social Research, 1923–1950.* Boston: Little, Brown.

Johnson, J., J. Christie, and F. Wardle. 2004. *Play, development, and early education.* Boston: Allyn and Bacon.

Johnson, J., J. Christie, and T. Yawkey. 1999. *Play and early childhood development.* New York: Longman.

Johnson, J., S. Eberle, T. Henricks, and D. Kuschner, eds. 2015. *Handbook of the Study of Play.* Lanham, MD: Rowman and Littlefield.

Kahler, E. 1956. *Man the measure: A new approach to history.* New York: George Braziller.

Kant, I. 2008. *Critique of pure reason.* Edited by M. Weigelt. New York: Penguin.

Klein, M. 1955. The psychoanalytic play technique. *American Journal of Orthopsychiatry* 25:223–37.

Kline, S. 1995. The promotion and marketing of toys: Time to re-think the paradox. In *The future of play theory: A multidisciplinary inquiry into the contributions of Brian Sutton-Smith,* edited by A. Pellegrini, pp. 165–86. Albany: SUNY Press.

Konner, M. 2010. *The evolution of childhood: Relationships, emotion, mind.* Cambridge: Harvard University Press.

Kuchler, T. 1994. *Post-modern gaming: Heidegger, Duchamps, Derrida.* New York: Peter Lang.

Kuschner, D., ed. 2009. *From children to Red Hatters: Diverse images and issues of play*. Play and Culture Studies 8. New York: University Press of America.

L'Abate, L. 2009. *The Praeger handbook of play across the life cycle: From infancy to old age*. Denver: Praeger.

Lambert, E. B., and M. Clyde. 2003. Putting Vygotsky to the test. In *Play and educational theory and practice*, edited by D. Lytle, pp. 59–98. Play and Culture Studies 5. Westport, CT: Praeger.

Lancy, D. 2008. *The anthropology of childhood: Cherubs, chattel, changelings*. Cambridge: Cambridge University Press.

Lash, S., and J. Friedman, eds. 1992. *Modernity and identity*. Cambridge, MA: Blackwell.

Lazarus, M. 1883. *About the attractions of play*. Berlin: F. Dummler.

Leakey, R., and R. Lewin 1991. *Origins: The emergence and evolution of our species and its possible future*. New York: Penguin.

LeDoux, J. 1996. *The emotional brain: The mysterious underpinnings of emotional life*. New York: Simon and Schuster.

Lefebvre, H. 1969. *The sociology of Marx*. Translated by N. Gutterman. New York: Vintage.

Lévi-Strauss, C. 1967. *Structural anthropology*. Garden City, NY: Doubleday Anchor.

———. 1969. *The savage mind*. Chicago: University of Chicago Press.

Levy, J. 1978. *Play behavior*. New York: Wiley.

Lieberman, J. N. 1977. *Playfulness: Its relation to imagination and creativity*. New York: Academic.

Lillard, A. S. 2007. *Montessori: The science behind the genius*. New York: Oxford University Press.

Lin, S.-H., and S. Reifel. 1999. Context and meanings in Taiwanese kindergarten play. In *Play contexts revisited*, edited by S. Reifel, pp. 151–76. Play and Culture Studies 2. Greenwich, CT: Ablex.

Lobman, C., and B. O'Neill, eds. 2011. *Play and performance*. Play and Culture Studies 11. New York: University Press of America.

Loy, J., ed. 1982. *The paradoxes of play*. West Point, NY: Leisure.

Lyotard, J. 1986. *The postmodern condition: A report on knowledge*. Manchester, UK: Manchester University Press.

Marks-Tarlow, T. 2010. The fractal self at play. *American Journal of Play* 31:31–62.

Marx, K. 1964. *Selected writings in sociology and social philosophy*. Edited and translated by T. Bottomore. New York: McGraw-Hill.

———. 1999. Economic and philosophical manuscripts. Translated by T. Bottomore. In *Marx's concept of man*, edited by E. Fromm, pp. 87–196. New York: Continuum.

McDonald, K., ed. 1993. *Parent-child play: Descriptions and implications*. Albany: SUNY Press.

Mead, G. H. 1964. *On social psychology*. Edited by A. Strauss. Chicago: University of Chicago Press.

Meares, R. 2005. *The metaphor of play: Origin and breakdown of personal being*. 3rd ed. New York: Routledge.

Messner, M. 1990. Boyhood, organized sports and the construction of masculinities. *Journal of Contemporary Ethnography* 4:416–44.

————. 1992. *Power at play: Sport and the problem of masculinity.* Boston: Beacon.

Messner, M., and R. Connell, eds. 2007. *Out of play: Critical essays on gender and sport.* Albany: SUNY Press.

Millar, S. 1968. *The psychology of play.* Baltimore: Penguin.

Miller, S. 1973. Ends, means, and galumphing: Some leitmotifs of play. *American Anthropologist* 75(1): 87–98.

Mitchell, R. 1990. A theory of play. In *Interpretation and explanation in the study of animal behavior: Interpretation, intentionality, and communication*, edited by M. Bekoff and D. Jamieson, pp. 197–227. Boulder: Westview.

Montessori, M. 1992. *The secret of childhood.* New York: Ballantine.

Nagel, M. 1998. Play in culture and the jargon of primordiality: A critique of Homo Ludens. *Play and Culture Studies* 1:19–30.

Newman, F., and L. Holzman. 1993. *Lev Vygotsky: Revolutionary scientist.* London: Roultedge.

————. 2006. *Unscientific psychology: A cultural-performatory approach to understanding human life.* 2nd ed. New York: iUniverse.

O'Brien, J., ed. 2006. *The production of reality: Essays and readings on social interaction.* 4th ed. Thousand Oaks, CA: Pine Forge.

Olds, A. 2000. *Child care design guide.* New York: McGraw-Hill.

Opie, I., and P. Opie. 1959. *The language and lore of schoolchildren.* Oxford: Oxford University Press, Clarendon Press.

Paley, V. 1992. *You can't say you can't play.* Cambridge: Harvard University Press.

————. 2005. *A child's work: The importance of fantasy play.* Chicago: University of Chicago Press.

Panksepp, J. 1998. *Affective neuroscience: The foundations of human and animal emotions.* New York: Oxford University Press.

————. 2008. Play, ADHD, and the construction of the social brain: Should the first class each day be recess? *American Journal of Play* 1(1): 55–79.

————. 2010. Science of the brain as a gateway to understanding play: An interview with Jaak Panksepp. *American Journal of Play* 2(3): 245–77.

Parsons, T. 1966. *Societies: Evolutionary and comparative perspectives.* Englewood Cliffs, NJ: Prentice-Hall.

————. 1971. *The system of modern societies.* Englewood Cliffs, NJ: Prentice-Hall.

Patrick, G. 1916. *The psychology of relaxation.* Boston: Houghton Mifflin.

Patte, M. 2009. All in a day's work: Children's views on play and work at the fifth grade level. In *From children to Red Hatters: Diverse images and issues of play*, edited by D. Kuschner, pp. 113–30. Play and Culture Studies 9. New York: University Press of America.

Pellegrini, A. 2005. *Recess: Its role in education and development.* Totowa: NJ: Erlbaum.

————. 2009. *The role of play in human development.* New York: Oxford University Press.

Pellegrini, A., and P. Smith. 1998. Physical activity play: The nature and function of a neglected aspect of play. *Child Development* 69(3): 577–98.

————. 2003. Development of play. In *Handbook of developmental psychology*, edited by J. Valsiner and K. Connolly, pp. 277–91. Thousand Oaks, CA: Sage.

Pellis, S., V. Pellis, and H. Bell. 2010. The function of play in the development of the social brain. *American Journal of Play* 2(3): 278–96.

Pellis, S., V. Pellis, and I. Whishaw. 1992. The role of the cortex in play-fighting by rats: Developmental and evolutionary implications. *Brain, Behavior, and Evolution* 39:270–84.

Perry, J., and L. Branum. 2009. "Sometimes I pounce on twigs because I'm a meat eater": Supporting physically active play and outdoor learning. *American Journal of Play* 2(2): 195–214.

Piaget, J. 1955. *The child's construction of reality.* London: Routledge and Kegan Paul.

———. 1962. *Play, dreams, and imitation in childhood.* New York: Norton.

———. 1966a. *The moral judgment of the child.* New York: Free Press.

———. 1966b. *The psychology of intelligence.* Totowa, NJ: Littlefield, Adams.

Piaget, J., and B. Inhelder. 1972. *The psychology of the child.* New York: Basic.

Plumb, J. 1973. *The commercialization of leisure in eighteenth-century England.* Reading, UK: University of Reading Press.

Plutchik, R. 2003. *Emotions and life: Perspectives from psychology, biology, and evolution.* Washington, DC: American Psychological Association.

Power, T. 2005. *Play and exploration in children and animals.* Mahwah, NJ: Erlbaum.

Provenzo, E. 2009. Friedrich Froebel's gifts: Connecting the spiritual and the aesthetic to the real world of play and learning. *American Journal of Play* 2(10): 85–99.

Radin, P. 1987. *The trickster: A study in American Indian mythology.* New York: Schocken.

Rappaport, R. 1979. *Ecology, meaning, and religion.* Richmond, CA: North Atlantic.

Ratey, J. 2012. *Spark: The revolutionary new science of exercise and the brain.* New York: Little, Brown.

Reder, D., and L. Morra, eds. 2010. Troubling tricksters: Revisioning critical conversations. Waterloo, ON: Wilfred Laurier.

Reynolds, P. 1993. The complementation theory of language and tool use. In *Tools, language, and cognition in human development,* edited by K. Gibson and T. Ingold, pp. 407–28. New York: Cambridge University Press.

Riesman, D., with R. Denney and N. Glazer. 1950. *The lonely crowd: A study in the changing American character.* New Haven: Yale University Press.

Roberts, J., M. Arth, and R. Bush. 1959. Games in culture. *American Anthropologist* 61:597–605.

Roberts, J., and B. Sutton-Smith. 1962. Child training and game involvement. *Ethnology* 1(2): 166–85.

Roberts, J., B. Sutton-Smith, and A. Kendon. 1963. Strategy in folktales and games. *Journal of Social Psychology* 61:185–99.

Roberts, K. 2001. *Leisure in contemporary society.* New York: CABI.

Rojek, C. 1985. *Capitalism and leisure theory.* New York: Tavistock.

Roopnarine, J., J. Johnson, and F. Hooper, eds. 1994. *Children's play in diverse cultures.* Albany: SUNY Press.

Rosenau, P. 1992. *Post-modernism and the social sciences: Insights, inroads, intrusions.* Princeton: Princeton University Press.

Rubin, K., G. Fein, and B. Vandenberg. 1983. Play. In *Handbook of child psychology,* edited by E. M. Hetherington, vol. 4: *Socialization, personality, and social development,* pp. 693–774. New York: Wiley.

Sarama, J., and D. Clements. 2009. Building blocks and cognitive building blocks: Playing to know the world mathematically. *American Journal of Play* 1(3): 313–37.

Sattelmair, J., and J. Ratey. 2009. Physically active play and cognition: An academic matter? *American Journal of Play* 1(3): 365–74.

Sawyer, R. 2003. *Group creativity: Music, theater, collaboration.* Mahwah, NJ: Erlbaum.

Schaefer, C., ed. 1992. *The therapeutic powers of play.* Northvale, NJ: Aronson.

Schechner, R. 1995. *The future of ritual: Writings on culture and performance.* New York: Routledge.

———. 2002. *Performance studies: An introduction.* New York: Routledge.

Schiller, F. 1965. *On the aesthetic education of man.* Translated by R. Snell. New York: Ungar. (Orig. pub. 1795.)

Schwartzman, H. 1978. *Transformations: The anthropology of children's play.* New York: Plenum.

Seiger, J. 2005. *The idea of the self: Thought and experience in Western Europe since the seventeenth century.* Cambridge: Cambridge University Press.

Seligman, A., R. Weller, M. Puett, and B. Simon. 2008. *Ritual and its consequences: An essay on the limits of sincerity.* New York: Oxford University Press.

Sennett, R. 1992. *The fall of public man.* New York: Norton.

Simmel, G. 1950. Sociability. In *The sociology of Georg Simmel,* edited by K. Wolff, pp. 40–57. New York: Free Press.

———. 1971. *On individuality and social forms.* Edited by D. Levine. Chicago: University of Chicago Press.

———. 1984. *Georg Simmel: On women, sexuality, and love.* Translated by Guy Oakes. New Haven: Yale University Press.

Singer, D., P. Golinkoff, and K. Hirsh-Pasek, eds. 2009. *Playlearning: How play motivates and enhances children's cognitive and social-emotional growth.* New York: Oxford University Press.

Singer, D., and Singer, J. L. 1990. *The house of make-believe: Children's play and the developing imagination.* Cambridge: Harvard University Press.

———. 2005. *Imagination and play in the electronic age.* Cambridge: Harvard University Press.

Singer, J. A., and P. Salovey. 1999. Preface to *At play in the fields of consciousness: Essays in honor of Jerome L. Singer.* New York: Erlbaum.

Singer, J. L. 1980. *Mind-play: The creative uses of fantasy.* New York: Prentice-Hall.

Skinner, B. F. 1974. *About behaviorism.* New York: Vintage.

Smilansky, S. 1968. *The effects of sociodramatic play on disadvantaged preschool children.* New York: Wiley.

Smith, P. 1982. Does play matter? Functional and evolutionary aspects of animal and human play. *Behavioral and Brain Sciences* 5:139–84.

———, ed. 1984. *Play in animals and humans.* Oxford: Basil Blackwell.

———. 2010. *Children and play.* Malden, MA: Wiley-Blackwell.

Spariosu, M. 1989. *Dionysus reborn: Play and the aesthetic dimension in modern philosophical and scientific discourse.* Ithaca: Cornell University Press.

———. 1997. *The wreath of the wild olive: Play, liminality, and the study of literature.* Albany: SUNY Press.

Spencer, H. 1896. *Principles of psychology.* New York: Appleton.

Sperber, M. 2001. *Beer and circuses: How big-time college sports is crippling undergraduate education.* New York: Holt.

Steinsholt, K., and E. Traasdahl. 2001. The concept of play in Hans-Georg Gadamer's hermeneutics: An educational approach. In *Theory in context and out,* edited by S. Reifel, pp. 73–96. Play and Culture Studies 3. Westport, CT: Ablex.

Sternberg, R. 2008. *Cognitive psychology.* 5th ed. Belmont, CA: Wadsworth.

Stromberg, P. 2009. *Caught in play: How entertainment works on you.* Stanford: Stanford University Press.

Sutton-Smith, B. 1959. *The games of New Zealand children.* Berkeley: University of California Press.

———. 1966. Piaget on play: A critique. *Psychological Review* 73(1): 104–10.

———. 1997. *The ambiguity of play.* Cambridge: Harvard University Press.

———. 1999. Evolving a consilience of play definitions: Playfully. In *Play contexts revisited,* edited by S. Reifel, pp. 239–56. Play and Culture Studies 2. Stamford, CT: Ablex.

———. 2008. Play theory: A personal journey and new thoughts. *American Journal of Play* 1(1): 80–123.

Sutton-Smith, B., and D. Kelly-Byrne. 1984a. The idealization of play. In *Play in animals and humans,* edited by P. Smith, pp. 305–21. London: Blackwell.

———. 1984b. The phenomenon of bipolarity in play theories. In *Child's play: Developmental and applied,* edited by T. Yawkey and A. Pellegrini, pp. 29–47. Hillsdale, NJ: Erlbaum.

Swalwell, M., and J. Wilson, eds. 2008. *The pleasures of computer gaming: Essays on cultural history, theory, and aesthetics.* Jefferson, NC: McFarland.

Thelen, E. 1980. Determinants of amounts of stereotyped behavior in normal human infants. *Ethology and Sociobiology* 1:141–50.

Tinbergen, N. 1963. On aims and methods in ethology. *Zeitschrift fur Tierspsychologie* 20:410–33.

Tizard, B., J. Philps, and I. Plewis. 1976. Play in pre-school centers: II. Effects on play of the child's social class and of the educational orientation of the center. *Journal of School Psychology and Psychiatry* 17:265–74.

Turkle, S. 2005. *The second self: Computing and the human spirit.* Cambridge: MIT Press.

Turner, V. 1967. *The forest of symbols: Aspects of Ndembu ritual.* Ithaca: Cornell University Press.

———. 1969. *The ritual process: Structure and anti-structure.* Chicago: Aldine.

———. 1979. Frame, flow, and reflection: Ritual and drama as public liminality. *Japanese Journal of Religious Studies* 6(4): 465–99.

———. 1982. *From ritual to theatre: The human seriousness of play.* New York: Performing Arts Journal Publications.

Vanderschuren, L. 2010. How the brain makes play fun. *American Journal of Play* 2(3): 315–37.

Van Gennep, A. 1960. *The rites of passage.* Chicago: University of Chicago Press.

Veblen, T. 1934. *The theory of the leisure class: An economic study of institutions.* New York: Random House.

Vygotsky, L. 1976. Play and its role in the mental development of the child. In *Play: Its role in development and evolution,* edited by J. Bruner, A. Jolly, and K. Silva, pp. 537–54. Middlesex, UK: Penguin.

———. 1978. *Mind and society: The development of higher psychological processes.* Cambridge: Harvard University Press.

Walvin, J. 1978. *Leisure and society, 1843–1950.* London: Longmans.

Wardrip-Fruin, N. 2009. *Expressive processing: Digital fictions, computer games, and software studies.* Cambridge: MIT Press.

Washburn, S. 1960. Tools and human evolution. *Scientific American* 203(3): 63–75.

Weber, M. 1958a. *The Protestant ethic and the spirit of capitalism.* Translated by T. Parsons. New York: Charles Scribner's Sons.

———. 1958b. *The rational and social foundations of music.* Translated by D. Martindale. Carbondale: Southern Illinois University Press.

White, R. W. 1959. Motivation reconsidered: The concept of competence. *Psychological Review* 66:297–333.

Whiting, B., and C. Edwards. 1988. *Children of different worlds: The formation of behavior.* Cambridge: Harvard University Press.

Whiting, B., and J. Whiting. 1975. *Children of six cultures.* Cambridge: Harvard University Press.

Wiley, N. 1994. *The semiotic self.* Chicago: University of Chicago Press.

Williams, S. 2001. *Emotion and social theory: Corporeal reflections on the (ir)rational.* London: Sage.

Wilson, E. O. 1975. *Sociobiology: The new synthesis.* Cambridge: Harvard University Press, Belknap Press.

Wilson, F. 1998. *The hand: How its use shapes the brain, language, and human culture.* New York: Pantheon.

Wilson, P. 2009. The cultural origins and play philosophy of playworkers: An interview with Penny Wilson. *American Journal of Play* 1(3): 269–82.

Wing, L. 1995. Play is not the work of the child: Young children's perceptions of work and play. *Early Childhood Research Quarterly* 10:223–47.

Winnicott, D. W. 1971. *Playing and reality.* New York: Tavistock.

Wolf, M., ed. 2001. *The medium of the video game.* Austin: University of Texas Press.

———. 2008. *The video game explosion: A history from Pong to Playstation and beyond.* Westport, CT: Greenwood.

Wolfenstein, M. 1951. The emergence of fun morality. *Journal of Social Issues* 7(4): 15–25.

Wood, E. 2009. Conceptualizing a pedagogy of play: International perspectives from theory, policy, and practice. In *From children to Red Hatters: Diverse images and issues of play*, edited by D. Kuschner, pp. 166–89. Play and Culture Studies 9. New York: University Press of America.

Wright, T., D. Embrick, and A. Lukacs, eds. 2010. *Utopic dreams and apocalyptic fantasies: Critical approaches to researching video game play.* New York: Rowman and Littlefield.

Yerkes, R. 1982. *Caring spaces, learning places: Children's environments that work.* Redmond, WA: Exchange.

INDEX

Note: Page numbers in italics represent illustrative material.

academic performance-physical activity relationship, 159–160
accommodation adaptation style (Piaget), 91–92
Ackerman, Diane, 31–32
action and experience context model, 69–71
action sequences (starting and stopping play), 223
activity instigation, 154–155
"adaptability," 78–79
adult play: Bakhtin, M., 197–198; Caillois, Roger, 191–193; civilizing process, 193–195; contemporary environment, 9–14; Elias, Norbert, 193–194; evolution of physical experience, 193–194; evolution of play,190–195; Geertz, Clifford, 198–199; Handelman, Don, 201–202; Huizinga, Johan, 190–191; medieval and early modern play, 197–198; modernity, 190–191; play as performance, 202–205; rituals, 199–205; Schechner, Richard, 202–205; Turner, Victor, 199–201; Weber, Max, 193
advanced industrial (postmodern) societies, 217–219
"The Adventurer" (Simmel), 83–84
adventures, 83–84
agon (Caillois), 35, 44, 70, 149, 190, 192
alea (Caillois), 35, 70, 191–192, 196
Allen, Marjorie (Lady), 154

The Ambiguity of Play (Sutton-Smith), 110
anchoring social function (Goffman), 172
animal behavior research: all species, 116–117; behavior ranges, 118–119; Bekoff, Marc, 29; Burghardt, Gordon, 38; complexities, 119; compulsivity v. subjectivity, 117; *contestiveness*, 44–45; "core consciousness," 135–136; creative activity, 117–118; developmental aspects, 120; duality, 117–118; maturation role, 120; physical v. symbolic engagement, 117–118; play presence in animal species, 116–117; Tinbergen, Niko, 117; *unpredictability*, 45
Animal Play Behavior (Fagen), 119–120
anthropological factors, 138–144, 213. *See also* evolution of human beings
anxiety transmutation, 13
ascending-descending pattern, 52
ascending meaning, 50, 52, 76–77, 221–222
assertive play, 211
assimilation adaptation style (Piaget), 91
associational self, 216
"attentional structure" (Bruner), 144–145
"autobiographical self" (Damasio), 136
autocosmic play (Erikson), 105

Bakhtin, M., 187, 197–198, 215
basic theories of play, 6–13

Bataille, Georges, 43–44
Bateson, Gregory, 19, 72, 80, 203
Beck, Ulrich, 12–13
behaviorism, 124–125
Bekoff, Marc, 29, 45
Bentham, Jeremy, 199
Berger, Peter, 161–162
Berlyne, Daniel, 124–125, 126
biochemistry of brain, 133–134
biomechanics of play. *See* nature (human body) and play
Bjorklund, David, 146–148
blessedness, 61
bottom-up and nonlinear qualities of play (Marks-Tarlow), 49
Bourdieu, Pierre, 182–183, 184
Boyd, Brian, 146
brain, 130–134
brain biochemistry, 133–134
brain neurocircuitry, 134
brain stem, 132
Branum, Lisa, 154–155
British Cultural Studies, 182
Brown, Fraser, 154
Brown, Stuart, 37, 47–48
Bruner, Jerome, 106–107, 144–146
Buber, Martin, 87–88
Burghardt, Gordon, 38, 46, 118–119, 128–129, 131

Caillois, Roger: characteristics of play, 35; cultural articulation and play, 28; cultural conditioning, 192; culture-resisting play, 196–197; "free" or "voluntary" quality of play, 46; as Huizinga theory extension, 191–192; ingestion processes of play, 43–44; play as culture-building, 191–193; risk-taking, 69, 70; ritual-play comparison, 54–55; simplest form of play, 49; stimulation-satisfaction and play, 187; traditional societies, 205; transformative power of the sacred in ritual, 58. See also *agon*; *alea*; *diagonal science*; *ilinx*; *psychasthenia*
carnival and carnivalesque (Bakhtin), 197–198
cerebellum, 132

characteristics of play varieties: as action, 43–44; as activity, 45–47; chart, *63*; combinations and refinements, 62–66; *communitas* relationship, 58–61; as context, 49–50; as disposition, 47; distinguishing qualities, 42–50; as experience, 47–49; as interaction, 44–45; overviews, 42–43, 67; ritual relationship, 58; work relationship, 50–53
childhood, 8–9. *See also* immaturity purposes; *specific theories*; *specific theorists*
childhood socialization, 188–190
children's playground culture, 189
chimpanzees, 145
choice-making in play. *See* framing decisions for play
Christie, James, 36, 48
"class fractions" (Bourdieu), 182–183
classic theories of physical play, 121–128. See also s*pecific theories*; *specific theorists*
Clements, D., 158–159
codification (rules) moral development stage (Piaget), 93
cognitive-moral behavior theory (Piaget), 91–95
combinations and refinements of play, 62–67
communal play, 66, 149–150
communication development, 26, 146
communitas (Huizinga), 58–61, 66–67, 211
communities commentary, 2
compulsivity v. subjectivity, 117
conclusion determination, 224
concrete operational cognitive development stage (Piaget), 92
"conflict enculturation," 190
conflict theory, 178–181
conformity, 60
conscious guidance, 24
consciousness, 134, 135–136
constructive play (Smilansky), 158
consummation, 43–44, 50, 51, 55, 59–60, 126, 213
contemporary environment and adult play, 9–14

contestiveness (Huizinga), 44–45, 51, 55, 66–67, 70, 77

"continuation desire" (Brown), 30–31, 47

controlling action sequences (for play), 224

Cooley, Charles, 86–87

"core consciousness" (Damasio), 135–136

"core self" (Damasio), 136

creative activity, 117–118

creativity, 162–164, 167–168, 205–206

cross-cultural studies of children's play, 189–190

Csikszentmihalyi, Mihalyi, 31–32, 47, 64, 125, 212

cultural articulation and play, 28

cultural conditioning, 192

cultural play: culture-guided play, 188–195; culture-play interrelationships, 185–188; culture-resisting play, 195–205; definition and explanation of culture, 184–185; as expression and resistance, 185–188; fundamental nature of play, 205–208; overviews, 184–185, 210; patterning relationships of culture and play, 205–208

culture-environment relationship, 186

culture-guided play, 188–190

culture-human body relationship, 186

culture-play interrelationships, 185–188

culture-play pattern types. *See* play-culture pattern types

culture-psyche relationship, 187–188

culture-resisting play, 195–197

curiosity, 47, 48, 50, 52, 213

Damasio, Antonio, 143

Darwin, Charles, 120, 121, 123, 127–128, 129, 132–133

deconstruction, 207

"Deep Play: Notes on the Balinese Cockfight" (Geertz), 198–199

"deferred adaptations" (Bjorklund), 147–148

defining play: as action, 23–26; as activity, 26–28; comprehensive description synthesis, 38–41; as context, 33–34; as disposition, 28–30; as experience, 30–33; multiplicity of meanings and manifestations, 19; overview, 19–20; paradoxes, 19–20; Sutton-Smith, 38–41; theories of play, 23–34; by theorist, 34–41; theory overview, 22; variation examples, 21–22. See also *specific theories; specific theorists*

Derrida, Jacques, 206–207

descending-ascending pattern, 52

descending meaning, 50, 76–77

developmental implications, 6

Dewey, John, 156, 213

"diagonal science" (Caillois), 196

dialogical play, 211

The Dialogic Imagination (Bakhtin), 198

différance (Derrida), 207

Distinction (Bourdieu), 182–183

Donald, Merlin, 143

Douglas, Mary, 186

dromenon (Huizinga), 54

Dunning, Eric, 13, 194, 216

Durkheim, Emile, 59, 93

duty, 52

early modern era play, 220–221

early modern societies, 217–219

Eberle, Scott, 30, 36–37, 46, 47, 48–49

Economic and Philosophical Manuscripts (Marx), 3

"educability" (Bruner), 66–67, 144–146

educational theory in object play, 154–160

ego mastery v. pleasurable release, 98–99

electronic media, 218–219

Elias, Norbert, 13, 193–194, 216

Ellis, M., 123

embedded self, 215

"embodied cognition" (Lillard), 157

"emotion-sequences" processes of play, 48–49

enchantment, 57

engagement of play, 25–26, 47

enjoyment v. pleasure, 31–32

episodic nature of play, 45, 46–47, 50, 60, 213

Erikson, Erik, 96–97, 105–106, 148–149

event assessment, 75

"evolution of educability" (Bruner), 144–146

evolution of human beings, 120–128, 139–144. *See also* animal behavior research; natural selection; *specific animal types*

"exercise play" (Pellegrini and Smith), 148

exhilaration, 48, 50, 52

expanded viewpoints about play, 13–15

expectation, 75

experiential meaning declaration, 225

expertise commitment in play, 216–217

exploratory play, 211

expressive behavior theory (Freud), 43–44, 95–100, 213

"extended consciousness," 135–136

externalization (Berger and Luckmann), 162–163

"fabrication" (Goffman), 173

Factor, June, 189, 222

Fagen, Robert, 118–120, 127–128

faith, 57

fantasy play, 162–163

Fein, G., 33–34

Fein, Greta, 107–108

"fields of relationships," 73–75

Fine, Gary Alan, 169

"flow" of play (Csikszentmihalyi), 31, 125

formal operational cognitive development stage (Piaget), 92

Foucault, M., 186–187

Frame Analysis (Goffman), 72, 171–175

framing behavior (Goffman), 73

framing decisions for play, 73, 222–225

Freud, Anna, 113

Freud, Sigmund, 43–44, 95–100, 195, 213. *See also* expressive behavior theory (Freud)

Freudian tradition, 111–112. *See also* expressive behavior theory (Freud)

Froebel, Friedrich, 155–156

Fromberg, Doris, 36, 46, 48

Frost, Joe, 151–152

fun, 50, 52

functionalism, 77–79, 181

functional play (Piaget), 158

fun-exhilaration-gratification, 213

"fun morality" (Wolfenstein), 11–12

The Future of Ritual (Schechner), 202–205

Gadamer, Hans-Georg, 207–208

game categorization, 190

game rule *norms* (Goffman), 175

games with rules category (Piaget), 94

game worlds, 175

"gates of evolution" (Fagen), 127–128

Geertz, Clifford, 198–199, 215

gender, 181

generalization (Piaget), 158

goal-attainment (Parsons), 79

Goffman, Erving: boundaries and play, 224; event framing, 80, 203; frame utilization, 72, 171–175; game world rules, 175; human positioning in social world, 169; play as experience of self, 212; play as presentation, 168–169; player identity v. personal identity, 32; separation feelings of play, 48; *setting of stakes*, 223; social functioning patterns, 171–175; *transformation rules*, 225

Gordon, Gwen, 36, 46, 47, 48, 49

gratification, 48–49, 50, 52

Groos, Karl: aesthetic implications, 226; classic theories of physical play, 120–121; description of play, 167; group orientation, 145–146; instinct refinement, 189; instinct satisfaction, 23–24, 130–131; surplus resource expression, 128

habitus (Bourdieu), 182–183, 184
Hall, G. Stanley, 122–123
The Hand (Wilson), 142
Handelman, Don, 201–202, 205, 215, 216
Heidegger, Martin, 207, 208
historical era classifications of play: advanced industrial (postmodern) societies, 217–219; early modern societies, 215–216; industrial (late modern) societies, 216–217; traditional societies, 214–215
Holzman, Lois, 167–168
hominid ancestors, 140–143
Homo faber, 3
Homo Ludens: A Study of the Play Element in Culture (Huizinga), 2–5, 191
hope, 60–61
The House of Make-Believe (Dorothy and Jerome Singer), 108–109
How We Think (Dewey), 156
Huizinga, Johan: aesthetic implications, 226; characteristics of play, 24–25; *communitas*, 58–61, 66–67, 211; *contestiveness*, 5, 44–45, 51, 70, 77; description of play, 35, 167; evaluation of play, 220–221; experience and play, 31; history/evolution of play, 191; industrial (late modern) societies play, 216–217; motivation for play, 77–78; order-disorder tension of play, 46; play as culture-building, 190–191; play-ritual contrast, 53–54; social and cultural implications of play, 2–5; *social skill building*, 149–150; traditional era gatherings, 214
human agency role in play, 221–225
human body. *See* evolution of human beings; nature (human body) and play
human brain development, 132–133

"The Idealization of Play" (Sutton-Smith and Kelly-Byrne), 110
ideal v. real play, 212–213
identity, 85

identity continuity, 32–33
identity interaction, 32–33
"idioculture," 187–188
*ilinx (*vertigo) (Caillois), 35, 69, 191–192, 196
imaginative-performance theory (Vygotsky), 100–104, 167, 169–170, 212
immaturity purposes, 144–150. *See also* childhood; *specific theories; specific theorists*
incipient cooperation moral development stage (Piaget), 92
individualism mythology, 1–2
individuality, 24–25
industrial (late modern) societies, 216–217
industrialism, 180
ingestion processes of play, 43–44
Inkeles, Alex, 7
institutionalization, 27–28
instrumentalization, 55
integration (Parsons), 79
integrativeness, 60
interdependence, 51–52, 56–57
interest, 52
interest-satisfaction, 52
internalization (Berger and Luckmann), 162–163
"inversions" (Turner), 199–201
"irrelevance" rules (Goffman), 175

James, William, 84–86, 134
Johnson, James, 36
Jung, Carl, 96

Kant, I., 91
Kelly-Byrne, Diana, 19, 110
"keys" (Goffman), 173
Klein, Melanie, 113
Kuchler, Tilmon, 12

latency (Parsons), 79
leaving the play setting, 225
Leiberman, Nina, 30
"leisure societies," 10–11
Lévi-Strauss, Claude, 55–56, 186–187
Levy, Joseph, 19
life expectancy, 10

lila (Schechner), 203–204
Lillard, Angeline, 157
limbic system, 132
"liminality" (Turner), 199–201
"liminoid" (Turner), 199–201
"locomotor" skill development (Pellegrini and Smith), 148
Luckmann, Thomas, 161–162, 163
ludus (Caillois), 49, 192

macrosphere (Erikson), 105–106
Mallory, George, 5
Man and the Sacred (Caillois), 54–55, 192
manipulative play, 211
Marks-Tarlow, Terry, 37–38, 46–47, 48, 49
Marx, Karl, 3, 50–51, 52, 178–181
maya (Schechner), 203–204
Mead, George Herbert, 86–87, 165–166
"mediascape" (Williams), 12
mediating contexts, 73–75
membership, 223
memory and anticipation, 133
methecticism (Huizinga), 54
microsphere (Erikson), 105–106
"mimetic culture" (Donald), 143
mimeticism (Huizinga), 54
mimicry (Caillois), 35, 70, 191–192, 196
"mirror neurons" (Boyd), 146
Mitchell, R., 118
mixed *ascending-descending* pattern, 52
modernism, 205
modernity, 215–216
modern play, 194–195
monkeys, 145
Montessori, Maria, 157, 213
Moral Education (Durkheim), 93

natural selection, 121, 123, 127–128, 129, 132–133. *See also* evolution of human beings
nature (human body) and play: affect, 132–134; animal behavior research, 116–120; brain role, 130–131;

consciousness, 134–137; overviews, 116, 137; stimulus-seeking, 123–128; surplus resource expression, 128–129. *See also* evolution of human beings
need, 52
"neotony" (Bjorklund), 147
"netting" (Schechner), 203
neurocircuitry, 134
"neuronal plasticity" (Bjorklund), 147
New Games movement, 150
Newman, Fred, 167–168
Nietzsche, Friedrich, 130, 187, 195

objectivation (Berger and Luckmann), 162–163
objective culture (Simmel), 185
object play in educational theory, 154–160. See also *specific theories; specific theorists*
"ontogenetic adaptation" (Bjorklund), 148
Opie, Peter and Iona, 189
optimism of play (Sutton-Smith), 47
order-seeking of play (Sutton-Smith), 110
"orienting reflex," 125
other behaviors v. play. *See* play v. other behaviors
other-regulation, 56, 60
outdoor play, 150–154
overview of book, 13–15

paidia (Caillois), 49, 192
Paley, Vivian, 162–163
Panksepp, J., 133–134
Parsons, Talcott, 78–79, 176
patterning relationships of culture and play, 205
pattern-maintenance (Parsons), 79
Pellegrini, Anthony, 148–149
Pellis, S., 131
Pellis, V., 131
"performances" (Schechner), 204–205, 219
"performance theory," 167–170
"permanent immaturity" (Bruner), 144

Perry, Jane, 154–155
personal control, 52
personal identity v. player identity, 32–33
personality as battleground, 99
personal situation comprehension, 80–84
physical and mental capacity development, 138–144
physical aspects of play. *See* nature (human body) and play
physical environment: childhood, 144–148; educational theory, 154–159; evolution of human capability, 138–144; immaturity functions, 144–148; object play, 154–159; outdoor play, 150–154; overviews, 138, 160; physical play patterns, 148–150
physical fitness-academic performance relationship, 159–160
physical play patterns, 148
physiology-play capacity relationship, 138–144
Piaget, Jean, 23, 91–95, 158, 213. *See also* cognitive-moral behavior theory (Piaget)
play as framing (Goffman), 173–175
play as human condition, 205–208
play as performance, 202–205
"play-as-progress" rhetoric (Sutton-Smith), 13
play as sense-making. *See* sense-making and play
play capacity-physiology relationship, 138–144
play combinations, 62–67, *63*
play-*communitas* combinations, 66–67
play-culture interrelationships, 185–188
play-culture pattern types: culture as *playing*, 205–208; play *within* culture, 185, 188–195; play *with* or *at* culture, 185, 195–205
player identity v. personal identity, 32–33
"play ethos" (Peter Smith), 6–7
play experience development, 47
playful communitas, 66–67

playfulness, 87–88
playful ritual, 65
playful work, 64
playgrounds, 151–154
Play of Animals (Groos), 120–121
play refinements, 62–67, *63*
play-ritual combinations, 64–65
play-self connection, 210–211
play v. other behaviors: combinations and refinements, 62–67; distinguishing qualities of play, 43–50; overviews, 42, 67; ritual-play comparison, 53–58; work-play comparison, 50–53
play-work combinations, 64
"playworker," 9, 153
pleasurable release v. ego mastery, 98–99
"pleasure industries," 11–12
pleasure v. enjoyment, 31–32
politicization of play, 217
"positive psychology" (Csikszentmihalyi), 31
possibility and play: aesthetic implications, 226; evaluation of play, 220–221; historical era classifications, 214–219; history/evolution of play, 191, 214–219; human agency role, 221–225; ideal v. real play, 213–214; overviews, 209, 225–227; positive-negative aspect juxtaposition, 226; real v. ideal play, 213–214; sense-making and play, 209–213
postmodern theory, 43–44, 206–208
post-structural theory, 206–208
power and privilege, 178–183
practice games category (Piaget), 94
predictability, 55–56
preoperational cognitive development stage (Piaget), 92
Presentation of Self in Everyday Life (Goffman), 168
"progress" and play development, 122–123
"proto-self" (Damasio), 136
psychasthenia (Caillois), 196
psychic pleasure, 23

psychoanalysis, 111–112
psycho-biological processes, 96
psychological theories: Bruner, Jerome, 106–107; cognitive-moral behavior theory (Piaget), 91–95; contemporary theories, 104–112; Erikson, Erik, 105–106; expressive behavior theory (Freud), 95–100; Fein, Greta, 107–108; Freud, Sigmund, 95–100; imaginative-performance theory (Vygotsky), 100–104; overviews, 90, 115, 210; Piaget, Jean, 91–95; play as therapy, 112–115; Singer, Dorothy and Jerome, 108–109; Sutton-Smith, Brian, 109–112; Vygotsky, Lev, 100–104
psychosexual development stages (Freud), 99–100
purpose of book, 13–15
purposes of play studies, 5–10

The Quest for Excitement (Elias and Dunning), 194
"quest for excitement" (Elias and Dunning), 13

Rappaport, Roy, 56
Ratey, J., 159–160
"rationalization," 193
reality construction, 75–77, 161–164
"realized resources" rules (Goffman), 175
real v. ideal play, 212–213
rebellion element of play, 76
rebellious play, 211
recess, 151–154
recognition and *response*, 75
recreation perspective, 122
"recursive" quality of play (Marks-Tarlow), 46
regimen and duty, 52
relaxation perspective, 122
"repetition compulsion" (Freud), 98
research purposes, 5–10
resource selection, 224
responses, 124–125
reverence, 57
rhetorics of play (Sutton-Smith), 38–40

"rhythmic stereotypies" (Pellegrini and Smith), 148
"risk society" (Beck), 12–13
ritual: Caillois, Roger, 205; Derrida, Jacques, 206–207; *dromenon*, 53–58; *enchantment*, 57; *faith*, 57; Geertz, Clifford, 198–199; Goffman, Erving, 204; Handelman, Don, 201–202, 205; *instrumentalization*, 55; *integration*, 55; *interdependence*, 56–57; negative emotion potential, 57–58; *other-regulation*, 56; *predictability*, 55–56; *reverence*, 57; Schechner, Richard, 202–205; sponsoring contexts, 58; stages or progressions, 57; *transformation*, 55; Turner, Victor, 199–200; Van Gennep, A., 200
ritualistic play, 64–65
ritual-play combinations, 64–65
ritual-play comparison, 53–58
The Ritual Process (Turner), 57
Roberts, John, 190
Romanticism, 195
"rough-and-tumble" play (Pellegrini and Smith), 148–149
Rubin, K., 33–34
rule administration, 224
rules. *See* framing decisions for play
rule-setting, 223

Sarama, J., 158–159
Sattelmair, J., 159–160
Schechner, Richard, 202–205, 213, 219, 224
Schiller, F., 121, 226
school recess, 151–154
Schwartzman, Helen, 189
The Secret of Childhood (Montessori), 157
self, 85–87
self-awareness, 145
self concept, 84–87
self-consciousness lessening, 47–48
self-development, 151–154
self-direction, 24
"self-domestication" (Bruner), 145
self-identity, 164–170

self-management development, 151
self-realization, 1, 80–82, 165–166, 179, 212–213
self-regulation, 45–46, 50, 51–52, 77, 213
sense-making and play: action and experience context model, 69–71; *assertive* play, 211; *dialogical* play, 211; examples, 69–71; *exploratory* play, 211; framing behavior, 71–75, 73; functionalism, 77–79; *manipulative* play, 211; overviews, 68, 89, 209–210; personal enterprise, 210–211; playfulness, 87–88; play-self connection, 210–211; reality construction, 75–77; *rebellious* play, 211; self concept expansion, 84–87; self-realization, 80–82; self-standing and play, 212–213; setting variability, 212; situation and altered identity, 82–84; *sensorimotor* cognitive development stage (Piaget), 92, 93
sequential choices of play. *See* framing decisions for play
setting for play, 223. *See also* physical environment
Shared Fantasy: Role-Playing Games as Social Worlds (Fine), 169
shared understandings, 26–27. *See also* ritual
Simmel, Georg: adventures, 83–84; boundaries, 224; distinct (separate) nature of play, 48; individual as subculture argument, 188; "objective culture" v. "subjective culture," 185; player-person interrelationships, 32–33; "play form" of association, 170–171; rule formation, 171; "subjective culture" v. "objective culture," 185
Singer, Dorothy and Jerome, 108–109
situation and altered identity, 82–84
situation comprehension, 80–84
Smilansky, Sara, 158
Smith, David, 7
Smith, Peter, 6–7, 148–149
sociability, 170–171

social conditions, 33–34
social functions, 176–178
social laboratory, 162–163
social life of play: overviews, 161, 183, 210; reality construction, 161–164; self-identity, 164–170; social laboratory, 162–163; social relationship, 170–176; social structure, 176–183
social play, 145–146
social relationship, 170–176
social skill building, 146–147, 149–150
social structure, 176–183
social units, 176–178
social workshop aspects, 6
S.O.R. (stimulus-organism response), 124–125
specifying play activity, 222
Spencer, Herbert, 105, 121
spirit, 28–29
sponsoring contexts of ritual, 58
sports, 176–181
stake-setting (Goffman), 223
stimulus-organism response (S.O.R.), 124–125
stimulus-seeking, 124–125
"stimulus-seeking" (Ellis), 123
Stromberg, Peter, 219
subjective involvement, 85
"subversions" (Turner), 199–201
"superego" (Freud), 99
surplus resource expression, 128–129
Sutton-Smith, Brian: adaptive layers, 110–111; character implications, 110; children's playground culture, 189; culture-resisting, 110, 195–196; disunity-unity juxtaposition, 226; equilibrial-disequilibrial tension, 46; excitement and optimism, 48; optimism, 47; order-seeking, 110; paradoxes, 19; "play-as-progress," 13; play stages, 110–111; positive-negative aspect juxtaposition, 226; rhetorics, 38–41
symbolic games category (Piaget), 94
"symbolic realities," 72–73

technological advancements, 205–206, 217–219

theories of play: as action, 23–25; as activity, 26–28; comprehensive synthesis, 38–41; as context, 33–34; as disposition, 28–30; as experience, 30; frameworks, 38–41; as interaction, 25–26; rhetorics (Sutton-Smith), 38–41; by theorist, 34–41; variation examples, 21–22. See also *specific theories; specific theorists*

The Theory of the Leisure Class (Veblen), 180

Tinbergen, Niko, 117

total absorption of play, 47

"Toys and Reasons" (Erikson), 105

traditional societies, 216–217

transformation, 43–44, 50, 51, 55, 77, 213

"transformation" rules (Goffman), 175

transformation social function (Goffman), 172–173

Truth and Method (Gadamer), 208

Turkle, S., 219

Turner, Victor, 57, 58–59, 63, 199–201

unpredictability, 44–45, 51, 55, 60

Vandenberg, B., 33–34

Van Gennep, A., 200

Veblen, Thorstein, 180

Vygotsky, Lev, 100–104, 167, 169–170, 212

Weber, Max, 193, 216

Whiting, Beatrice, 189

Whitshaw, I., 131

Williams, Simon, 12

will v. *skill* (Freud), 96–97

Wilson, E. O., 118–120

Wilson, Frank, 142, 144

Wilson, Penny, 153

Winnicott, D. W, 113–114

"wish fulfillment" (Vygotsky), 101

Wolfenstein, Martha, 11

Wood, Elizabeth, 36, 47

work, 51–52, 52, 54, 61

worklike play, 64

work-play combinations, 64

work-play comparison, 50–53

Yawkey, Thomas, 36, 48

"zone of proximal development" (Vygotsky), 103

THOMAS S. HENRICKS is the Danieley Professor of Sociology at Elon University and author of *Play Reconsidered: Sociological Perspectives on Human Expression.*

The University of Illinois Press
is a founding member of the
Association of American University Presses.

Composed in 9.5/12.5 Trump Mediaeval
at the University of Illinois Press
Manufactured by Sheridan Books, Inc.

University of Illinois Press
1325 South Oak Street
Champaign, IL 61820-6903
www.press.uillinois.edu